Excel for Windows Answers: Certified Tech Support

Mary Campbell

Osborne **McGraw-Hill**

Berkeley · New York · St. Louis
San Francisco · Auckland · Bogotá
Hamburg · London · Madrid · Mexico
City · Milan · Montreal · New Delhi
Panama City · Paris · São Paulo
Singapore · Sydney · Tokyo · Toronto

D1399748

Osborne **McGraw-Hill**
2600 Tenth Street, Berkeley, California 94710, USA

For information on software, translations, or book distributors outside of the U.S.A., please write to Osborne McGraw-Hill at the above address.

Excel for Windows Answers: Certified Tech Support

1234567890 DOC 9987654

ISBN 0-07-882054-5

Publisher
Lawrence Levitsky

Project Editor
Emily Rader

Computer Designer
Peter F. Hancik

Illustrator
Marla Shelasky

Series Design
Marla Shelasky

Quality Control Specialist
Joe Scuderi

Cover Designer
Ted Mader Associates

Contents
at a
Glance

Contents

Foreword

Few things are as frustrating as having a computer problem that you can't solve. Computer users often spend hours trying to find the answer to a *single* software question! That's why the tech support experts at Corporate Software Incorporated (CSI) have teamed up with Osborne/McGraw-Hill to bring you the **Certified Tech Support Series**—books designed to give you all the solutions you need to fix even the most difficult software glitches.

At Corporate Software, we have a dedicated support staff that handles over 200,000 software questions every month. These experts use the latest hardware and software technology to provide answers to every sort of software problem. CSI takes full advantage of the partnerships that we have forged with all major software publishers. Our staff frequently receives the same training that publishers offer their own support representatives and has access to vendor technical resources that are not generally available to the public.

Thus, this series is based on actual *empirical* data. We've drawn on our support expertise and sorted through our vast database of software solutions to find the most important and frequently asked questions for Excel for Windows. These questions have also been checked and rechecked for technical accuracy and are organized in a way that will let you find the answer you need quickly—providing you with a one-stop tech support solution to your software problems.

No longer do you have to spend hours on the phone waiting for someone to answer your tech support question! You are holding the single, most authoritative collection of answers to your software questions available—the next best thing to having a tech support expert by your side.

We've helped millions of people solve their software problems. Let us help you.

Randy Burkhart
Senior Vice President, Technology
Corporate Software Inc.

Acknowledgments

I would like to thank all the staff at Corporate Software who enthusiastically committed so much time and knowledge to this effort. So many of them spent time on weekends and after hours to search their data banks for the best questions and answers. They also spent untold hours reviewing manuscript and pages and responding to all of our requests for help. Without all of their hard work, this book would not exist. I would like to personally thank each of the following people for their assistance: Laura C., Mahin K., Matt M., Michael T., Pam V., Robert M., Rodney C., Roy A., and Wilfred H. Special thanks to Christopher L., John S., Joshua B., William C., Paul P., Brian K., Tom A., Jo-Anne A., Kim A., and Jan R.

The staff at Osborne was also an important part of this book. Without exception, everyone did more than their share to insure that we met all the important deadlines. I would like to extend special thanks to Larry Levitsky, Publisher, for the idea to do the series and all of his work with Corporate Software to make the idea a reality; Cindy Brown, Managing Editor, whose handling of this project was as flawless as ever; Emily Rader, Project Editor, who managed the editorial process and helped to polish the manuscript; and all of the Production staff, who each did everything possible to make this book the best source of technical support available.

I would also like to especially thank my assistants, Gabrielle Lawrence and Elizabeth Reinhardt. They contributed extensively to the book's content and art work. They also proofread the final manuscript to help catch technical and grammatical errors.

Introduction

There is no good time to have a problem with your computer or the software you are using. You are anxious to complete the task you started and do not have time to fumble through a manual looking for an answer that is probably not there anyway. You can forget about the option of a free support call solving your problems, since most software vendors now charge as much as $25 to answer a single question. *Excel for Windows Answers: Certified Tech Support* can provide the solution to all of your Excel problems. It contains the most frequently asked Excel questions, along with the solutions to get you back on track quickly. The questions and answers have been extracted from the data banks of Corporate Software, the world's largest supplier of third-party support. Since they answer over 200,000 calls a month from users just like you, odds are high that your problem has plagued others in the past and is already part of their data bank. *Excel for Windows Answers: Certified Tech Support* is the next best thing to having a Corporate Software expert at the desk right next to you. The help you need is available seven days a week, any time you have a problem.

Excel for Windows Answers: Certified Tech Support is organized into 14 chapters. Each chapter contains questions and answers on a specific area of Excel. An excellent index makes it easy for you to find what you need, even if you are uncertain which chapter covers the solution.

Throughout the book you will also find the following elements to help you sail smoothly through your Excel tasks, whether you are a novice or a veteran user:

Frustration Busters   Special coverage of Excel topics that have proven confusing to many users. A few minutes spent reading each of these boxes can help you avoid problems in the first place.

Tech Tips and Notes Short technical helps that provide additional insight into a topic addressed in one of the questions.

Tech Terrors Pitfalls you will want to steer clear of.

Top Ten Tech Terrors

Every computer user experiences technical difficulties at one time or another. We've tapped the data banks and consultant expertise at Corporate Software to identify and provide step-by-step solutions to the ten most common Excel for Windows problems. These are problems *thousands* of users have encountered. They've turned to the consultant expertise at Corporate Software for help and so can you!

In fact, you can probably avoid these problems altogether simply by reviewing this list as a preventive measure. If for some reason, however, you still run into any of them, you'll know just how to fix them.

I'm having problems printing a specific area of my worksheet. How do I specify what I want to print?

There are several ways to specify the print area in Excel. If you want to always print the same area of the worksheet or you want to specify titles to appear at the left or top of each page, the best approach is to define a print area.

Follow these steps to define a print area:

1. Choose Page Setup from the File menu.

2. Click the Sheet tab to display the options shown here:

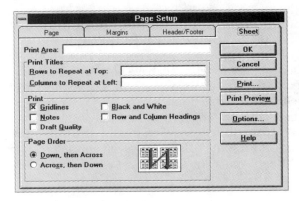

3. Move the insertion point to the Print Area box, and either select the area in the worksheet that you want to print or type its address.

4. If you want to display titles at the top of each printed page, move the insertion point to the Rows to Repeat at Top box and either select the range in the worksheet that contains the titles or type its address.

5. If you want to display titles in the leftmost column of each printed page, move the insertion point to the Columns to Repeat at Left box and either select the range in the worksheet that contains the titles or type its address.

6. Click OK.

If, on the other hand, you want to specify a different print area each time you print the worksheet, you can expedite the process by adding the Set Print Area button to the Standard toolbar. You can add this button to any toolbar you display regularly; we suggest the Standard toolbar here, because most users show it whenever they work in Excel.

To add the Set Print Area button:

1. Display the Toolbar dialog box by clicking any toolbar with the right mouse button and then choosing Toolbars from the shortcut menu, or by choosing <u>T</u>oolbars from the <u>V</u>iew menu.

2. Select Standard in the Toolbars list box, if necessary, and then click the <u>C</u>ustomize button to display the Customize dialog box, shown here:

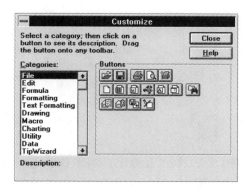

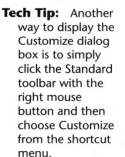

Tech Tip: Another way to display the Customize dialog box is to simply click the Standard toolbar with the right mouse button and then choose Customize from the shortcut menu.

3. Select File in the <u>C</u>ategories list box.

4. Click the fifth button in the first row in the Buttons section. The button looks like a miniature printer with lines above and to the left of it.

5. Drag the button to the desired position on the toolbar.

6. Click the Close button.

Once this toolbar button is available, you can reassign the print area by selecting the cells you want to print and clicking the button.

If you plan to print different areas of your worksheet each time, you can specify the print range in the Print dialog box by following these steps:

1. Select the range you want to print.

2. Choose <u>P</u>rint from the <u>F</u>ile menu to display the Print dialog box, as shown here:

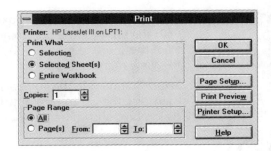

Tech Tip: This doesn't set a print area default; it simply lets you indicate a different area of your worksheet each time you print.

3. Select the Selectio<u>n</u> option button.

4. Click OK.

Excel prints the selected area.

Whenever I enter a number on my worksheet, Excel adds a decimal point even though I select a number format that doesn't include one. What is wrong?

The Fi<u>x</u>ed Decimal option is turned on. This option automatically adds a decimal point at a specific location in an entry. For example, if you enter the number 2, Excel may display it as .02 or .2, depending on the setting. You might use this option when you enter prices to convert an entry such as 4999 to 49.99.

Tech Tip: You can easily tell whether this option is on by looking at the right end of the status bar; if FIX appears there, this option is enabled.

To turn off the Fi<u>x</u>ed Decimal option:

1. Choose <u>O</u>ptions from the <u>T</u>ools menu.

2. Click the Edit tab to display the options shown here:

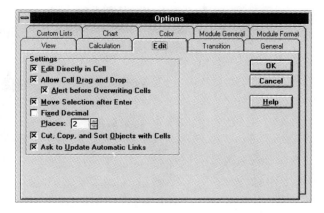

3. Clear the Fi<u>x</u>ed Decimal check box.

Excel should now display values exactly as you enter them.

Tech Tip: You can override the Fi<u>x</u>ed Decimal option by typing a decimal point as part of your entry.

3 I have a corrupted file. Is there any way that I can recover the data from it?

You can create a link to recover the values in the damaged sheet. This procedure will almost certainly take less time than retyping all of your data. However, any formulas in the corrupt file are permanently lost. The only way to restore both your data and formulas is by opening an existing backup copy of the file.

To create a link to recover your data:

1. Choose <u>N</u>ew from the <u>F</u>ile menu twice to create two new workbooks.

2. Select an area in the first workbook to link to the second workbook. For example, highlight A1:Z250 on Sheet 1 of Book 1.

3. Choose <u>C</u>opy from the <u>E</u>dit menu.

4. Switch to Book 2 by choosing it from the <u>W</u>indow menu.

5. Choose Paste <u>S</u>pecial from the <u>E</u>dit menu to display the Paste Special dialog box, shown here:

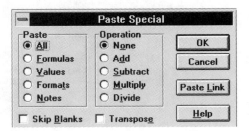

6. Click the Paste <u>L</u>ink button.

The two workbooks are now linked together. For example, the formula in A1 is {=[Book1]Sheet1!$A$1:$Z$250}. Because there is no data in Book 1, zeros appear in the cells in Book 2.

In the next several steps, you will change the links to refer to the damaged workbook.

1. Choose Lin<u>k</u>s from the <u>E</u>dit menu.

2. Click the <u>C</u>hange Source button.

3. Select the damaged file from the File <u>N</u>ame list box in the Change Links dialog box that appears.

4. Click OK.

The data from the corrupted file displays in the cells in Book 2. However, each cell still contains a link formula.

To break the link and save the values themselves in the new workbook:

1. Select the entire data range.

2. Choose <u>C</u>opy from the <u>E</u>dit menu to place the data on the Windows Clipboard.

3. Choose Paste <u>S</u>pecial from the <u>E</u>dit menu, select the <u>V</u>alues option button, and click OK.

This procedure removes the link to the corrupted file and pastes the results of the formulas into the new workbook.

4 Formatting a chart to include more than one chart type was a difficult task in Excel 4.0. Is there an easier method in Excel 5.0?

Yes. In Excel 5.0, you can specify a different type for each series in your chart. First, create the chart itself and then follow these steps to use multiple types:

1. Select the series whose format you want to change.

2. Choose Chart Type from the Format menu.

3. Make sure that the Selected Series option button is selected.

Tech Tip: If this option is not selected, the overall chart type you used cannot be combined with other chart types. In this case, you must reset the initial chart type before you change individual series. Some chart types cannot be combined at all. For example, you cannot combine any type of 3-D chart with any other type of chart.

4. Select the desired chart type for the designated series and click OK.

Excel instantaneously displays the series using the new chart type, as shown in Figure 1-1.

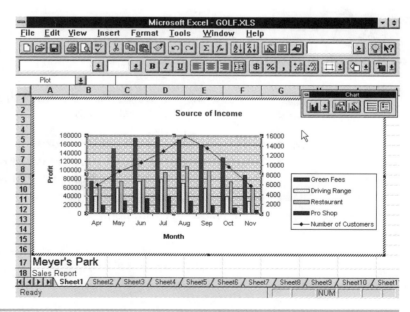

FIGURE 1-1   A chart that includes different types of series

5 Except for a few cells, I want to prevent any changes to my worksheet. I protected the worksheet but now I can't enter data in any cell. How can I make entries in some of the locked cells?

When you protect a worksheet, Excel *locks* every cell by default. However, you can selectively remove this property from the cells you want to change by following these steps:

1. If the worksheet is currently protected, unprotect it by choosing Protection from the Tools menu, selecting either Unprotect Sheet or Unprotect Workbook, and then clicking OK.

2. Select the cells in the worksheet that you want to be able to edit even when the rest of the sheet or workbook is locked.

3. Choose Cells from the Format menu.

4. Click the Protection tab and clear the Locked check box.

5. Click OK to accept the changes.

6. Repeat steps 2 through 5 to unlock any other cells that you want to be able to change.

Tech Tip: A quick way to repeat the procedure after you've done it once is to select the next group of cells and press F4.

To protect the sheet or workbook and activate the locked property on all but the designated cells:

1. Choose Protection from the Tools menu.

2. Select either Protect Sheet or Protect Workbook, depending on the extent of protection you want.

3. If desired, enter a password in the Password box, shown in the following illustration.

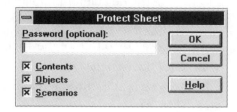

4. Click OK to enable protection.

Tech Tip: You can limit the type of protection applied to a sheet or workbook by selecting the Contents, Objects, or Scenarios check box in the Protect Sheet or Protect Workbook dialog box.

How do I designate my default font and directory in Excel 5.0?

You can set numerous defaults in Excel, most of which you specify by choosing the Options command from the Tools menu. The font and directory defaults are the ones you're most likely to change: the font that Excel uses to display your entries, and the directory in which Excel opens and saves workbooks.

You can change the default font for just the current workbook or for all workbooks you open in Excel 5.0. To change the default font for the current workbook:

1. Choose Style from the Format menu. The Normal style name appears in the Style Name box.

This named style determines the appearance of each entry, unless you apply a different style or modify the individual cell's format.

2. Click Modify and then click the Font tab.

3. Select the desired font in the Font, Font Style, and Size list boxes.

4. Select any other attributes you wish to apply, such as Color, Underline, or one of the options in the Effects section.

5. Click OK twice to return to the current workbook.

To change the default font for all future workbooks created in Excel:

1. Choose Options from the Tools menu.
2. Click the General tab.
3. Select a font in the Standard Font drop-down list box and click OK.

Excel prompts you to quit and then restart Excel to implement your changes.

To specify the directory from which Excel opens files and to which it saves them:

1. Choose Options from the Tools menu.
2. Click the General tab.
3. Type the path for your new default directory in the Default File Location box; for example, **C:\EXCEL\MYFILES**.

This change takes effect the next time you start Excel and overrides any default directory set in Windows.

Alternatively, you can set a default directory in Windows that Excel will use unless you specify otherwise from within the application. To change the default directory in the Program Manager:

1. Select the Microsoft Excel program icon.
2. Choose Properties from the File menu to display the Program Item Properties dialog box, shown here:

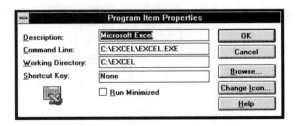

3. Type a new path in the Working Directory box.
4. Click OK.

7

Can I increase all of the values in a worksheet by 10% without re-entering them?

You can use this quick-and-easy method to have Excel increase formulas and numeric constants:

1. Enter a value, such as **110%** or **1.1**, in a blank cell.

2. Choose <u>C</u>opy from the <u>E</u>dit menu.

3. Select the data that you want to increase.

4. Choose Paste <u>S</u>pecial from the <u>E</u>dit menu.

5. Select <u>M</u>ultiply in the Operation section and click OK.

Excel multiplies all your constants by 110% and adds *1.1 to every formula. By using a percentage, the results correctly reflect a 10% increase.

For example, to create the worst and best scenarios based on current data depicted in column B of the worksheet in Figure 1-2, you first copy the numbers in column B to columns C and D. Then, you use the foregoing procedure to multiply each value in column C by .75 and each value in column D by 1.1. For the worst case numbers, you copy the 75% in C11 to the Clipboard and select the numbers in C12:C18 before you choose Paste <u>S</u>pecial from the <u>E</u>dit menu to multiply the numbers in C12:C18 by .75. For the best case numbers, you copy the 110% in D11 to the Clipboard and select the numbers in D12:D18 before you choose Paste <u>S</u>pecial from the <u>E</u>dit menu to multiply the numbers in D12:D18 by 1.1. The percentage number format is copied to these new values in C12:D18. The final results you see in Figure 1-2 show the numbers after the number format for these new values is returned to the previous setting.

Tech Tip: To view the results of this procedure, you may want to increase the number of decimal places Excel displays in the worksheet, since multiplying by a percentage often changes the number of digits after the decimal point.

	Microsoft Excel - TUNEDTMS.XLS					
File	Edit	View	Insert	Format	Tools	Data Window Help

C13 = 118140.75

	A	B	C	D	E	F
1						
2						
3						
4						
5						
6	TUNED TIMES					
7	Division of Brickerbrack Publishing					
8	Budget Projections					
9						
10	Expense Category	Current Budget	Worst Case	Best Case		
11			75%	110%		
12	Salary	$ 358,245	$ 268,684	$ 394,070		
13	Wages	157,521	118,141	173,273		
14	Benefits	245,641	184,231	270,205		
15	Supplies	208,721	156,541	229,593		
16	Rent	115,200	86,400	126,720		
17	Utilities	97,563	73,172	107,319		
18	Travel	105,489	79,117	116,038		
19	Total	$ 1,288,380	$ 966,285	$ 1,417,218		
20						

Sheet1 / Sheet2 / Sheet3 / Sheet4 / Sheet5 / Sheet6

Ready — NUM

FIGURE 1-2   You can use a shortcut to have Excel calculate percentage increases or decreases

8   **In Excel 5.0, how do I select a database and extract data from it?**

Excel 5.0 handles database tasks slightly differently than Excel 4.0 and introduces some new terminology. For example, Excel 5.0 uses the term *lists* to refer to what used to be called databases and it doesn't include the Set Database option. In addition, when you choose a database-related command, Excel 5.0 automatically tries to identify the appropriate area in your sheet to use for database purposes:

- If a previously defined range includes the current selection and has the name Database, Excel uses this named range as the list.

- If a blank cell is selected, Excel either opens the Advanced Filter dialog box indicating that the range is not valid, or gives a dialog saying, "No list found," depending on which database command you chose.
   You can select the range containing the list in the List Range box.

■ If a contiguous range of cells is selected, Excel assumes it's the list.

■ If a single cell is selected, Excel defines the current region surrounding the cell as the list.

When you perform an extract, Excel copies data from a list to another location. You must define three ranges in order to extract data: the list range, the criteria range, and the copy to range.

The *list range* is the data source, which was called a database range in Excel 4.0. For example, in Figure 1-3, the list range is A3:D13. Excel would automatically recognize this area as the list based on the worksheet entries.

The second range you must set is the *criteria range*. The criteria range must include the column headings of the list and any conditions to be met when filtering. In Figure 1-3, this range should be defined as F1:G3. This criteria range tells Excel to search for the list entries with 4 in the Price column or ABC in the Supplier column.

The *copy to range* is the location to which Excel should copy the data that meets the criteria. It was called an extract range in Excel 4.0. In Figure 1-3, F5:H5 is designated as the copy to

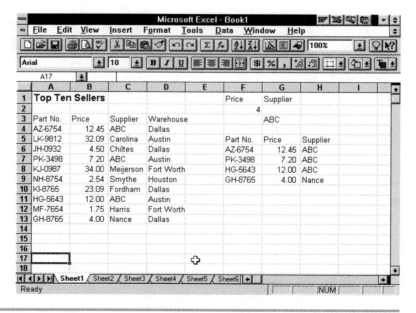

FIGURE 1-3   A worksheet set up to extract data from a list

range and displays the extracted data. You select only one row, but Excel uses as many rows as it needs to copy all of the matching data.

Follow these steps to define the appropriate database ranges and extract the data in a worksheet:

1. Choose Filter from the Data menu.

2. Choose Advanced Filter.

3. Select the Copy to Another Location option button, as shown here:

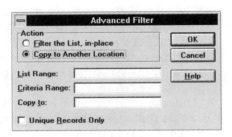

4. Move the insertion point to the List Range box and either select the desired range in the worksheet or type its address.

5. Move the insertion point to the Criteria Range box and either select the desired range in the worksheet or type its address.

6. Move the insertion point to the Copy to box and either select the desired range in the worksheet or type its address.

7. Click OK.

Excel copies all the data that meets the criteria to the specified range.

How do I create a trendline in Excel 5.0?

You can add a *trendline* to an Excel 5.0 chart to indicate the overall pattern of a data series, as well as forecast a future or past trend based on the given data. This option is directly built into Excel 5.0 and eliminates the Linest, Logest, and Trend functions used in earlier versions.

To add a trendline to any chart:

1. Select the series for which you want to produce a trendline.

2. Choose Trendline from the Insert menu to display the Trendline dialog box shown here:

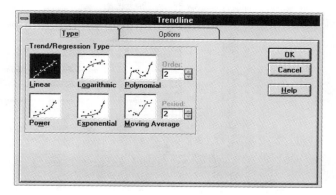

3. Click the Type tab.

4. Select the type of trendline you would like to create.

5. Click the Options tab and set any specific options for the trendline, such as intercepts and forecasting, if necessary.

6. Click OK.

10 I always double-clicked an embedded chart to display a chart "window" in Excel 4.0. This doesn't seem to work in Excel 5.0. What happened?

You no longer "blow up" a chart so that it appears full size in a separate window the way you did in Excel 4.0. You can now edit charts directly in the worksheet window. This eliminates the distortion that occurred in earlier versions when you made formatting changes to an enlarged chart and then switched back to the worksheet window.

When you modify an embedded chart in Excel 5.0, it remains the same size to allow true WYSIWYG (what you see is what you get) editing. As shown in Figure 1-4, there are only a few minor changes to the screen display once you select the chart: the

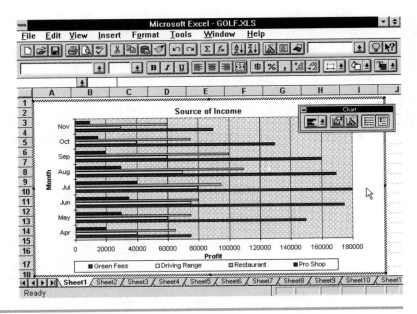

FIGURE 1-4   An embedded chart that is currently selected

chart border thickens, the Chart toolbar appears, the Data menu is no longer visible, and the workbook's Control-menu box disappears. Also, when you select the chart, certain commands that do not apply to charting become unavailable or aren't listed on the menus, and a number of new commands for features that apply to chart formatting are added.

Installing and Starting Excel

It's easy to install Excel 5.0 for Windows—just let the Excel Setup program do it for you! All you have to do is insert the first Setup disk into your A drive (or whichever drive is appropriate for the type of disk you're using), choose Run from the Program Manager's File menu, type **A:\SETUP** in the Command Line box (or substitute another letter for A, if appropriate), and click OK. Setup takes it from there! Once installed, you can start Excel by simply double-clicking its program icon in the Program Manager.

FRUSTRATION BUSTERS!

Excel 5.0 is a comprehensive spreadsheet application that offers many new and sophisticated features. Consequently, it requires more of your computer's resources, and you may want to make a few changes to your setup to improve Excel's performance. Depending on the Excel features you are using, try one or more of the following techniques to enhance productivity:

- Close any open Excel windows you are not currently using.

- Divide large worksheets into smaller ones.

- Close other applications you are running.

- Remove any RAM drives, unless you have at least 8MB of RAM.

- Increase the amount of RAM on your computer.

- Add a Windows graphics card if your monitor's resolution is more than 800 × 600 or you are using a 256-color 1-N mode video driver.

- Make sure your Windows swap file is a permanent swap file.

- Use a disk cache such as SMARTDrive.

- Reduce the numbers in the SMARTDRV line in your AUTO-EXEC.BAT file, unless you have at least 8MB of RAM.

- Set the Desktop wallpaper to None in the Desktop dialog box, which you access from the Windows Control Panel.

What are the requirements to run Excel on my computer?

To run Excel 5.0 for Windows, your computer must meet the following minimum hardware and operating system requirements:

- The MS-DOS operating system version 3.1 or later
- One of the following versions of Windows: Microsoft Windows version 3.1 or later, Microsoft Windows for Workgroups version 3.1 or later, Microsoft Windows for Pen Computing, or Microsoft Windows NT version 3.1 or later
- A 286 or higher microprocessor
- 4MB of RAM memory
- Sufficient hard disk space to hold the Excel program files. (The amount you need depends on the installation option you select. You need approximately 6MB for a laptop installation, approximately 16MB for a typical installation, and up to 24MB for a complete installation.)
- A 3.5-inch or 5.25-inch disk drive
- An EGA or higher resolution monitor compatible with Microsoft Windows
- A Microsoft Mouse or compatible pointing device (mouse recommended)

These requirements reflect the *minimum* configuration you need to install and use Excel 5.0 for Windows; exceeding these requirements will make Excel run faster and better.

What do the options in the Microsoft Excel Setup program mean?

Excel provides three options in t Setup program that determi Excel features are installe

- The Complete/Custom option ins Microsoft Excel components. disk space Excel requires, then click the Change only those compo
- The Typical setu Data Access optio Show add-in.
- The Laptop setup optic necessary to run Microso

Why do my name and company display automatically when I use Setup?

You have installed Excel 5.0 previously. Setup writes your name and company to the Setup disk. Because this information is "hard coded" on the disk, there is no way to clear it. Excel's Setup program also adds this data to the [MS User Info] section in your WIN.INI file, just as Microsoft Office 4.0 and Word for Windows 6.0's Setup programs do.

When installing Excel, I get the message, "Disk write error on drive A:." What does this mean and how do I fix it?

Excel writes the registration information to the first Setup disk. This message displays if this disk is write-protected. To correct this problem, hold this 3.5" disk so the sliding metal part is at the bottom and you're looking at the label, then pull down the plastic write-protect tab behind the hole in the top right-hand corner. The Excel Setup program should now be able to write the registration information to the disk and complete the installation.

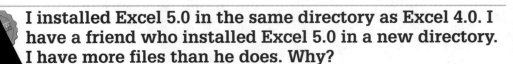

I installed Excel 5.0 in the same directory as Excel 4.0. I have a friend who installed Excel 5.0 in a new directory. I have more files than he does. Why?

There are some files that were part of Excel 4.0 but are not included in Excel 5.0, such as the Q+E program. Setup does not automatically remove these files when you upgrade to Excel 5.0. In most cases, the features and functions performed by these files are built into Excel 5.0. However, they may have new names and work somewhat differently. For example, Crosstabs are replaced by Pivot Tables in Excel 5.0.

I installed Excel 5.0 over Excel 4.0. It left some Excel 4.0 files that are no longer needed. How can I determine which files are from Excel 4.0 so I can delete them?

The date for all of the Excel 5.0 files is 12/14/93; Excel 4.0 files have an earlier date. You can use the Windows File Manager to examine the files in your Excel directory and delete those with dates prior to 12/14/93. (Keep in mind, however, that .XLS files may be your own spreadsheet files.) When you upgrade to Excel 5.0, Setup only adds and replaces files. Because it doesn't delete any previously stored files, it leaves some of your Excel 4.0 files intact.

Also, the FILELIST.TXT file on the first Excel 5.0 Setup disk indicates the three possible types of installations and the files that each one copies to your computer. Figure 2-1 shows the beginning of this file. You can compare this list to your Excel program directory; it should be safe to delete any file in your directory that does *not* appear in FILELIST.TXT.

```
=                    Notepad - FILELIST.TXT                    ▼ ≑
 File  Edit  Search  Help
 A list of files, their location and size (in bytes) installed with Microsoft ▲


 LOCAL/FLOPPY INSTALLATIONS
                                    COMPLETE
                                    or CUSTOM      TYPICAL       MINI
 \EXCEL
 cnf2ini.exe                        23667
 excel.exe                          4185600        4185600       4185
 excel5.reg                         9903           9903          9903
 filelist.txt                       12702          12702         1270
 macrofun.hlp                       936351
 mainxl.hlp                         2972069        2972069
 network.txt                        21809          21289         2128
 trans.exe                          159152
 trans123.xlm                       18930
 transmp.xlm                        17309
 vba_xl.hlp                         2044758        2044758
 xlconvmp.dll                       45600
 xlen50.olb                         229376         229376        2293
 xlhelp.dll                         13728          13728         1372
 xlintl.dll                         489456         489456        4894
 xlpss.hlp                          77332          77332         7733
 xlreadme.hlp                       28204          28204         2820
 \EXCEL\EXAMPLES
 bookst.xls                         89600          89600         8960
 sales.xls                          13824          13824
 samples.xls                        139264         139264        1392 ▼
 ◄ |                                                              ► |
```

FIGURE 2-1   FILELIST.TXT shows the files that Excel installs on your computer

What is the compliance checker that comes with Excel 5.0?

When you run Setup to install either a regular Excel upgrade or a competitive upgrade, the compliance checker first examines your computer for any signs of a previous version or a competitor's product. If it finds no evidence of either application, it displays an error message. The compliance checker only runs the first time Excel is installed. Therefore, if you are installing Excel to replace a prior version of Excel or of another competitor's spreadsheet, do not remove the other application until you run Excel's Setup program.

Tech Tip: The compliance checker does not run when you install a full version of Excel.

Once I install Excel, why do I need the Setup program?

After you install Excel 5.0 the first time, a Setup program icon appears in the Program Manager. Microsoft provides this version of Setup as an added convenience to help you maintain and customize the application. This Setup program provides three options:

- Add/Remove adds and removes optional parts of the Excel program.

- Reinstall automatically reinstalls all of the currently installed components of Excel, overwriting any corrupt files. A reinstallation does not affect any customized toolbars or overwrite your existing data.

- Remove All deletes all of the files for the modules associated with Excel 5.0. If you need to remove Excel 5.0 from your computer, use this method rather than deleting the entire Excel directory. This option is preferable both because it leaves any files that you created intact and it gets rid of *every* Excel 5.0 component, including those located in other directories.

I did a minimal installation when I first set up Excel on my computer. Do I have to perform the entire setup procedure to add the Help files?

Tech Tip: If you do not have an MS Excel Setup icon, you can start Setup by inserting the first Excel Setup disk in drive A, choosing Run from the File menu, typing **A:\SETUP** in the Command Line box, and clicking OK.

When you first installed Excel, a version of the Setup program was copied to your computer. You can use this program to selectively install the Help files or any other component of the Excel application that you did not add initially.

To install the Help files:

1. In the Program Manager, display the program group that contains your Excel icons.

2. Double-click the MS Excel Setup icon.

3. Click the Add/Remove option to display a dialog box like the one shown in Figure 2-2.

4. Select the Online Help and Lessons check box. You can also remove any components you initially installed by clearing the appropriate check box.

5. Click Continue.

6. When prompted, insert the requested Excel Setup disks.

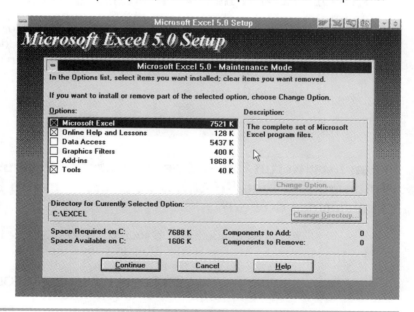

FIGURE 2-2   Setup allows you to selectively add and remove Excel components

7. Click OK when Setup finishes installing the desired components.

I saved some queries in the MSQUERY directory. Even though I removed Microsoft Query using the Setup program's Add/Remove option, the directory still exists. Is this a bug?

Setup is designed so that it only removes files it puts on the system. Therefore, the files you created and saved in this directory remain; Setup will not delete the MSQUERY directory even if it is empty. If you wish, you can use the Windows File Manager to remove the directory.

Excel added the line C:\DOS\SHARE.EXE /l:500 /f:5100 to my AUTOEXEC.BAT file. Do I need this line and, if so, why?

You need this line to run Excel 5.0. It is required for OLE 2.0 support. OLE 2.0 allows in-place editing of embedded objects. Because both the source application and Excel can use the embedded object at the same time, they must be able to share the file that contains it.

When I try to run Excel, I get this error: "You must exit Windows and load SHARE.EXE in order to run Microsoft Excel." What do I do?

You need to add a line to your AUTOEXEC.BAT file to load SHARE.EXE. The SHARE program allows more than one program to access the same file at a time.

Follow these steps to examine and edit your AUTOEXEC.BAT file:

1. Choose <u>R</u>un from the Program Manager's <u>F</u>ile menu.

2. Type **SYSEDIT** in the Command Line box and click OK.

3. When the System Configuration Editor opens, move to the window that displays your AUTOEXEC.BAT file, if necessary.

4. Check the line that loads SHARE.EXE to make sure that it is loaded using the correct settings. The line should read:

```
C:\DOS\SHARE.EXE /L:500 /F:5100
```

5. Edit or add this line, as necessary.

Tech Note: If your DOS files are located in a directory other than C:\DOS, substitute a different path for C:\DOS.

6. Save your edited AUTOEXEC.BAT file by choosing Save from the File menu.

7. Exit Windows, reboot your computer, start Windows, and open Excel.

When I set up Excel, I get the message "Cannot find SHARE.EXE." I loaded SHARE.EXE in my AUTOEXEC.BAT file. What is going wrong?

Examine the Path statement in your AUTOEXEC.BAT. It should list the directory that contains the DOS files, including the drive letter. For example, this path is correct:

```
PATH=C:\WINDOWS;C:\DOS;C:\
```

but this one would cause problems:

```
PATH=C:\WINDOWS;\DOS;C:\
```

When I open Excel, I get an error that says, "Cannot find Opennow, which has been assigned to run each time [book1.xlw]Sheet2 is opened. Continuing could cause errors. Cancel opening [book1.xlw]Sheet2?" I know the macro Opennow is there, so how do I fix this problem?

There are two reasons why this error message may appear:

- Excel cannot find the macro, as the error message states.
- Excel locates the macro but it contains a mistake, such as a syntax error.

To resolve this problem, first make sure the macro is located in the proper place by opening the workbook containing the macro and finding the macro in the workbook. Assuming that you have found the macro, it probably has an error. To find the error:

1. Choose Macro from the Tools menu.
2. Select the macro that produced the error in the Run list box. In this case, you would select Opennow.
3. Click OK.

Excel tries to run the macro and displays an error message that describes the specific problem, which will make it easier for you to debug the macro.

When I try to open Excel 5.0, I get the message "An Error Occurred Initializing VBA Libraries." Then it displays, "The timer driver is not installed." Why can't I open Excel 5.0?

To start Excel, there are three files that must be stored in your WINDOWS\SYSTEM directory: TIMER.DRV, MMSYSTEM.DLL, and VTDAPI.386. In addition, these files must appear in the proper place in your SYSTEM.INI file, which is located in your Windows program directory.

To check your SYSTEM.INI file:

1. Choose Run from the Program Manager's File menu.

2. Type **SYSEDIT** in the <u>C</u>ommand Line box and click OK.

3. When the System Configuration Editor opens, move to the window that displays your SYSTEM.INI file.

4. Double-check that the following line appears in the [boot] section; if not, add it:

```
drivers=mmsystem.dll
```

You may also need to specify other drivers for Windows, such as drivers=mmsystem.dll pen penwindows.

5. Move to the [drivers] section and make sure it lists this statement:

```
timer=timer.drv
```

6. Check whether the [386Enh] section includes this line:

```
device=vtdapi.386
```

7. Choose E<u>x</u>it from the System Configuration Editor's <u>F</u>ile menu.

8. Click <u>Y</u>es if you are prompted about saving the SYSTEM.INI file.

If you find the appropriate lines in the proper places in your SYSTEM.INI, use the File Manager to check whether TIMER.DRV, MMSYSTEM.DLL, and VTDAPI.386 are all stored in the SYSTEM subdirectory of the Windows program directory. If one is missing, expand it from your Windows 3.1 Setup disks. If all three appear, expand them all again from the Windows disks.

I just installed Excel 5.0 over Excel 4.0. Now, whenever I try to open Excel, it begins to open and then just hangs. Why?

More than likely, there are macros in your XLSTART subdirectory. The Excel 5.0 Setup program will not overwrite these files. Many of these macros were probably placed there by third-party applications, such as fax or sound software. These macros are compatible with Excel 4.0, but not Excel 5.0. Use the File Manager to delete any macro (.XLA) files in your EXCEL\XLSTART directory or move them to another location. Then try to open Excel 5.0 again.

If this doesn't solve the problem, use Notepad to open the EXCEL5.INI file in your Windows program directory. Search for a line that reads as follows:

```
AltStartUp=
```

This setting should either be missing or should have nothing after the = sign. If this setting indicates a directory after the = sign, delete the directory and resave the file. Now you can start Excel.

Why does Excel 5.0 take so much longer to load than Excel 4.0?

Excel 5.0 offers so many enhancements and additional capabilities that its program files are significantly larger than those for Excel 4.0. Accordingly, it takes longer for your computer to load these files into memory.

Does Excel 5.0 offer any startup options?

Yes. Excel provides several startup options that you can use to specify how the application runs, as shown in the following table.

Startup Option	Effect
filename	Opens the specified Excel file once the application is loaded; you must include the path information if the file is not in the default data directory
/r *filename*	Opens the specified Excel file as read-only so you cannot save it again with the same filename
/p *directory*	Sets the directory in which Excel looks for your data files
/e	Starts Excel without opening an empty workbook

To use these options once:

1. Choose Run from the Program Manager's File menu.
2. Type **C:\EXCEL\EXCEL** followed by a space and the desired startup options in the Command Line box.
3. Click OK.

If you want to use one or more startup options on a regular basis:

1. Click the Excel program icon in the appropriate window in the Program Manager to select it.
2. Choose Properties from the File menu or press ALT+ENTER.
3. Add the startup option(s) to the end of the entry in the Command Line box.
4. Click OK.

I have Office 4.0 with the Microsoft Office Manager toolbar. How can I get the toolbar to start my new version of Excel instead of the old one?

Excel Startup button

Since Microsoft Office 4.0 included Excel 4.0, the Excel button on the Microsoft Office Manager toolbar tries to start Excel 4.0. To change the button's function, start Excel 5.0 from the Program Manager. With Excel running, click the Microsoft Excel button on the Microsoft Office Manager toolbar—it's the second one from the left, as shown in the illustration. This procedure "retrains" the toolbar button so that it will launch Excel 5.0 the next time you click it.

I accidentally deleted the Excel 5.0 icon in the Windows Program Manager. How do I get it back?

Microsoft
Excel

You can recreate the Excel icon, shown to the left, by following these steps:

1. Choose New from the Program Manager's File menu.

2. Select Program Item and click OK.

3. Move the insertion point to the Command Line box and click the Browse button.

4. Switch to the EXCEL directory in the Browse dialog box, select the EXCEL.EXE file, and click OK.
   The Program Item Properties dialog box redisplays, and an entry such as C:\EXCEL\EXCEL.EXE appears in the Command Line box.

5. Type a name for the icon, such as **Microsoft Excel 5.0**, in the Description box.

6. Enter the directory in which your data files are stored in the Working Directory box.

7. Click OK.

Tech Tip: You can also add the Excel program icon by opening the File Manager and dragging the EXCEL.EXE file to the appropriate program group window in the Program Manager.

Can I tell Excel to automatically open a particular workbook whenever I start it?

There are several ways to set up Excel so that it opens a specified workbook every time you launch the application:

- You can add the filename startup option to the end of the Command Line box in the Program Items Property dialog box.

- You can move the workbook to the EXCEL\XLSTART subdirectory. If you want to open multiple workbooks, save several as a workgroup and store the workgroup in XLSTART.

- Create separate Excel program icons that open different workbooks.

To create separate Excel icons, first create several Excel program icons by following the procedure outlined in the previous question. Then select each one in turn and perform these steps to modify its properties:

1. Select one of the Excel program icons you created in the Program Manager.

2. Choose <u>P</u>roperties from the Program Manager's <u>F</u>ile menu, or press ALT+ENTER.

3. Enter a space at the end of the entry in the Command Line box and then type the path and filename of the document you want to open automatically.
   For example, you might add **D:\DATA\BUDGET.DOC** so that the entry reads C:\EXCEL\EXCEL.EXE D:\DATA \BUDGET.DOC.

4. Click OK to save the properties.

Now whenever you double-click a particular Excel icon, it automatically displays the workbook you specified.

Tech Tip: You can also add these additional icons by simply dragging each filename (for example, BUDGET.DOC) from the File Manager window into the Program Manager.

When I try to load Excel 5.0, I get a message that there isn't enough space on the destination drive. I know that I have enough free space, so why can't I start Excel?

If DOS 6.0's Undelete Protection was active when you deleted files in the past, all of the space is "available" but protected; this is also a problem with other undelete utilities. Undelete protection reserves the disk space previously used by the deleted files in case you change your mind and want to undelete them. To see the *actual* amount of available disk space, type **CHKDSK** at the DOS prompt.
   To make this protected disk space available:

1. Start the File Manager.

2. Choose the Undelete command from the File menu in the File Manager to open the Microsoft Undelete for Windows utility.

3. Choose Purge Delete Sentry File from the File menu to free this space for installation.

4. Choose Exit from the File menu to leave Microsoft Undelete.

5. Choose Exit from the File menu to leave the File Manager.

6. Start Excel.

How do I install Microsoft Excel for Windows on a network server?

The NETWORK.TXT file on Setup Disk 1 provides instructions for setting up Excel on a network. You can view and print this file by following these steps:

1. Switch to the Accessories group in the Program Manager.

2. Start Notepad.

3. Choose Open from the File menu.

4. Switch to the drive that contains your Microsoft Excel 5.0 Setup disk and select the NETWORK.TXT file.

5. Click OK.

6. Choose Word Wrap from the Edit menu to make the text easier to read.

7. Choose Print from the File menu to print the file.

8. Choose Exit from the File menu to close the NETWORK.TXT file and quit Notepad.

I performed a network installation of Office 4.0, which contained Excel 4.0, using SETUP /a. How can I upgrade to Excel 5.0?

Use the SETUP /a command to install Excel 5.0 on the network server in a directory other than the directory containing Microsoft Office. (If you install the new version to the same directory as the one that came with Microsoft Office, you will overwrite the Office setup file.) You can then perform the Excel workstation installations.

Tech Tip: Microsoft Office 4.2 includes Excel 5.0, so if you have Office 4.2 you won't need to perform this upgrade.

When I installed Excel on a network, Setup didn't give me a chance to input my name. Why?

When you use the SETUP /a command to perform a server installation of Excel, you are prompted to enter your company's name. When you install Excel on the separate workstations, it asks you to enter the user's name. Separating these two pieces of user information allows individuals to enter their names on their own copies of Excel.

Workbooks

Excel 5.0 offers "new and improved" workbooks that make it even easier to organize your data. For starters, all Excel 5.0 data files are workbooks and contain multiple worksheets, greatly increasing the amount of related information you can store together. If you have used previous versions of Excel, take a moment to review the new features provided in Excel 5.0 to help you work with your data more effectively.

FRUSTRATION BUSTERS!

Here are just a few of the many new features provided in Excel 5.0 workbooks:

- You can enter and edit data directly in a cell as well as in the formula bar.

- You can name a range by simply selecting it and then typing an entry in the *name box* on the left end of the formula bar.

- You can not only select and name three-dimensional ranges but reference them in formulas.

- You can sum values in your worksheet by moving to the cell in which you want the total to appear and clicking the AutoSum button.

- You can use Full Screen view to get a better look at your worksheets. Full Screen view removes the scroll bar, title bar, formula bar, toolbars, status bar, and all other screen elements to provide more room to display your data.

- You can save the identity and arrangement of the open workbooks in a *workspace file*. When you reopen the file, it displays the same workbooks in exactly the same way they appeared when you saved the file. This feature is helpful when you work on projects that involve numerous workbooks.

- You can easily customize toolbars to remove buttons for features you rarely use and add ones for those you use frequently. You can even create new toolbars! You can also edit the images that appear on toolbar buttons so they are more meaningful to you.

- You not only can save workbooks as templates to use as the basis for new files, but you can create autotemplates. *Autotemplates* are templates that have specific names and are stored in the startup directory, which is usually EXCEL\XLSTART. Excel automatically uses these templates whenever you create a new sheet or workbook. Excel uses BOOK.XLT for new workbooks, SHEET.XLT for new worksheets, CHART.XLT for new charts, MACRO.XLT for new Excel 4.0 macro sheets, and DIALOG.XLT for new dialog sheets.

- Excel 5.0 includes a new Find File feature that can help you locate workbook files even if you have forgotten their names. You can use Find File to search for files and then delete, rename, copy, or open them. Find File's preview feature displays the upper-left corner of the active sheet in a workbook file so that you know that you are working with the correct one.

- You can add auditor arrows to your workbook to help you find errors in your models. The auditor arrows can show which cells are referenced in a specific formula or which formulas reference a particular cell.

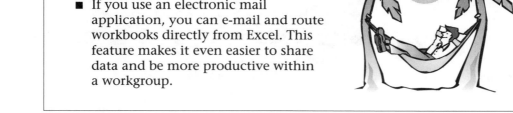

- If you use an electronic mail application, you can e-mail and route workbooks directly from Excel. This feature makes it even easier to share data and be more productive within a workgroup.

I opened a new workbook and the sheets are named Sheet1, Sheet2, and so on. How do I change the names?

You can assign a name to a sheet within an Excel 5.0 workbook in any of three ways:

- Double-click the tab of the sheet you want to rename to open the Rename Sheet dialog box. Type the desired name in the Name box and click OK.

- Click the sheet tab with the right mouse button and choose Rename from the shortcut menu. Enter the new name and click OK.

- Choose Sheet from the Format menu, and then choose Rename. In the Rename Sheet dialog box, enter the name and click OK.

When you copy Excel 4.0 worksheets to a new Excel 5.0 workbook, the sheet tabs reflect the names of the original files, as shown in Figure 3-1.

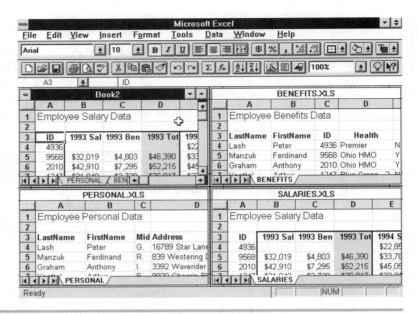

FIGURE 3-1   Excel 4.0 worksheets copied to an Excel 5.0 workbook

When I open my old Excel 4.0 worksheets in Excel 5.0, they appear as workbooks with only one worksheet. Is there any way to consolidate these workbooks?

Follow these steps to combine your single sheet workbooks into a multiple page one:

1. Open all of the workbooks.

2. Choose <u>A</u>rrange from the <u>W</u>indows menu.

3. Select the <u>T</u>iled option button and click OK so you can see all of your workbooks on the screen at one time.

4. One by one, move each sheet to the destination workbook. You move a sheet from one workbook to another by dragging the sheet's tab to the new location.

5. Repeat step 4 as necessary to move each additional sheet to the destination workbook.

6. Save the destination workbook with an appropriate name.

Tech Tip: If you press CTRL while you drag the sheet tab, you copy the sheet to the other workbook instead of moving it. A copy remains in the original workbook.

Another way to move or copy sheets is to right-click the sheet tab and then select the appropriate command from the shortcut menu. Enter the location and name of the workbook to which you want to copy or move the sheet.

If you move a sheet to a workbook that already contains a sheet with the same name, Excel adds a number to the new sheet to distinguish it, such as *Name (2)*. In this case, you may want to assign unique names to the worksheets after you have all of them in the same workbook.

Tech Tip: Another method for moving and copying sheets from one workbook to another is described in the question "How do I move sheets within a workbook?," which appears later in this chapter.

How can I see more than one sheet at a time?

Excel lets you open the workbook in more than one window and display a different sheet in each. Similarly, you can also display different areas of the same sheet at the same time.

To display multiple windows:

1. Choose <u>N</u>ew Window from the <u>W</u>indow menu. Excel opens a second window with the same workbook. The new window's title bar displays the same filename followed by :2.

2. Choose <u>A</u>rrange from the <u>W</u>indow menu, select the <u>T</u>iled option button, and click OK.

Both copies of the workbook are displayed in the Excel application window at the same time, as shown in Figure 3-2.

You can activate either window by clicking it and then moving to whichever part of the workbook you want to display. This technique lets you look at widely separated data in the same workbook at the same time.

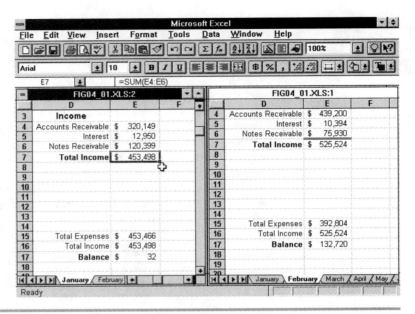

FIGURE 3-2 You can display multiple copies of a single workbook

---

Can I prevent Excel from prompting me for summary info whenever I save a workbook for the first time?

You can easily disable the automatic prompt for summary information by following these steps:

1. Choose Options from the Tools menu.

2. Click the General tab.

3. Clear the Prompt for Summary Info check box.

4. Click OK.

Tech Tip: If you do not save summary information, you cannot preview the workbook by using the Find File command on the File menu.

How many sheets can I have in a workbook?

Excel does not inherently limit the total number of sheets in a given workbook; the maximum is determined by the amount of available memory on your system. However, the maximum number of sheets you can place in a new workbook is 255.

How do I move sheets within a workbook?

Excel provides several methods for moving sheets within a workbook.

To move a sheet with the mouse:

1. Click the tab of the sheet you want to move.

2. Drag the sheet to the new location.

As you drag the sheet, an upside down triangle appears just above the sheet tabs to indicate where the sheet will appear if you release the mouse button:

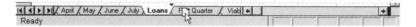

To change a sheet's position by using the keyboard:

1. Choose <u>M</u>ove or Copy Sheet from the <u>E</u>dit menu to display the Move or Copy dialog box. (You can also display this dialog box by clicking the sheet tab with the right mouse button and choosing Move or Copy from the shortcut menu.)

2. Highlight the sheet before which you want to place the selected one in the <u>B</u>efore Sheet list box.

3. If you wanted to copy the sheet instead of moving it, select the <u>C</u>reate a Copy check box.

4. Click OK to move or copy the sheet to the position you specified.

Tech Tip: You can also use this method to move or copy a worksheet to another open workbook. Simply select the name of the workbook to which you want to move or copy the sheet in the <u>T</u>o Book drop-down list box.

When you move a sheet, it keeps the same name. Therefore, if you move Sheet4 before Sheet2, your sheet tabs will be in this order: Sheet1, Sheet4, Sheet2, and so on. If you move numbered sheets, you may want to rename them.

When I pressed DEL in Excel 4.0, I got to choose what I wanted to delete; in Excel 5.0, it just deletes my data. Is this feature gone?

This feature still exists, but only when you delete information using the menus. By default, Excel 5.0 deletes formulas and data when you press DEL, but not formatting or notes. If you choose Clear from the Edit menu, however, you can choose to delete everything or just the formats, contents, or notes. This feature was changed to make deleting faster, because most of the times you press DEL, you want to clear only the contents of the cell.

Is there an easy way to provide documentation in complex worksheets?

Excel 5.0 lets you add *cell notes*, which make it easy to document your work. Cell notes can be either sound or text. They are attached to the individual cells, but are not actually part of their contents. In a sense, cell notes are like the removable "sticky" notes you add to printed documents—they are attached to but separate from the actual work.

To attach a note to a cell:

1. Move to the cell to which you want to attach the note.

2. Choose Note from the Insert menu to open the Cell Note dialog box. Alternatively, press SHIFT+F2 or click the Attach Note button in the Auditing toolbar, as shown here:

The current cell's address appears in the Cell box.

3. Type the text you want to attach to the cell in the Text Note box, or click either Import or Record to attach a sound note.

4. Click OK to attach the note to the cell.

Tech Tip: If you frequently add notes to cells, you may want to add the Attach Note button to the Standard or Formatting toolbar.

A red dot appears in the upper-right corner of the cell to indicate that a note is attached, as shown here:

You can print these cell notes by following the instructions given in the question "How do I print cell notes?," later in this chapter.

If you want to display your documentation directly in the worksheet, you can use *text boxes* instead of cell notes. You add a text box by clicking the Text Box button on either the Standard or Drawing toolbar, and dragging the mouse across the worksheet to create the box itself. You then type the text for the note right in the box. Because a text box is a drawing object, it appears "on top" of the worksheet, as you can see here:

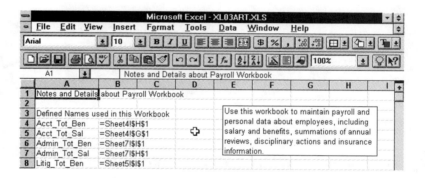

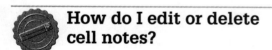 **How do I edit or delete cell notes?**

At times, you may find you want to edit or remove cell notes entirely. Because they are not part of the cells' normal contents, you modify and delete cell notes differently than data.

To edit a cell note:

1. Open the Note dialog box by selecting <u>N</u>ote from the <u>I</u>nsert menu, pressing SHIFT+F2, or clicking the Attach Note button.

2. Edit the text in the <u>T</u>ext Note box and click OK.

Tech Tip: You cannot edit a sound note. You must either re-record the note or edit the sound clip using the application with which you created it. You then re-attach the note to the cell.

To delete a cell note:

1. Select the cell containing the note.

2. Choose Clear from the <u>E</u>dit menu, and then choose <u>N</u>otes.

Tech Tip: You can also delete a note by opening the Cell Note dialog box, as described above, selecting the note to delete in the <u>N</u>otes in Sheet list box, and clicking <u>D</u>elete.

How can I see the notes I have added?

You can view the notes you have added to a particular worksheet by opening either the Cell Note dialog box or an Info window.

To open the Cell Note dialog box:

1. Press SHIFT+F2 or choose <u>N</u>ote from the <u>I</u>nsert menu.

2. Select the cell whose note you want to see in the <u>N</u>otes in Sheet box.

The <u>T</u>ext Note box displays the contents of the note for the selected cell, as shown here:

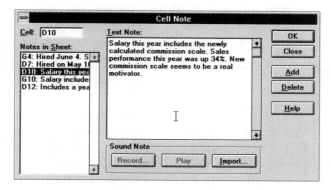

3. When you have finished reviewing the note, either select another cell whose note you want to see or click Close.

An Info window displays a variety of information about a particular cell, including any of the following, if they exist: a note, formatting, its formula, and an assigned name. Figure 3-3 shows an Info window.

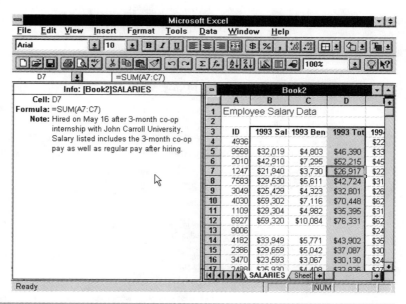

FIGURE 3-3   Info window shows notes and other information about the current cell

To display an Info window:

1. Choose <u>O</u>ptions from the <u>T</u>ools menu.
2. Click the View tab.
3. Select the Info <u>W</u>indow check box.
4. Click OK.

Alternatively, you can display the Info window by clicking the Info Window button on the Auditing toolbar.

You can add and remove information to and from the Info window by choosing items from the <u>I</u>nfo menu that appears when the Info window is active.

How do I print cell notes?

You can print cell notes when you print the cells to which they're attached or you can print them separately from the Info window. To print the notes along with the cells:

1. In the worksheet, select the cells you want to print.
2. Choose <u>P</u>rint from the <u>F</u>ile menu.
3. Click Page Set<u>u</u>p.
4. Click the Sheet tab.
5. Select the <u>N</u>otes check box in the Print section.
6. Click OK twice to print the cells with their notes.

A page that contains just the notes prints after the last page of the print area. A preview of such a page appears here:

SALARIES

Note: Hired June 4. Salary includes pay for three-month co-op internship with Case Western Reserve University - Accounting Dept.

Note: Hired on May 16 after 3-month co-op internship with John Carroll University. Salary listed includes the 3-month co-op pay as well as regular pay after hiring.

Note: Salary this year includes the newly calculated commission scale. Sales performance this year was up 34%. New commission scale seems to be a real motivator.

As you can see, the printed notes do not indicate the cells to which they're attached.

You can print the contents of the Info window, shown in Figure 3-3, including any note, by choosing Print from the File menu and clicking OK. To print the contents of multiple cells, simply select them in the worksheet before switching to the Info window.

Tech Tip: You can quickly select all the cells in a sheet that have notes attached to them by choosing Go To from the Edit menu, clicking Special, selecting the Notes option button, and clicking OK. Alternatively, you can use the CTRL+SHIFT+? shortcut key.

Is there a quick way to switch to another sheet in a workbook?

Excel 5.0 offers a keyboard shortcut for switching among the sheets in a single workbook. To switch from the current sheet to the next one, press CTRL+PGDN. To switch from the current sheet to the previous one, press CTRL+PGUP.

Tech Tip: You can also simply click the tab of the sheet to which you want to switch.

When I try to replace a word such as "go," Excel replaces the letters "go" in words like "gone" and "good" as well. What can I do to prevent this?

When you use this feature, Excel replaces every occurrence of the letters "g" and "o" when they appear together. Therefore, if a cell contains this combination, even as part of another word, Excel substitutes the replacement text. However, you can tell Excel to only recognize and replace the designated text if it constitutes the entire contents of the cell. For example, you could tell Excel to replace "go" when it is the only entry in the cell, but not if the cell contains other data. In this case, Excel would neither find nor replace entries such as "gone" because additional characters exist in the cell.

To replace text only if it is the entire contents of a cell:

1. Choose Replace from the Edit menu.

2. Type the appropriate entries in the Find what and Replace with boxes.

3. Select the Find Entire Cells Only check box and proceed as usual.

Tech Tip: Because the text you are looking for with the Find Entire Cells Only check box selected must be the entire contents of a cell, you could not tell Excel to use this feature to replace "go" with the word "goes" in a phrase such as "go to the bank." To do this, you would search for "go" without this check box selected, and then click Replace rather than Replace All when Excel finds this particular cell.

My password doesn't work, even though I've double-checked it and I'm definitely typing it correctly. Why?

Passwords in Excel are case-sensitive. More than likely, you had CAPS LOCK on the opposite setting when you originally entered the password. If CAPS LOCK is currently on, turn it off; if it's off, turn it on. Then, try entering the password again. To eliminate this problem in the future, make a practice of entering passwords in either all uppercase or all lowercase.

My Excel 4.0 workbook had unbound sheets that brought information into a bound sheet. When I open it in Excel 5.0, the unbound sheets aren't listed with the bound sheet's tab, but the data is accurate. Where are those sheets?

Excel 5.0 does not use bound or unbound sheets; instead, a worksheet is always stored in its entirety in a workbook. The Excel 5.0 equivalent of unbound sheets are separate files that are linked to the sheet in your workbook. To see the links and the names of the files to which they connect, choose Links from the

Edit menu. If you open one of the linked files, it appears as a one-sheet workbook.

You can keep these links to other files, or you can combine all these sheets into one workbook by moving the "unbound" sheets from the new workbooks to the original.

Tech Tip: See the question "When I open my old Excel 4.0 worksheets in Excel 5.0, they appear as workbooks with only one worksheet. Is there any way to consolidate these workbooks?," earlier in this chapter, for information about moving worksheets from one workbook to another.

My file is large even though I have only a few rows and columns of data in the worksheet. Why?

Each cell you use in a worksheet occupies memory—about 8 bytes per cell. Sometimes, Excel considers some of the blank rows and columns as part of your worksheet and saves them, even though they are blank. To conserve memory, you can delete these blank rows and columns from the file.

To delete blank cells:

1. Move to the row immediately below the last row in your worksheet that contains data.

2. Select all the remaining rows in the sheet by pressing SHIFT+END+DOWN ARROW.

3. Choose Clear from the Edit menu and Select All to clear the selected rows.

4. Move to the column to the right of the last column of data in your worksheet.

5. Select all the remaining columns in the sheet by pressing SHIFT+END+RIGHT ARROW.

6. Choose Clear from the Edit menu and Select All to delete the contents of the selected columns.

7. Choose Save from the File menu. Excel reduces your file size accordingly.

My worksheet displays arrows between a couple of cells and I can't get rid of them. When I try to select an arrow, nothing happens except sometimes the cell at the end of the arrow becomes active. What can I do?

You are describing an *auditing arrow*, like those shown in Figure 3-4. You can add auditing arrows to trace the cells to which a specific formula refers or to identify the formulas that refer to a specific cell. These auditing arrows can be particularly useful in helping you determine the source of any errors in your worksheet. To remove the arrows, choose <u>A</u>uditing from the <u>T</u>ools menu, and then choose Remove <u>A</u>ll Arrows. If the Auditing toolbar is displayed, you can also click the Remove All Arrows button, shown here:

		Car	1st Bank-1	1st Bank-2	XYZ Loan	Totals
1	*Personal Debt Repayment Plan*					
2						
3		Car	1st Bank-1	1st Bank-2	XYZ Loan	Totals
4	9-Feb-95	$12,349	$1,203	$5,638	$2,102	$21,292
5	Rate	0.33%	0.83%	0.67%	0.81%	
6	Payment	$240	$80	$120	$60	$500
7	Final Date	Oct-99	Jun-96	Oct-99	Jul-98	
8	1-Jul-96	$8,877		$4,160	$1,323	
9	Payment	$240		$120	$140	$500
10	Final Date	Sep-99		Jul-99	Apr-97	
11	1-May-97	$6,741		$3,209		
12	Payment	$250		$250		$500
13	Final Date	Aug-99		May-98		
14	1-Jun-98	$4,431				
15	Payment	$500				$500
16	Final Date	Feb-99				
17						

Microsoft Excel - FIG04_02.XLS

<u>F</u>ile   <u>E</u>dit   <u>V</u>iew   <u>I</u>nsert   F<u>o</u>rmat   <u>T</u>ools   <u>D</u>ata   <u>W</u>indow   <u>H</u>elp

D11   =FV(D5,(MONTH($A$11)-MONTH($A$8))+((YEAR($A$11)-YEAR($A$8))*12), D9,-D8)

LOANS

Ready

FIGURE 3-4   Auditing arrows help you track where errors might appear in a formula

Can I hide a worksheet?

Yes. With Excel, you can hide or display sheets in your workbook. You may want to hide sheets in your workbook that contain sensitive material. For example, in a workbook used to compute expenses, you might hide the sheet that contains the payroll data and show the cumulative totals on another sheet to make it harder for people walking by to see the confidential information.

To hide a sheet:

1. Move to the sheet you want to hide.
2. Choose Sheet from the Format menu.
3. Choose Hide.

To redisplay a hidden sheet:

1. Choose Sheet from the Format menu.
2. Choose Unhide.
3. Select the sheet that you want to display again in the Unhide Sheet list box and click OK.

What is the box on the left side of my formula bar?

The box on the left side of the formula bar is the *name box*, as shown below. It displays the name of the current cell or range, if one exists; otherwise, it displays the current cell's reference. You can also use it to quickly assign names to ranges and move to named ranges.

Name box   *Formula box*

To use the name box to define a new range name in your worksheet:

1. Select the new range.
2. Enter a name for this range in the name box to define it.

Tech Tip: Any names you define with the name box are automatically global names unless you explicitly make them local names, as described later in this chapter.

To use the name box to move to a named range:

1. Click the down arrow next to the name box to display a list of all the defined names in your worksheet.

2. Select a name from this list to go to that range, or type a name in the name box.

Can I delete a defined name using the name box in the formula bar?

No, you cannot delete a defined name using the name box at the left-hand side of the formula bar. To delete a defined name, choose Name from the Insert menu and then choose Define, or press CTRL+F3. Select the name you want to remove and choose Delete.

What's the difference between local and global names and how do I define them?

Names, whether local or global, are assigned to cells or ranges of cells in a worksheet. You can use them in formulas or functions to refer to the cells to which they apply. Using names can make formulas easier to understand. For example, you might refer to Results instead of A1:X1203 in a formula.

The difference between local and global names is where you can use them. *Local names* can only be used in the sheet in which they are defined; *global names*, on the other hand, are available to all the sheets in the workbook. Most likely, your workbooks already include one or more local names. For example, the area that Excel prints when you select Print from the File menu is defined with the local name Print_Area.

Suppose you had twelve sheets in a workbook, each one of which calculated the total expenses and income for a particular month. You could use the same local name on each of the twelve sheets for the cell that contains the total benefits expenditures. To total these expenditures on the last sheet, you would need to reference each sheet with an exclamation point separator followed by the defined name. For example, Sheet1!Expenditures refers to the name Expenditures on Sheet1.

To define a local name:

1. Move to the cell or select the range of cells you want to name.

2. Choose Name from the Insert menu, and then choose Define. You can also press the CTRL+F3 shortcut keys.

3. In the Names in Workbook box, type **Sheet1!Test**, assuming that you want to use Test as a local name for Sheet1.

4. Click OK.

To define a global name:

1. Choose Name from the Insert menu, and then choose Define. You can also press the CTRL+F3 shortcut keys.

2. Type a name, such as **Test**, in the Names in Workbook box without a sheet reference.

3. Click OK.

Tech Tip: When you name a range or cell with the name box in the formula bar, you can make the name a local name by typing the sheet name and an exclamation point before the name.

Can I select only the blank cells in a range of a worksheet?

Yes, Excel 5.0 lets you select only the cells within a range that are blank. To do so:

1. Select the range.
   If you do not preselect a range, Excel will select all the blank cells on the sheet from A1 to the last active cell, which is the one Excel moves to when you press CTRL+END.

2. Choose Go To from the Edit menu or press F5.

3. Choose Special.

4. Choose the Blanks option button and click OK.

Is there an easy way to make a sheet into its own workbook?

Excel offers a shortcut for making a sheet into its own workbook file. To do so with the mouse, first arrange your Excel window so that part of it does not show a workbook, such as by tiling the windows or reducing the size of the workbook. Then drag the sheet's tab to the area of the Excel application window that is not part of a workbook. Excel automatically converts the sheet to a single-sheet workbook. You can now save this workbook just as you would any other file.

To create a new workbook from a single sheet by using the keyboard:

1. Select the sheet.
2. Choose <u>M</u>ove or Copy Sheet from the <u>E</u>dit menu.
3. Select (new book) in the <u>T</u>o Book drop-down list box.
4. To copy the sheet instead of moving it, select the <u>C</u>reate a Copy check box.
5. Click OK to move or copy the sheet to a new workbook.

Tech Tip: If you simply drag the sheet to create a new workbook, Excel deletes it from the original workbook. If you want to keep the sheet in the original workbook as well as create a copy in a separate file, press CTRL while dragging it.

Can I select the same range of cells on several different sheets?

Excel 5.0 lets you select three-dimensional ranges. To do so:

1. Select the range on the first sheet.
2. Press CTRL while clicking the tabs of the other sheets on which you want to select this same range. You can also press SHIFT and click the tab of the last sheet to select all of the sheets in between.

Tech Tip: You can also group the sheets first and then select the cells.

For example, you can select the range B2:C9 on the first sheet in your workbook, press CTRL, and click the tabs of the next four sheets to select the range on all five sheets. (You could also press

SHIFT and click the tab of the fifth sheet.) You can now format them as a group, if desired.

Can I select cells that aren't next to each other as part of the same range?

Yes. In Excel 5.0 you can create *nonadjacent ranges*, which consist of single cells or ranges that are not next to each other. To select a nonadjacent range:

1. Select the first cell or range of adjacent cells.

2. Press CTRL while you select the other cells or ranges of adjacent cells that you want to include in the range.

Figure 3-5 shows a selected nonadjacent range. You might refer to these cells collectively in a formula or format them all at once.

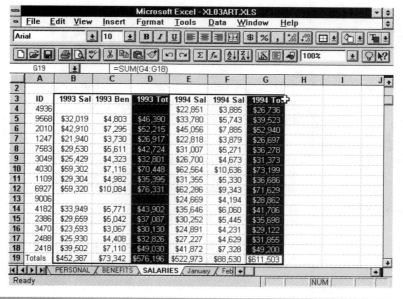

FIGURE 3-5   A selected nonadjacent range

Is there a quick way to copy entries in my sheet?

Excel offers several shortcuts for duplicating an entry or other object in your sheet. You can use the Clipboard or you can drag the entries.

To copy your data with the Clipboard:

1. Select the range you want to copy.

2. Click the range with the right mouse button to display the shortcut menu.

3. Choose Copy to copy the range to the Clipboard.

4. Move to where you want the copy to appear.

5. Press ENTER, right-click the cell, and choose Paste from the shortcut menu; or choose <u>P</u>aste from the <u>E</u>dit menu to paste the Clipboard contents in the worksheet.

Alternatively, you can use the Copy and Paste buttons on the Standard toolbar, as shown here, to copy a range:

Copy   *Paste*

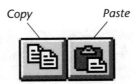

You simply select the range, click the Copy button, move to the place you want the copy to appear, and then click the Paste button.

Tech Tip: You can also press CTRL+C to copy to the Clipboard, CTRL+X to cut to the Clipboard, and CTRL+P to paste from the Clipboard.

To copy data by dragging it:

1. Select the range you want to copy.

2. Point to the border of the range so that the mouse pointer becomes an arrow.

3. Press the right mouse button and drag the range to a new location.

Excel displays an outline of the range as you drag it, as shown here:

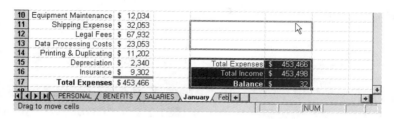

4. Release the mouse when the outline appears where you want to place the entries.

5. Choose Copy from the shortcut menu that displays.
   This menu also includes commands for moving the range, copying formats, copying values, or shifting the existing entries down or to the right.

If you have used Microsoft Word 2.0 or 6.0, you may be familiar with their *drag-and-drop* feature. Drag-and-drop also works in Excel. The drag-and-drop feature works just like dragging except that you use the left mouse button instead of the right one and no shortcut menu appears. Unlike Word, you must point to the border when you drag the range rather than its contents. If you want to copy the entries, hold down CTRL while you drag the border of the range to a new location.

Is there a shortcut for selecting an entire column without a mouse?

To select an entire column at once, move to any cell in the column and press CTRL+SPACEBAR.
   Similarly, you can select an entire row with SHIFT+SPACEBAR or the entire worksheet with CTRL+SHIFT+SPACEBAR.

Is there a shortcut for inserting cells in my sheet?

To quickly insert cells:

1. Move to a cell next to which you want to insert new cells.
2. Press CTRL+SHIFT++ (plus sign) to open the Insert dialog box.

3. Select the appropriate option button to indicate where you want to insert the cells.

4. Click OK.

Tech Tip: To quickly delete cells, columns, or rows, press CTRL+ – (minus sign) to display the Delete dialog box.

In Excel 4.0, I chose Select Special from the Formula menu to select cells containing constants. Can I still do this in Excel 5.0?

Yes. This capability still exists in Excel 5.0—you just need to use a different command.

1. Choose Go To from the Edit menu.

2. Click Special.

3. Select the Constants option button and click OK.

How do I edit links in Excel 5.0?

You can edit a link to change the file to which it refers; you can also edit a link to update it so that your worksheet contains the most recent data.

To edit a link:

1. Choose Links from the Edit menu to display the Links dialog box.

2. Select the link you want to edit in the Source File list box.

3. If you want to redirect the link to a different file, click Change Source to display the Change Links dialog box. If you want to retrieve the current data, click Update Now.
   You can also click Open to open the source document or select either Manual or Automatic to determine how Excel updates the link.

4. Click OK when you have finished to return to your worksheet.

Tech Tip: The Links dialog box lists all the links that the current workbook has to other files, including non-Excel documents. You can create these links by including formulas or by embedding objects.

Is there a way to insert another workbook into the current one?

Excel does not include an Insert File command, but you can copy the data from one workbook and paste it into another. To do so:

1. Select the data you want to insert in the other workbook.
2. Choose Copy from the Edit menu or click the Copy button on the Standard toolbar.
3. Switch to the workbook in which you want to insert the data and move to the location where you want it to appear.
4. Select Paste from the Edit menu or click the Paste button on the Standard toolbar.

When I press CTRL+END, the insertion point sometimes moves far beyond the lower-right corner of my worksheet. How can get it to go to the right place?

Excel maintains a pointer to the last cell in your worksheet that contains data. When you press CTRL+END, Excel should move to this cell. If it no longer points to the right place, as in your case, you can readjust it by clearing all of the cells that do not contain data.

For example, suppose you have a worksheet in which the last cell containing data is J57. To readjust the pointer:

1. Choose Go To from the Edit menu to display the Go To dialog box.
2. Enter **K58:IV16384** in the Reference box and then click OK to select everything but your data.
3. From the Edit menu, choose Clear and then All.
4. Choose Close from the File menu.
5. Click Yes when Excel prompts you about saving the changes.

When you next open the file, the pointer works correctly.

Can I drag a selection from one workbook to another in Excel 5.0?

No. You cannot move cell entries between workbooks by dragging. However, you can drag an object such as a chart or a worksheet between workbooks. To move entries from one workbook to another, copy them to the Clipboard and then paste them to the other workbook.

How can I see more of my worksheet than currently appears?

You can change the zoom factor to see more of your worksheet in the window. You can change the zoom by using a menu command or a toolbar button.

To change the zoom using the menus:

1. Choose Zoom from the View menu to display the Zoom dialog box.

2. Select the option button for the desired percentage of zoom. The default is 100%. Figure 3-6 shows a spreadsheet at 200% zoom. You can also enter a percentage by selecting Custom and typing a percentage as large as 400% or as small as 10%.

3. Click OK.

To reset the zoom using the toolbar, enter a percentage in the Zoom Control box on the Standard toolbar, or click the arrow next to it and select a percentage in the drop-down list that appears.

Changing the zoom percentage has no effect on the worksheet's size when you print it.

Tech Tip: You can set the zoom percentage to be as large or small as necessary to fit a range by selecting Fit Selection in the Zoom dialog box or Selection in the Zoom Control box's drop-down list.

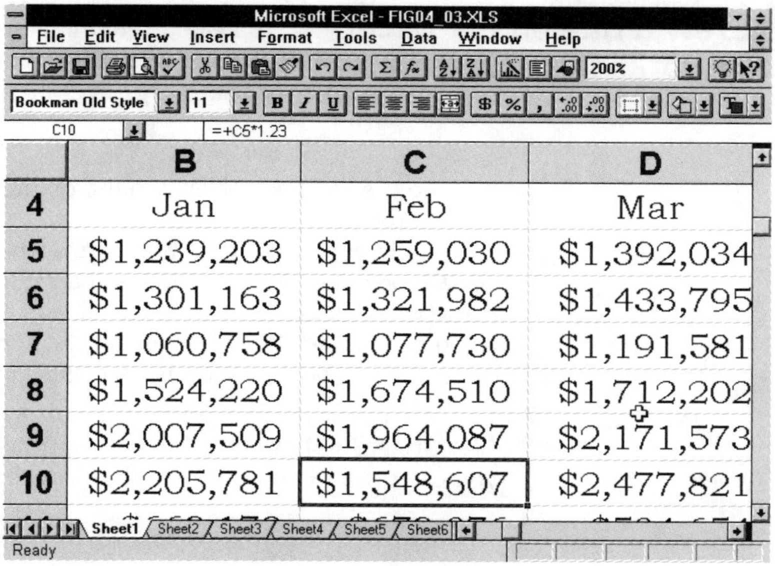

FIGURE 3-6   A worksheet at 200% zoom

I had a hidden macro sheet in my Excel 4.0 workbook. After I opened this workbook in Excel 5.0, I chose Unhide from the Window menu but my hidden macro sheet was not listed. What happened to it?

Because of the new structure of workbooks in Excel 5.0, the Unhide command on the Window menu only unhides workbooks. To unhide or hide a sheet within a workbook, you need to choose Sheet from the Format menu then choose Unhide or Hide. When you choose Unhide, Excel lists all of the hidden sheets in the active workbook; your hidden macro sheet should appear in this list.

I drew a line on my Excel 5.0 worksheet. How do I delete it?

You can delete this line or any other drawing object by following these steps:

1. Point to the line and click when the pointer becomes a white arrow.
   The pointer changes to a white arrow when you are actually pointing at the line, rather than at the cells under it. Black boxes, called *handles*, appear at either end of the line when it's selected. (The handles can also appear around other drawing objects, such as a rectangle or circle.)

2. Click the line with the right mouse button and choose Clear from the shortcut menu that appears. Alternatively, you can press DEL to remove a drawing object.

Can I view a workbook without opening it?

Excel 5.0 lets you view a portion of a workbook before opening it, so you can make sure you are retrieving the correct file. To preview the file:

1. Choose Find File from the File menu to display the Find File dialog box. You can also click the Find File button in any dialog box that lets you open a file.

2. Click Search to open the Search dialog box.

3. Enter the name of the file you want to view in the File Name box and its location in the Location box, and click OK.

4. Select the filename in the Listed Files list box.

The upper-left corner of the active sheet appears in the Preview of box, as shown in Figure 3-7.
   If file or summary information appears instead of the worksheet, select Preview in the View drop-down list box to display it.

Tech Tip: The preview of the workbook is saved as part of the summary information. If you turn off the prompt for entering summary information when you initially save your workbooks, you will not be able to preview them.

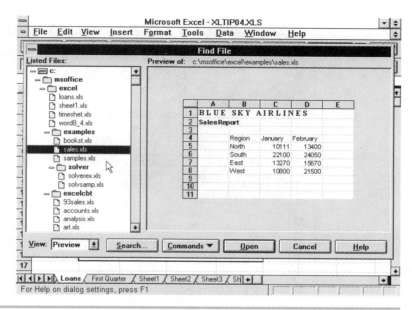

FIGURE 3-7   You can preview a workbook before opening it

Can I do anything to speed up Excel when I am working on a sheet with many graphics?

The reason Excel runs so slowly when your worksheet contains a lot of graphics is that it must redraw them each time you move to another location. To speed up this process, you can hide the graphics while you work on other data in your sheet. If you need to know where the graphics are located on the sheet, you can display *placeholders* instead, as shown in Figure 3-8. Redrawing placeholders is much faster than redrawing pictures. After you have finished working with the sheet, you can change the setting to display the objects again without any problems.

To change how Excel displays graphics:

1. Choose Options from the Tools menu.

2. Click the View tab.

3. In the Objects section, select Hide All to completely hide the graphics or Show Placeholders to display placeholders instead.

4. Click OK.

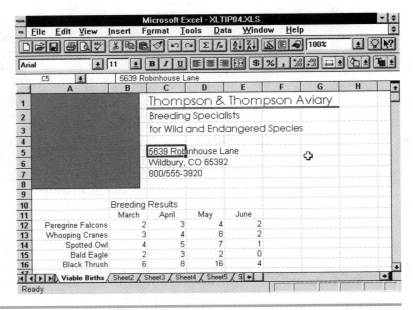

FIGURE 3-8   Placeholders indicate where graphics appear but are faster to redraw

Changing the display of graphics also affects how some embedded or linked objects appear. Excel will print the graphics even if you hide them or display placeholders instead.

To redisplay the graphics:

1. Choose Options from the Tools menu.

2. Click the View tab.

3. Select Show All In the Objects section and click OK.

Can I get Excel to add a list of all of the worksheet's defined names in my worksheet?

You can tell Excel to insert in the sheet a list of all the defined names accessible in that sheet and what they refer to by following these steps:

1. Move to where you want the list to appear.

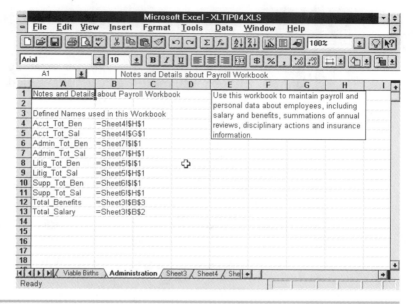

FIGURE 3-9   A list of defined names in a worksheet

>   **2.** Choose <u>N</u>ame from the <u>I</u>nsert menu, and then choose
>   Paste.
>
>   **3.** Click Paste <u>L</u>ist.
>
>   Starting at the current cell, Excel pastes a two-column list of the
>   defined names and the cells to which they refer, as shown in
>   Figure 3-9.

 Can I close all of my open workbooks without exiting Excel?

>   To close all of your workbooks and leave Excel open:
>
>   **1.** Press SHIFT and open the <u>F</u>ile menu with the mouse or
>   keyboard.
>
>   **2.** Choose <u>C</u>lose All (which replaces <u>C</u>lose when you open
>   the menu in this way) to close all of the open workbooks
>   without exiting Excel.

Can I delete all the values in my sheet except the formulas and text?

Yes, you can delete just the values in your sheet. By retaining the formulas and text, you make it easy to use the worksheet as a model for a new one.

To remove only the values:

1. Choose <u>G</u>o To from the <u>E</u>dit menu.
2. Click <u>S</u>pecial.
3. Select the <u>C</u>onstants option button.
4. Clear the <u>T</u>ext check box.
5. Click OK to select all of the cells containing values, but none of the cells containing text or formulas.
6. Choose Cle<u>a</u>r from the <u>E</u>dit menu, and then choose <u>C</u>ontents. You can also press DEL.

What am I saving when I choose Save <u>W</u>orkspace from the <u>F</u>ile menu?

When you use this command you save a workspace file, not your workbook data. A *workspace file*, which has a .XLW extension, stores information about what files are open and where they are located on the screen. You can open a workspace file to return to a particular set of open workbooks in a specific arrangement.

I don't use all the columns in my worksheets, but I keep needing more rows. Can I increase the number of rows?

No. You cannot increase the number of columns or rows in your worksheet. Excel's file structure allows for 256 columns and 16,384 rows. You cannot have more rows, even if some columns are empty, and vice versa. In your case, you may simply want to use another sheet in the same workbook. However, this won't help if you are using Excel's data management features to work with lists, because a list cannot span worksheets. If you are maintaining a list of more than 16,384 records, you might want transfer it to a database management application, which is designed to work with large sets of data.

Formulas and Functions

Formulas are the backbones of most worksheets. They let you perform all types of calculations and projections using the data in cells. The formulas that Excel calculates are identical to those that you would do yourself—the advantage is that you don't have to do the computation! Using Excel not only saves time but lowers the risk of making basic mathematical errors.

Functions are prerecorded formulas that are stored as part of Excel. You tell Excel to use a function by entering its keyword followed by *arguments* that specify the data to use in performing the computation.

If you use many formulas, you may want to add additional formula buttons to your Standard or a Custom button bar. The following Frustration Buster box describes the formula buttons that are available in Excel 5.0.

FRUSTRATION BUSTERS!

Entering a lot formulas can be a tedious job, especially when many of them are similar. To expedite this process, you can add one or more of Excel's formula buttons to an existing toolbar or create a custom one to suit your needs. These buttons help set up the formula properly and then let you enter the additional data or references.

To edit a toolbar:

1. Choose <u>T</u>oolbars from the <u>V</u>iew menu.

2. Select the toolbar you want to edit in the <u>T</u>oolbars list box, and then click <u>C</u>ustomize.

3. Select Formula in the <u>C</u>ategories list box to display the formula buttons in the Buttons section of the Customize dialog box.

4. To add a button to a toolbar, drag it from the dialog box to the position at which you want it to appear. To create a new toolbar, simply drag a button out of the dialog box but not to a toolbar.

5. Repeat step 4 to continue adding buttons, as desired, and then click OK.

Button	Name	Action
"="	Equal Sign	Inserts an equal sign (=) in the formula bar or cell
"+"	Plus Sign	Inserts a plus sign (+) in the formula bar or cell
"−"	Minus Sign	Inserts a minus sign (−) in the formula bar or cell
"*"	Multiplication Sign	Inserts a multiplication sign (*) in the formula bar or cell
"/"	Division Sign	Inserts a division sign (/) in the formula bar or cell

Button	Name	Action
"^"	Exponentiation Sign	Inserts an exponentiation sign (^) in the formula bar or cell
"("	Left Parenthesis	Inserts a left parenthesis (( ) in the formula bar or cell
")"	Right Parenthesis	Inserts a right parenthesis ( )) in the formula bar or cell
":"	Colon	Inserts a colon (:) in the formula bar or cell
","	Comma	Inserts a comma (,) in the formula bar or cell
"%"	Percent Sign	Inserts a percent sign (%) in the formula bar or cell
"$"	Dollar Sign	Inserts a dollar sign ($) in the formula bar or cell
Σ	AutoSum	Inserts the SUM function and selects a range to use as the argument
f_x	Function Wizard	Starts the Function Wizard to let you enter or edit a function
=ab	Paste Names	Opens the Paste Name dialog box that lets you choose a name to add to the formula bar or cell
42⁄	Constrain Numeric	If you are using Windows for Pen Computing, constrains the pen so that it only recognizes numeric or formula characters

I'm not sure of the syntax of a specific function. Where do I find this information?

Excel 5.0 provides extensive online Help that details the syntax of each function. Excel also includes a new tool, called the Function Wizard, that enables you to enter functions quickly and correctly.

To enter a function using the Function Wizard:

1. Choose <u>F</u>unctions from the <u>I</u>nsert menu, or click the Function Wizard button on the Standard toolbar.
Excel opens the first of two Function Wizard dialog boxes, as shown here:

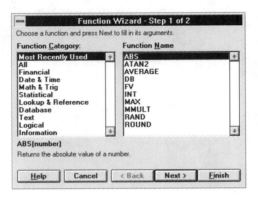

2. Select the category of the function you want to use in the Function <u>C</u>ategory list box.
If you are not sure which category the function is in, select All. If it is a function you use frequently, try selecting Most Recently Used.

3. Select the function you want in the Function <u>N</u>ame list box.
The function and the arguments it takes appear at the bottom of the dialog box, along with an explanation of its purpose.

4. Click Next to move to the next dialog box, in which you can specify the appropriate arguments, as shown here:

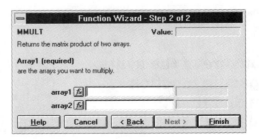

Required arguments appear in boldface, while optional arguments are in normal type.

5. Enter each argument in the appropriate box, or move the insertion point to the box and then select the cell or range in the worksheet with the mouse.

   As you enter each argument in the correct box, Excel displays the current value in the upper-right corner of the dialog box.

6. After entering all of the arguments, click Finish.

The completed function appears in the current worksheet cell.

Some of my functions recalculate automatically even though I selected the manual recalculation option. Why?

Excel has some functions that are considered *volatile*—they always recalculate, even when manual recalculation is specified. Two such functions are RAND and NOW. The only way you can prevent recalculation is to replace the function or the formula in which it appears with its current value.

   To replace a formula entry with a calculated value:

1. Select the cell.

2. Choose Copy from the Edit menu.

3. Choose Paste Special from the Edit menu.

4. Select the Values option button and click OK.

Excel replaces the formula containing the volatile function with its current value.

Tech Tip: If your volatile function is part of a formula, you may want to move it to a cell by itself and then simply reference the cell in the formula. This method allows you to replace only the function, not the other components of your calculation.

How can I quickly fill all of the cells in a range with the same value?

Using the same entry for many cells can be the quickest way to generate many similar entries. Once the cells are filled with identical values, you can edit them to make minor changes.

   The entries in column A of Figure 4-1 were created quickly by duplicating the entry "Wooden Desk -" and then editing the contents of each cell in the range.

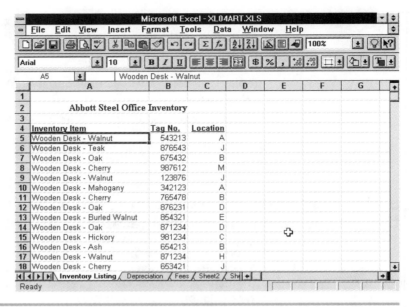

FIGURE 4-1   Inventory item entries were duplicated automatically and then edited

To duplicate an entry:

1. Highlight the range that you want to fill.

2. Enter the value and press CTRL+ENTER.

The value in the first cell is placed in every cell in the entire highlighted range.

What is an array formula and why would I want to use one?

Array formulas are formulas that work with ranges of data. They frequently produce a range of results, not just an entry in a single cell. Array formulas not only simplify worksheet layout by compressing data but they can produce results not readily available using single-value formulas.

Figure 4-2 illustrates one way that array equations can simplify a worksheet's layout and calculations. In this example, an array formula multiplies each item in the first array, which lists hours per item, by the second array, which contains the hourly rate for

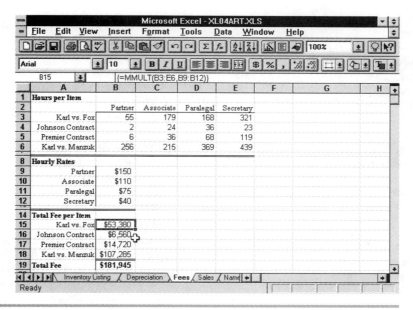

FIGURE 4-2   Using array formulas can simplify your calculations

each type of employee. To create this calculation using single-value formulas, you would enter four formulas such as =SUM(B3*B9,C3*B10,D3*B11,E3*B12) and hope that you didn't type anything incorrectly. By using the single array formula of =MMULT(B3:F7,B9:B12) instead, you simplify the calculation, reduce the likelihood of mistakes, and make it easier to understand the model at a glance.

Because of their special characteristics, you enter array formulas in a somewhat different manner than normal single-value formulas. To enter an array formula correctly:

1. Select the entire range that will display the array formula's results.

   Not all array formulas return a range as a result. For those that simply return a single value, you can just select the correct cell. If you don't know how much room to leave for the results, select a range that is much larger than any of the arrays used in the calculation.

2. Enter the array formula.

3. Press CTRL+SHIFT+ENTER (not ENTER) to input the array formula.

When you press CTRL+SHIFT+ENTER, you tell Excel to copy the entry to all of the selected cells and to enclose it in curly brackets ({})to indicate that it is an array formula.

If you selected more cells than Excel needs to display the array formula's results, #VALUE! appears in the extra ones. To remove this error indicator, reselect the entire results range and delete the array formula. Then select only the cells needed, and re-enter the formula.

Tech Tip: If you use the Function Wizard to create a formula, Excel inserts a regular formula when you click Finish. To convert it to an array formula, select all of the cells necessary to display the results, press F2 to edit the function, and then press CTRL+SHIFT+ENTER.

Array size is described in terms of the number of rows and columns it contains. For example, an array that is three rows deep and four columns high is called a 3 by 4 array. When you work with arrays, the order in which you enter the arrays as arguments is very important. For example, Excel can only multiply arrays when the first array listed as an argument contains the same number of columns as the second array has rows. For example, if you entered **=MMULT(B9:B12,B3:F7)** as the array formula in Figure 4-2, Excel would return the #VALUE! error indicator because the first array would have only one column while the second one would have four columns.

Tech Tip: If you are working with business and economic projections, you may want to explore the array formulas available to you. Array formulas are often used in such calculations because they offer capabilities that you cannot perform otherwise.

Why does #NAME? appear when I enter a function?

The most common reason this error indicator appears is that the function name is misspelled. To avoid this problem, use the Function Wizard to avoid typos when inserting functions.

I want to average only some of the cells in my range. How can I do this?

You need to use two functions, instead of just AVERAGE. You can combine AVERAGE with the IF function to tell Excel to average only the cells you specify. For example, suppose you list salespeople in column A and their respective sales in column B, as shown in Figure 4-3. You want to average only Carol Brandt's sales, whose name appears in many places because she has

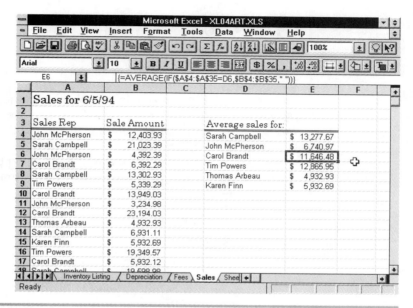

FIGURE 4-3   You can combine two functions to selectively average entries

made numerous sales. To do so, you might enter the array formula

    =AVERAGE(IF(A4:A18="Carol Brandt",B4:B18," ")).

   If, on the other hand, you want to find the average sales for each salesperson, you could enter the names in column D and then enter the formula

    =AVERAGE(IF($A$4:$A$18=D4,$B$4:$B$18))

in column E. Because this formula is an array formula, press CTRL+SHIFT+ENTER after typing it.

In Excel 4.0, I double-clicked a formula's cell to trace the values the formula used. In Excel 5.0, double-clicking just lets me edit directly in the cell. Can I change back to the old way?

You can revert to double-clicking's former functionality by following these steps:

1. Choose <u>O</u>ptions from the <u>T</u>ools menu.

2. Click the Edit tab.

3. Clear the <u>E</u>dit Directly in Cell check box and click OK.

When you disable this option, double-clicking has the same effect that it did in Excel 4.0. Figure 4-4 shows the results of turning off this setting and then double-clicking the formula in B15 to see the cells it references.

Excel 5.0 also provides a new method of tracing the entries, called *precedent cells*, that are referenced by a formula. To use this technique:

1. Select the formula.

2. Choose <u>A</u>uditing from the <u>T</u>ools menu.

3. Choose <u>T</u>race Precedents.

Excel displays one or more arrows to identify the cells that a formula uses in its calculations, as shown in Figure 4-5. You can remove these arrows by choosing <u>A</u>uditing from the <u>T</u>ools menu and then choosing Remove <u>A</u>ll Arrows.

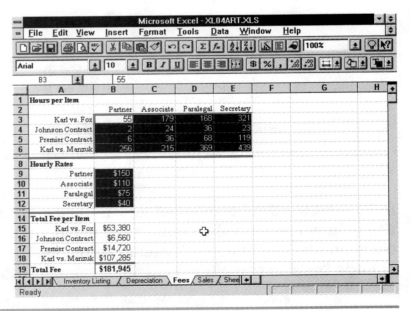

FIGURE 4-4 Highlighted cells referenced in the formula

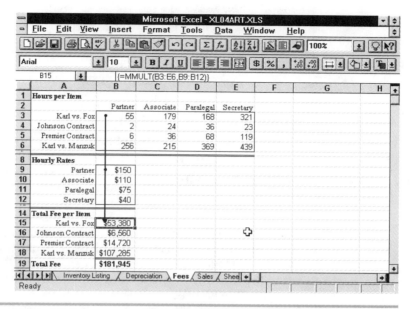

FIGURE 4-5 In Excel 5.0, you use auditing arrows to indicate precedent cells.

The AVERAGE function returns the wrong value when text is included in the calculation range. How can I avoid this?

The AVERAGE function is not designed to work with text entries and may not return the correct results if a range contains them. For example, you might have these entries in a worksheet:

A1=4
A2=2
A3=*text*

If you enter the formula **=AVERAGE(A1:A3)**, and the Transition Formula Entry option is turned on, Excel returns 2 instead of the correct result, which is 3. To avoid this problem, you need to edit the formula so that it doesn't reference the cell containing text.

Frequently this problem occurs when you open a Lotus 1-2-3 file in Excel because the Transition Formula Evaluation option is selected by default. When this option is in effect, Excel interprets a text entry as a zero and uses this value in formula calculations. To disable this option and fix the problem:

1. Choose <u>O</u>ptions from <u>T</u>ools menu.

2. Click the Transition tab.

3. Clear the Transition <u>F</u>ormula Evaluation check box and click OK.

I have a formula in a cell that works fine, but when I copy it to another cell, the #REF! error appears. Why?

Your formulas probably use *relative cell references*. This means that the cell or range referred to by the formula is defined based on its position in relation to the formula. When you use a relative cell reference, it's like describing the location of a house as "two houses to the left of mine." For example, a relative cell reference might simply indicate that the cell being referenced is two cells up and four cells to the left of the formula. When you copy a formula that contains relative cell references, the cell references change to refer to the cell in the same position relative to the formula's new location.

To move your formulas without changing the cells they reference, you need to use *absolute cell references*. As their name implies, absolute cell references refer to specific cells, such as A4 and D19, and don't change even when you copy the formula. Using this type of reference is like giving someone the exact address of a house on your street, rather than just saying where it is in relation to yours. To create an absolute cell reference, you place a dollar sign ($) before each of its components. For example, A1 is a relative reference whereas $A$1 is an absolute reference. You can insert these dollar signs by highlighting the formula in the formula bar or cell and then pressing F4.

Tech Tip: You can also create mixed cell references by putting a dollar sign only in front of a row or column. For example, when you copy a formula that contains the reference $A1, it always refers to the first column but the row number changes. Similarly, A$1 always denotes the first row but the column letter varies.

All of my cell references are relative. Can I change them to absolute cell references without retyping them?

It's easy to change a relative cell reference (such as A1:A10) to an absolute or mixed one ($A$1:$A$10 or $A1:$A10, respectively) in Excel. To do so, highlight the reference you want to change in the cell or formula bar and press F4. If you press F4 more than once it cycles through all the reference options. Within a macro, you can also use the FormulaConvert command from Visual Basic.

I want to combine the contents of two cells that contain text. Can I do this without re-entering the text?

Yes, Excel has an operator that works just like a plus sign (+) for text. That symbol is the ampersand (&). It *concatenates*, or joins, two text entries. For example, suppose cell A3 contains a last name and B3 contains a first name. You want both to appear in cell C3. To achieve this, you would enter **=B3&" "&A3** in C3. The " " adds a space between the two names to make them easier to read. The worksheet shown in Figure 4-6 uses this formula to combine the entries in columns A and B in column C.

After combining the entries, you could copy the formulas in column C and then use the Paste Special command from the Edit menu to paste the values the formulas return into the worksheet. You could then delete the data in columns A and B, if desired.

Tech Tip: Excel also provides a CONCATENATE function that works the same way as the concatenation operator.

Tech Tip: You can use any text string between double quotes. Two other popular characters to insert in strings are the hyphen (-) and the slash (/).

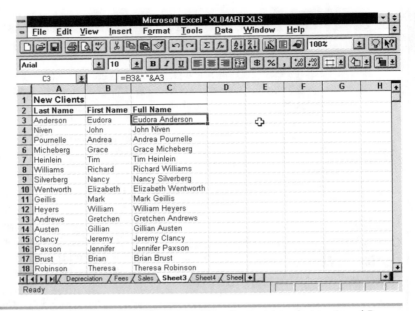

FIGURE 4-6 You can use a text formula to combine the text in columns A and B

When I enter my dates as YYMMDD, Excel treats them as numbers. Is there any way to tell Excel to see them as dates instead?

You can create a formula that uses functions to extract the different parts of the number and then create a date from them. For example, suppose you enter the date 940201 in cell A1. In cell B1, you might enter this formula:

```
=DATEVALUE(MID(TEXT(A1,"##"),3,2)&"/"
&RIGHT(TEXT(A1,"##"),2)&"/"&LEFT(TEXT(A1,"##"),2))
```

Once you enter the formula Excel returns the date serial number for the date you entered that is stored as a number.

This formula works because the DATEVALUE function returns the serial number of a date that is in text format. The appropriate parts of the date were obtained as text using LEFT, RIGHT, and MID functions. The & operator joins the components with the slashes to provide the common U.S. date format.

Tech Tip: If you entered the number as text, you would use the formula =DATEVALUE(MID(A1,3,2)&"/"&RIGHT(A1,2)&"/"&LEFT(A1,2)) instead.

When I enter a date before 1920, Excel assumes that it is in the next century. Can I get around this?

When you enter a date using two digits for the year and the digits are less than 20, Excel assumes that you are talking about the 21st century. To enter dates earlier than 1920, you need to use four digits for the year.

For example, if you type **1/1/19** Excel interprets the date as January 1, 2019; if you type **1/1/1919**, Excel recognizes the date as January 1, 1919.

When I start typing in a cell, I see a new button on the formula bar. What does it do?

You are probably seeing the Function Wizard button. This button opens the Function Wizard, which makes it easier for you to insert functions. You can also start the Function Wizard by clicking the Function Wizard button on the Standard toolbar or by choosing <u>F</u>unction from the <u>P</u>aste submenu.

Is there an easy way to determine what is causing a formula error?

To trace a formula error back to its source:

1. Choose <u>A</u>uditing from the <u>T</u>ools menu.

2. Choose Trace <u>E</u>rror.

Figure 4-7 shows the trace arrows that Excel displays.

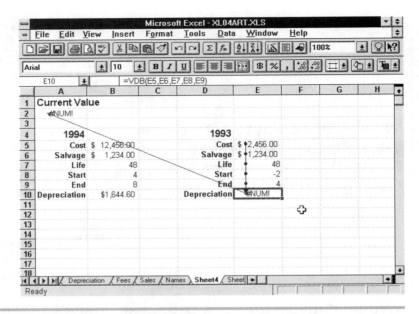

FIGURE 4-7 Excel displays trace arrows when you choose Trace Error

Does Excel handle relative references in the same way when you copy and paste as when you cut and paste?

No, the two procedures handle relative references very differently. When you copy and paste formulas containing relative references, the references are adjusted. When you cut and paste the same formula, the relative references are not adjusted.

Can I enter the current time without using the NOW function?

You can enter the current time by pressing the CTRL+SHIFT+; key combination. Unlike NOW, which creates an entry that updates every time the worksheet is recalculated, CTRL+SHIFT+; enters the current time as a constant. You can enter the current date in a similar fashion by pressing the CTRL+; key combination.

Whenever I enter a function with more than one parameter, the message "Error in Formula" appears. What's wrong?

You have changed the list separator in the Windows Control Panel to a character other than a comma. Consequently, Excel cannot recognize that you have entered more than one parameter. Although you can use another separator in your functions, you should probably change the default back to a comma since it is the standard one used.

To respecify the list separator:

1. Start the Control Panel by double-clicking its program-item icon in the Main program group in the Windows Program Manager.
2. Double-click the International icon.
3. Change the character in the List Separator box to a comma.
4. Click OK.

How can I resolve circular references in Excel 5.0?

Circular references occur when two formulas refer to each other and thus make it impossible to compute the results. To locate the cause of the circular reference:

1. Highlight one of the cells you think contains a circular reference.
2. Choose Auditing from the Tools menu.
3. Choose Trace Precedents.

Excel draws an arrow to the other cell involved in the circular reference.

Tech Tip: These steps work when only two cells are involved in a circular reference. If three or more cells are involved, you need to repeat these steps for each until the circular reference is revealed.

I am trying to create a custom function but the error message "Expected procedure, not module" appears. What's the problem?

This message indicates that you attempted to run a custom function to which you assigned the same name as a Visual Basic procedure in the same workbook. Instead of using a custom function, you can avoid the problem by creating a subprocedure with the same name as the module. Alternatively, you can simply give the custom function a different name.

I've created a formula to calculate a value. Is there any way to place the current formula result in the cell as a value and eliminate the formula?

Replacing a formula with its result is quite easy. However, you might want to save a copy of your workbook with the formula intact in case you'd like to use it to perform a new set of calculations at a later date.

To make the change:

1. Select one or more cells that you want to convert from formulas to results.

2. Choose Copy from the Edit menu.

3. Choose Paste Special from the Edit menu to open the Paste Special dialog box, shown here:

4. Select the Values option button.

5. Click OK.

I want to write a formula that sums certain numbers in a column based on the text in the previous column. Since I want to use multiple conditions, should I use the SUMIF function or a macro?

SUMIF cannot meet your needs. This function does not allow you to check more than one condition. However, Excel does offer an easy solution to the problem. You can use multiple IF statements in one formula. This technique, called *nesting*, uses one IF function to determine whether a second level of IF functions is evaluated. You can nest up to seven IF statements in one formula.

For example you may have four columns of data, as shown in Figure 4-8. Column A contains dates, column B indicates car models, column C lists salespeople, and column D shows the numbers of the specific models of cars sold on a given date. You could enter this formula, which consists of three nested IF functions, to sum all the luxury models sold by Bob after January 1,1994:

=SUM(IF(A2:A18>Datevalve(1/1/94),IF(B2:B18="Luxury", IF(C2:C18="Bob",D2:D18,0),0)))

Microsoft Excel - XL04ART.XLS			
File Edit View Insert Format Tools Data Window Help			

G5 {=SUM(IF($A$2:$A$18>=6/4/94,IF($B$2:$B$18=$F$4,IF($C$2:$C$18=F5,$D$2:$D$18,0)))))

	A	B	Salesperson	Number Sold			
1	Date	Model	Salesperson	Number Sold			
2	6/4/94	Luxury	Will	1	Total Sales		
3	6/4/94	Luxury	Bob	2	6/4/94		
4	6/4/94	Luxury	Sue	2	Luxury		
5	6/4/94	Sporty	Kim	1		Bob	3
6	6/4/94	Luxury	Bob	1		Will	1
7	6/4/94	Sporty	Bob	2		Sue	5
8	6/4/94	Sporty	Sue	1		Kim	1
9	6/4/94	Compact	Will	3	Compact		
10	6/4/94	Compact	Sue	3		Bob	4
11	6/4/94	Sedan	Kim	3		Will	3
12	6/4/94	Compact	Kim	2		Sue	3
13	6/4/94	Sporty	Will	1		Kim	2
14	6/4/94	Luxury	Sue	3	Sedan		
15	6/5/95	Sedan	Bob	2		Bob	2
16	6/5/95	Luxury	Kim	1		Will	0
17	6/5/95	Compact	Bob	4		Sue	0
18	6/5/95	Sporty	Sue	1		Kim	3

Errors \ **Sales2** \ Grades \ Fees2 \ Times \ Sheet9 \ S

Ready

FIGURE 4-8   You can test conditions by using multiple IF functions

Press CTRL+SHIFT+ENTER to enter this as an array. When you do so, Excel places brackets around the formula.

When I entered a 19-digit number into a cell and pressed ENTER, Excel turned the last four digits into zeros. What is happening?

Excel only maintains numbers up to 15 digits. Any digit beyond the 15th is displayed as a zero.

What is the order in which formulas are calculated?

The order of operation is as follows:

1.	( )	Operators within parentheses
2.	–	Negation
3.	%	Percent
4.	^	Exponentiation
5.	* and /	Multiplication and division
6.	+ and –	Addition and subtraction
7.	&	Concatenation (text joining)
8.	=, <, >, >=, <=	Comparison

For example, observe how Excel computes the results of these equations:

- $=4+3*5\wedge2+1= 4+3*25+1= 4+75+1=80$
- $=4+3*5\wedge(2+1)= 4+3*5\wedge(3)= 4+3*125= 4+375=379$
- $=(4+3)*5\wedge(2+1)= (7)*5\wedge(3)= 7*125=875$

I tried to use the FREQUENCY function to find out how many students got each letter grade, but Excel only showed the result for As. What am I doing wrong?

You probably set up your worksheet like the one shown in Figure 4-9. However, you neglected to enter the FREQUENCY function correctly. The FREQUENCY function's results are an array, which means the results appear in several cells. To enter an array function, you need to enter the formula in all of the cells required

Microsoft Excel - XL04ART.XLS											

File Edit View Insert Format Tools Data Window Help

J3 `{=FREQUENCY(F3:F18,I3:I6)}`

	A	B	C	D	E	F	G	H	I	J	K	L
1	Grades											
2		Test A	Test B	Test C	Final	Final Grade			Grade Distribution			
3	Brown	83%	69%	76%	66%	73%		A	90%	4		
4	Bush	42%	64%	42%	68%	54%		B	80%	1		
5	Connors	86%	81%	85%	78%	83%		C	70%	5		
6	Crabtree	89%	77%	82%	96%	86%		D	60%	4		
7	Fox	13%	64%	84%	90%	63%		F	50%	2		
8	Green	100%	85%	94%	95%	94%						
9	Hoskins	97%	87%	63%	95%	86%						
10	Howard	52%	78%	71%	48%	62%						
11	Luck	59%	74%	70%	63%	66%						
12	Meshenberg	67%	52%	66%	59%	61%						
13	Newberg	38%	65%	54%	52%	52%						
14	Parks	62%	56%	65%	69%	63%						
15	Parsenella	95%	73%	100%	71%	85%						
16	Perkins	92%	99%	79%	90%	90%						
17	Stout	45%	74%	46%	58%	56%						
18	Stratter	52%	53%	63%	57%	56%						

Errors / Sales2 / **Grades** / Fees2 / Times / Sheet9 / S

Ready

FIGURE 4-9   Using FREQUENCY to count items in categories

to display the results. To do so, first select the necessary cells, which are C1:C5 in this example, and type the formula again. Then, press CTRL+SHIFT+ENTER to enter the formula as an array formula.

I like the Function Wizard but I'm comfortable enough with some functions that I don't need to go through all the steps. How can I enter them more quickly?

You can type the function directly into the cell or you can skip the last step in the Function Wizard. To type the function directly into the cell, simply enter = followed by the function name and the arguments in parentheses. To bypass the second step of the Function Wizard, you can click Finish once you select the function name.

How can I round the number 12.41 up to 13?

There are two functions that can handle this task: CEILING and ROUNDUP.

CEILING uses the syntax CEILING(*number,significance*) where *number* is the number you want to round, and *significance* is the multiple you want the number rounded to. For example, you could enter **=CEILING(12.41,1)** to round up to 13 while **=CEILING(12.41,5)** will round to 10.

ROUNDUP uses the syntax ROUNDUP(*number, num_digits*) in which *number* is the number you want to round and *num_digits* is the number of digits you want to use. For example, you could enter **=ROUNDUP(12.41,0)** to round up to 13.

Is there a way to simplify complex formulas to help track errors?

If you highlight part of a formula and then press F9, Excel only evaluates that part. You can also use numbers instead of cell references in a formula to make it easier to debug.

Tech Terror: Only use actual numbers in your formulas as a temporary step in your testing phase! If you use numbers instead of references in your final computations, you aren't taking advantage of two of Excel's most important capabilities: the ability to copy a single formula for use in many places and to vary the data a formula uses.

I used the Paste Special command on the Edit menu to transpose my data. Is there any way to also create a link to the source data?

You can use the TRANSPOSE function to transpose the data as well as update it each time the source data changes. This function uses the syntax TRANSPOSE(*array*).

For example, the first set of fees in Figure 4-10 change regularly. To create a second, linked set:

Tech Tip: This is an array function, as described earlier in this chapter.

1. Select B10:B15.

2. Type **=TRANSPOSE($B$4:$G$4)**.

3. Press CTRL+SHIFT+ENTER to enter the formula.

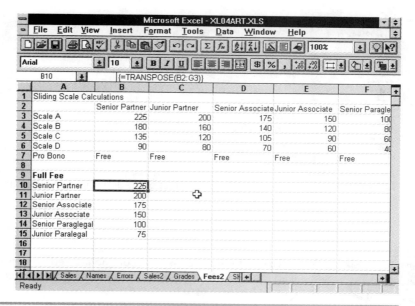

FIGURE 4-10 Transposing and linking data

Is there a function I can use to determine if the entries in two cells are exact matches?

The EXACT function can handle this task for you. It compares the entries in two cells and only returns True as a result when their contents are exactly the same, right down to capitalization. For example, if you enter **=EXACT(A1,H1)**, the function returns True if the entries in A1 and H1 match exactly, including upper- and lowercase; it returns False if they are not identical.

Can Excel determine if a number in a cell is entered as text or a value?

You can use the TYPE function to tell Excel to evaluate a cell's contents. For example, to check if the number you see displayed in A1 is text or a value, enter **=TYPE(A1)** in cell B1. The function returns a number that represents the type of data in cell A1, as described in the Table 4-1. For example, if cell A1 contains a number, then the function in cell B1 returns 1.

Result	Entry Type
1	Number
2	Text
4	Logical value, such as TRUE or FALSE
8	Formula
16	Error value
64	Array

TABLE 4-1   You can use the TYPE function to determine whether an entry is text or a value

Tech Tip: This function is most commonly used in macros where you need to make sure that the correct type of entry was recorded in a cell in order for the macro to proceed.

I maintain a department time sheet. When people work past midnight, my results are incorrect. Is there a way to calculate this correctly?

You can use the IF function in a formula to help manage this situation. For example, Figure 4-11 depicts the time schedule for the nurses on a hospital ward. The formula entered in D5 is =C5-B5+IF(B5>C5,1). When the end of the shift, in column C, is an earlier hour than the beginning, in column B, then the IF statement adds a 1 to the time serial number. This calculates the correct elapsed time, as you can see.

Tech Tip: To correctly display the results of this formula, you must format the cell with the HH:MM format. Otherwise, the entry appears as a time serial number.

Microsoft Excel - XL04ART.XLS								

File Edit View Insert Format Tools Data Window Help

D5 | =C5-B5+IF(B5>C5,1)

	A	B	C	D	E	F	G	H	I
1	Work Schedule for 6/4/94 - Evening								
2									
3	Ward 6								
4		In	Out	Hours					
5	Connor	3:00 PM	11:00 PM	8:00					
6	Bridges	7:00 PM	11:00 PM	4:00					
7	Samson	11:00 PM	7:00 AM	8:00					
8	Delphin	3:00 PM	3:00 AM	12:00					
9	Malcolm	4:30 PM	12:30 AM	8:00					
10	Straight	3:00 PM	11:00 PM	8:00					
11	Calais	3:00 PM	11:00 PM	8:00					
12	Short	7:00 PM	11:00 PM	4:00					
13	Johnson	3:00 PM	11:00 PM	8:00					
14	Sanders	7:00 PM	3:00 AM	8:00					

Names / Errors / Sales2 / Grades / Fees2 \ Times / S

Ready

FIGURE 4-11   Calculating elapsed time

I would like to know the date exactly 24 months from today. Is there a function to calculate this?

The EDATE function calculates a date that falls a given number of months away from the start date. For example, suppose the date in cell B4 is 1/1/94. To calculate the ending date of a 24-month loan that started on this date, enter the formula **=EDATE(B4,24)** in cell B5. This function returns the serial number of the date that is exactly 24 months from 1/1/94.

Tech Tip: The EDATE function is only available when you have installed the Analysis ToolPak add-in. See the online Help to learn about installing this add-in.

To determine the date that is exactly 24 months from the current one, use the TODAY function to provide the starting date within the EDATE function, as in =EDATE(TODAY(),24).

Can I easily discover the largest and smallest values in a range?

Use the MAX and MIN functions to find the maximum and minimum values within a range. For example, to find the maximum value in the range B1:B105, enter the formula **=MAX(B1:B105)**. To find the minimum value in the range B1:B105, enter the formula **=MIN(B1:B105)**.

Is there a function that rounds to the nearest 5 rather than the nearest 10?

The MROUND function lets you round to any multiple you want. This function uses the syntax MROUND(*number, roundto*) where *number* is the number you want to round, and *roundto* is the multiple to which you want to round. For example, to round to the nearest 5, use the formula =MROUND(623,5) to return 625. If you enter **27** in this same formula, the result is 25.

How do I keep a running total in a cell on a worksheet?

You can calculate a running total by setting up a circular reference in a cell. You then tell Excel to allow the circular reference and keep recalculating it. For example, suppose you want to keep a total of the numbers entered in cell B1. To do so:

1. Enter the formula **=A1+B1** in A1.
2. Click OK when Excel displays the error message "Cannot resolve circular references."
3. Choose Options from the Tools menu.
4. Click the Calculation tab.
5. Select the Iteration check box.
6. Enter **1** in the Maximum Iterations box, and then click OK.

Excel will now keep a running total in A1 as you enter different values in B1.

Can I specify ranges that use more than one worksheet in my formulas?

You can select a *three-dimensional range*, which includes cells in more than one worksheet. For example, suppose you have a workbook containing worksheets 1, 2, and 3 and you want to sum A1:A5 on all three sheets. You can enter the formula:

=SUM(Sheet1:Sheet3!A1:A5)

To use a 3-D range, your reference must specify the range of sheets just as you would a range of cells.

Can I base the contents of a text box on the contents of a cell?

You can create a text box, which is a drawing object that appears on top of a worksheet, whose contents are determined by a cell entry in the worksheet. To create the text box and base its contents on a cell's entry:

1. Click the Text Box button on the Standard toolbar, as shown here:

2. Click the worksheet and drag across the area where you want the text box to appear.

3. With the text box selected, click the formula bar and enter = followed by the cell reference, such as **=A1**.
   If you edit the cell's entry, the text box's contents change accordingly.

I've used the formula =""&A1&"" to store numbers as text in a .WK1 worksheet after importing it into Excel 5.0. I get a #VALUE! error although the formula works fine in my Excel worksheets. Why is this happening?

By default, when you import a Lotus 1-2-3 spreadsheet, Excel selects an option that lets you enter formulas just as you would in 1-2-3. This formula you mention, which works correctly in Excel, would not work the same way in the Lotus application. Therefore, you need to turn this option off so that you can use this Excel–style formula.

To clear this option:

1. Choose <u>O</u>ptions from the <u>T</u>ools menu.

2. Click the Transition tab.

3. Clear the Transition Form<u>u</u>la Entry check box and click OK.

Tech Terror: When you have the Transition Formula Entry option turned on, you cannot enter dates in the normal fashion because Excel will interpret them as calculations. For example, instead of interpreting 1/8/94 as a date, Excel will actually perform the calculation; it will divide 1 by 8 and then divide the result by 94.

Excel displays the error message "Cannot change part of an array" when I try to edit my array formula. How can I modify it?

To edit an array formula, you need to select all of the cells in which the array formula appears, not just one cell of the array's results. A shortcut for selecting all of the cells used by an array formula is to place the insertion point in any one of the cells used in the array formula and then press the CTRL+/ key combination.

Are there shortcut keys that I can use to find precedents or dependents?

Excel provides shortcut keys to select the cells that contain precedents or dependents of the current cell's formula or value.

- Press CTRL+[to select the cells that are named in the formula in the current cell.

- Press CTRL+] to select the cells with formulas that directly name the current cell.

- Press CTRL+SHIFT+{ to select all of the precedent cells.

- Press CTRL+SHIFT+} to select all of the dependent cells.

Precedent cells are those cells that are used by the formula in the current cell. If one of the cells referenced is a formula, then any cells it references are also considered precedent cells of the original formula. *Dependent cells* are those that reference the contents of the current cell. If the dependent cell is also referenced by another formula, then the second formula is another dependent cell.

My company's fiscal year runs from October to September. I sometimes need to know the current fiscal month. Is there a function that can calculate this?

Excel does not have a built-in function for this purpose, but you can write a formula to perform the calculation. The following formula returns the month in the fiscal year.

=IF(MONTH(*date_value*)>9,MONTH(*date_value*)–9, MONTH(*date_value*)+3)

For October, November, and December, this formula subtracts 9 from the date's month, which gives 1,2,3 for these months. For all other months, this formula adds 3 from the date's month to return 4 through 12. Of course, if your fiscal year were different, such as from June to July, you would be subtracting and adding a different number of months.

Can I test for two conditions in one IF function like =SUM(IF(OR(*range=value1*, *range=value2*),1,0))?

No. Excel cannot accept a formula that attempts to check two conditions in one IF function. This is a limitation of Excel. In order to check two conditions, you need to use two nested IF functions. For example, you could enter

=SUM(IF(*range=value1*,1,IF(*range=value2*,1,0))

This formula is the equivalent of the one suggested in the question. Essentially, this formula adds 1 to the total any time the value of *range* equals either *value1* or *value2*.

Tech Tip: Remember, because this is an array function, you must press CTRL+SHIFT+ENTER to enter it.

Can I look up an entry in a table that isn't sorted?

Tech Tip: You can also use this feature of the VLOOKUP and HLOOKUP functions to force Excel to find an exact match, instead of simply finding the closest match.

By using a special option, you can use the VLOOKUP and HLOOKUP functions in Excel 5.0 to look up an entry in an unsorted lookup range. In Excel 4.0, you could not use these functions with an unsorted lookup range without running the risk of returning the wrong answer.

Both of these functions use the syntax HLOOKUP or VLOOKUP(*lookup_value*, *table_array*, *index_num*, *range_lookup*) in which *lookup_value* is the value the function tries to find in the header row or column, *table_array* is the table in which you want to find a value, *index_num* is the row or column whose value you want to return, and *range_lookup* specifies whether the table's header row or column contents are sorted (*range_lookup* equals True) or are in any order (*range_lookup* equals False).

If *range_lookup* is True, Excel knows that the *table_array* is sorted in ascending order by the header row or column. If *lookup_value* is not actually found in the header row or column, then Excel returns a value from the row or column headed by the closest previous value. For example, if *lookup_value* is 5, and 5 does not appear in the header column or row, Excel returns the value from the row or column headed by 4. If *range_lookup* is False, Excel knows that the *table_array* is not sorted, and won't return any value at all if it cannot find the *lookup_value* itself in the header row or column. For example, if the *lookup_value* is 5 and 5 does not appear in the header row or column, Excel displays the #N/A error instead of a value.

Tech Tip: In Excel 4.0, you had to use a complicated combination of the INDEX and MATCH functions to look up an exact value rather than approximate value in a table. This new feature for the HLOOKUP and VLOOKUP functions is designed to avoid this confusion.

Can I turn off the Most Recently Used List in the Function Wizard ?

No, you cannot disable this feature. The Most Recently Used List is controlled by a line in the EXCEL5.INI file that begins with MRUFuncs=221,3,45, and so on. If you delete or add a semicolon in front of this line, causing Excel to ignore it, Excel 5.0 just creates a new line using the ten most commonly used functions.

Formatting

Today's spreadsheet applications are no longer judged simply by how quickly they perform your calculations—they now must also present data attractively. Well-designed spreadsheets not only look more professional but are easier to understand. Excel provides as many features for formatting your data as most word processing or desktop publishing products.

FRUSTRATION BUSTERS!

You can access Excel's most frequently used formatting features from the Formatting toolbar. If you have used Word for Windows, the left half of the Formatting toolbar should seem very familiar. These buttons and any equivalent key combinations are described in the following table.

Button	Name	Key Combination	Action
Arial	Font	CTRL+SHIFT+F	Lets you set the font of the current cell
10	Font Size	CTRL+SHIFT+P	Lets you set the font size of the current cell
B	Bold	CTRL+B	Applies boldface
I	Italic	CTRL+I	Applies italics
U	Underline	CTRL+U	Adds an underline
≡	Align Left		Left aligns the cell entry
≡	Center		Centers the cell entry
≡	Align Right		Right aligns the cell entry
⊞	Center Across Columns		Centers cell entries over several columns
$	Currency Style	Press ALT+', select Currency in the Style Name box, and click OK	Applies the Currency style

Button	Name	Key Combination	Action
%	Percent Style	Press ALT+', select Percent in the Style Name box, and click OK	Applies the Percent style
,	Comma Style	Press ALT+', select Comma in the Style Name box, and click OK	Applies the Comma style
+.0 .00	Increase Decimals		Increases the number of decimal digits displayed by 1
.00 +.0	Decrease Decimals		Decreases the number of decimal digits displayed by 1
⊡ ▼	Borders		Adds a border to the sides of cells
◱ ▼	Color		Sets the background color of the cell
T ▼	Font Color		Sets the color of text

Why do I get a flashing bar in a cell when I double-click it?

The flashing bar indicates that you are in Edit mode and can edit the contents of the cell directly.

With this option selected, you no longer need to activate the formula bar to change an entry. However, you can turn it off by following these steps:

1. Choose Options from the Tools menu.
2. Click the Edit tab.
3. Clear the Edit Directly in Cell check box.
4. Click OK.

Tech Tip: If you are accustomed to editing in the formula bar, try leaving this option on for awhile. It's like beginning a new exercise regimen—after awhile it grows on you. One advantage of editing directly in the cell is that you can hide the formula bar if you want to free up some room in the Excel application window.

Can Excel format my data for me?

Yes, to an extent. Excel has an AutoFormat feature that applies formatting to a range of cells. However, Excel can only guess how you want the data formatted. Sometimes, it may not look exactly as you want it, and you will need to make some modifications.

To apply AutoFormat:

1. Move to a cell in the range that you want to format. AutoFormat determines which range you want to format based on the data surrounding the current cell. AutoFormat assumes that the data to format has either a border or at least one empty row and column around it to separate it from any other data.

2. Choose <u>A</u>utoFormat from the F<u>o</u>rmat menu. Excel highlights the data that it will format and displays an AutoFormat dialog box like the one shown here:

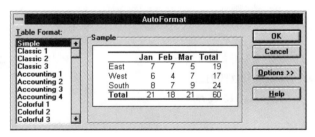

3. Select the format you wish to apply in the <u>T</u>able Format box.

4. If you only want to apply some but not all of the attributes of the format you selected, click <u>O</u>ptions to expand the dialog box. Clear the <u>N</u>umber, <u>B</u>order, <u>F</u>ont, <u>P</u>atterns, <u>A</u>lignment, and <u>W</u>idth/Height check boxes, as desired.

5. Click OK to format the range.

The following is an example of a range that was formatted with AutoFormat only:

	A	B	C	D	E	F	G	H	I
1			Sales Projections						
2									
3		1995	1996	1997	1998	1999			
4	Product A	1000	1080	1166.4	1259.712	1360.489			
5	Product B	2000	2240	2508.8	2809.856	3147.039			
6	Product C	700	780	869.28	968.928	1080.161			
7	Total	3700	4100	4544.48	5038.496	5587.688			

If you use AutoFormat frequently, you may want to add the AutoFormat button to a toolbar. You can click this button to apply the AutoFormat table format you last used to another range of data. Alternatively, you can hold down SHIFT while you click the AutoFormat button to apply the next AutoFormat table format to the data.

I am entering part numbers with the format 12-345. Excel either transforms them into a date or evaluates them as an equation. How do I stop this?

You need to tell Excel to consider your entries as text. If you have only a few part numbers to enter, you can simply start your entry with a single quotation mark ('). Excel will accept your entry as typed without trying to evaluate it as a number, date, or formula.

If you plan to enter part numbers in a large range of cells, you can preformat the range so that Excel treats the entries as text rather than as numbers or dates.

To format the range before entering the numbers:

1. Highlight the range in which you will enter the numbers.
2. Choose Cells from the Format menu.
3. Click the Number tab.
4. Select Text in the Category list box.
5. Click OK.

Tech Tip: You can set the format of any cell by clicking it with the right mouse button and choosing Format Cells from the shortcut menu that appears, or by pressing CTRL+1.

Tech Terror: Make sure you use this method if you plan to enter phone numbers or social security numbers in your worksheet; otherwise, you may get unexpected results!

Can you edit directly in a cell with Excel 5.0?

You can edit the contents of the current cell by double-clicking it. You can also edit a cell's contents in the formula bar, as you did in previous versions.

Tech Terror: If this feature isn't working, you may have turned off the option that enables it. In this case, choose <u>O</u>ptions from the <u>T</u>ools menu, click the Edit tab, select the <u>E</u>dit Directly in Cell check box, and then click OK.

In previous versions of Excel, I could only have one font and font size per cell. Is this still the case in Excel 5.0?

No, in Excel 5.0, you may have more than one font and font size per cell. You can apply formatting to the individual characters in the cell in addition to the overall formatting you apply to the cell.

For example, you make some of the characters in a cell superscript by following these steps:

1. Highlight the characters within the cell that you want to format.

2. Choose C<u>e</u>lls from the F<u>o</u>rmat menu or press CTRL+1. The Format Cells dialog box displays with only the options from the Font tab since this is the only additional formatting you can apply to the characters.

3. Select the font, style, size, and effect you prefer. In this case, you would select the Sup<u>e</u>rscript check box in the Effects section.

4. Click OK for the changes to take effect.

Tech Tip: You cannot apply character formatting to individual characters in the cell if the cell contains the results of a formula.

Some of my entries appear as # signs. What happened to them?

These entries are numbers or formula results that are too wide to display in the column. These entries will redisplay if you do one of the following:

- Double-click the right border of the column heading. Excel widens the column enough to display all of its entries in their entirety.

- Select a range of cells that includes the ones with the # signs. Choose <u>C</u>olumn from the <u>F</u>ormat menu and then click <u>A</u>utoFit Selection to widen the column to accommodate the selected entries.

- Apply a different number format that uses less space so that the values fit within the current column width.

Tech Terror: None of these tips will work if you have formatted a cell containing a negative number as a date or time. In this case, the number appears as ###### regardless of the width of the column.

How much data can I fit in my Excel workbooks?

Although generous, Excel does limit how much data a workbook can hold. These restrictions are part of Excel, so you cannot change them. An Excel workbook can contain up to 255 sheets. An Excel worksheet has 16,384 rows and 256 columns. Each cell can contain up to 255 characters, regardless of font size. If you attempt to enter more characters than this in a single cell, Excel displays a warning message and will not accept them. If you import a file from another program that attempts to put more than 255 characters in a single cell, the additional characters are truncated. You may have a maximum row height of 409 points and a maximum column width of 255 characters based on the Normal style font.

In reality, the real limitation on the size of your workbook is the amount of memory on your system. While Excel requires only 4MB, you may need more if you use advanced features. If you often run multiple programs or use data files larger than 250K, you probably need at least 8MB of memory. Although you can manipulate large files with less than 8MB, Excel will run very slowly.

What shortcuts exist for adding number formats?

When you enter numbers, you can include formatting characters to specify their format. For example, if you type a number with a dollar ($) sign, Excel applies a Currency format. Similarly, entering 50% sets a Percentage format.

However, this method only works when you initially enter a number—you can't use it to change an existing number format. Instead, you can use one of the key combinations shown in the following table:

Number Format	Key Combination
General	CTRL+SHIFT+~
Currency with two decimal places	CTRL+SHIFT+$
Percent with no decimal places	CTRL+SHIFT+%
Exponential with two decimal places	CTRL+SHIFT+^
D-MMM-YY	CTRL+SHIFT+#
H:MM AM/PM	CTRL+SHIFT+@
Comma with 2 decimal places	CTRL+SHIFT+!

Tech Tip: You cannot use formatting characters to format formula results.

Can I display text on several lines within a single cell?

You can enter a multiline cell entry, but not by pressing ENTER, since that key moves you to the next cell. To make Excel wrap text within a cell:

1. Select the cell in which you want the entry to wrap.

2. Choose Cells from the Format menu.

3. Click the Alignment tab.

4. Select the Wrap Text check box.

5. Click OK.

Excel wraps the entry within the cell, as shown here:

A2	±	Loan
A	**B**	Number

1	**Overdue Loans**					
2	**Loan Number**	**Branch**	**Origination Date**	**Principal Amount**	**Principal Remaining**	**Last Payment Date** **Loan Officer**

If you want to force Excel to wrap a cell entry at a specific point, move to that position in the cell entry and then press ALT+ENTER. This procedure inserts a carriage return, or an end of line code, forcing Excel to move the remainder of the entry to the next line. Pressing ALT+ENTER in a cell automatically selects the Wrap Text check box for the cell.

Tech Tip: When you have multiple lines in a cell and you want the bottom line underlined (as in the example shown above), add the Single Accounting or Double Accounting underlining style to the cells. Regular Single or Double underlining underlines all the lines in the cell, not just the last one.

I want to add a double underline under my numbers. Is that possible?

Yes. Excel 5.0 has added double underlining. To apply it:

1. Select the cells to be underlined.
2. Choose Cells from the Format menu.
3. Click the Font tab.
4. Select Double or Double Accounting in the Underline box. Double places an underline under every character in every line in the cell whereas Double Accounting omits the double underline under certain formatting symbols, such as the dollar sign, and underlines only the last line in a cell with several lines.
5. Click OK to add a double underline in the selected cells.

How do I remove an object, such as a circle or a line, from a worksheet?

There are two ways to delete an object:

- Click the object with the right mouse button, and then choose Clear from the shortcut menu.

- Select the object and press DEL or choose Cle<u>a</u>r and then <u>A</u>ll from the <u>E</u>dit menu.

Tech Tip: You can tell whether you are pointing to a cell or an object by the shape of the mouse pointer. The pointer looks like a large plus (+) when you point to a cell; it appears as an arrow when you point to a drawing object.

When I print out my sheet, the hard copy displays ######### in a cell even though the data shows up fine on the screen. Is my file corrupted?

No, the pound signs simply indicate that the data in the cell is wider than the column width. Widening the column in which the cell is located will make the contents print correctly. The difference between the screen display and the printed output is caused by the fonts you are using. You have probably formatted the cell with a screen font such as MS Sans Serif. The closest printer font is substituted for this one when you print the worksheet, which can increase the width of the cell's contents beyond that of the column.

Tech Tip: You may have the same problem if you format your document with a printer font, since Windows still substitutes the most similar screen font when it displays the data on the screen.

Windows uses three types of fonts: screen fonts, printer fonts, and TrueType fonts. TrueType fonts are designed to print the same way they display on the screen. Therefore, you can use TrueType fonts to prevent this problem and provide WYSIWYG (what you see is what you get) capabilities.

You can see what type of font you have chosen just by looking at the font list:

```
System
Terminal
T Times New Roman
Univers (WN)
T Wide Latin
T Wingdings
```

A True Type font displays TT to the left of its name. A miniature printer appears to the left of a printer font's name. A screen font displays nothing to the left of the name. You can see examples of how these fonts are shown by this section of a font list.

Do I have to repeat all the selections I made if I want a cell in a different location to look just like one I've already formatted?

No. Excel provides two ways to quickly duplicate the formatting you applied to the current cell. The simplest method is to move to the formatted cell and click the Format Painter button on the Standard toolbar. When you click this button, Excel outlines the current cell to remind you which formats you are copying. The mouse pointer also displays a small paintbrush next to the oversized plus sign. You can then select the cells to which you want to apply the formatting, as shown here:

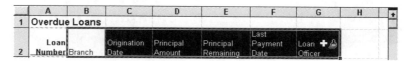

The other method is to copy a formatted cell to the Clipboard and then paste just the formatting to the other cells. To paste only the formatting, choose Paste Special (instead of Paste) from the Edit menu, select the Formats option button in the Paste Special dialog box, click OK, and press ENTER or ESC.

Tech Tip: You can double-click the Format Painter button if you want to copy the current cell's format to multiple locations. The Format Painter button remains selected until you click it again.

How can I take the style from one sheet and apply it to another without changing one element at a time?

You can copy the formatting of named styles from one workbook to another. This feature allows you to have multiple workbooks that have the same appearance without reapplying the formatting to each one.

To copy the styles from one workbook to another:

1. Open the source workbook from which you want to take the style.

2. Open the target workbook to which you want to apply the style.

3. With the target workbook active, choose <u>S</u>tyle from the F<u>o</u>rmat menu.

4. Click the M<u>e</u>rge button.

5. Select the source workbook in the Merge Styles dialog box.

6. Click OK.

7. Click Close to leave the Style dialog box.

 **Tech Tip:** You can copy a style from one workbook to another by copying a cell formatted with the style to the other workbook.

 ## I use styles in my word processing documents so that all my text has the same appearance. Can I create styles in Excel?

Yes. Styles are sets of formats that you can apply to your data. The advantage to using styles instead of applying the formats directly is that you can modify the formatting in your entire workbook by simply changing the attributes assigned to a particular style. Styles are like a paint-by-number set. Excel applies the same formats to all the cells with the same style, just as you would apply the same paint to all the areas of a paint-by-number set with the same number. The formatting used for a specific style is like the color applied to a specific number. You can create very different looks by changing the formatting a style represents, just as you can change how a paint-by-numbers set looks if you apply green instead of blue to areas with the number 1.

To set the formatting that a style represents:

1. Select a cell that looks the way you want all the cells with the style to look.

2. Choose <u>S</u>tyle from the F<u>o</u>rmat menu, or press the ALT+' key combination.

3. Type a name for the style in the <u>S</u>tyle Name box.

The rest of the dialog box reflects the different formatting that exists in the selected cell, as shown here:

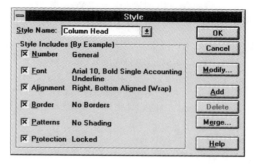

4. Make any changes to the formats that this style represents. You can remove formatting from a style by clearing one of the check boxes. You can also change one or more settings by clicking <u>M</u>odify to display the same Format Cells dialog box that you see when you format individual cells.

5. Click <u>A</u>dd.

To modify an existing style:

1. Choose <u>S</u>tyle from the F<u>o</u>rmat menu, or press the ALT+' key combination.

2. Select the style name in the <u>S</u>tyle Name box. The Style dialog box shows the settings that the style name represents.

3. Make the desired changes to the formats that this style represents. You can remove formatting from a style by clearing one of the check boxes. You can also change one or more settings by clicking <u>M</u>odify to display the same Format Cells dialog box that you see when you format individual cells.

4. Click OK.

The appearance of all the cells that use the modified style changes to reflect the new formatting selections.

Tech Tip: When you want to change the appearance of all the cells to which you have not made formatting changes, modify the Normal style. By default, all cells start out with this style and continue to use it until you assign a different one. When you alter the Normal style, it changes in only the active workbook, not all your other workbooks.

To apply the styles you have created:

1. Select the cells to which you want to apply the style.

2. Choose <u>S</u>tyle from the F<u>o</u>rmat menu, or press the ALT+' combination.

3. Select the style in the <u>S</u>tyle Name box. You can limit which features of the style are applied to the selected cells by clearing the check boxes for the different formatting features that the style represents.

4. Click OK to apply the style to the cells.

If you later modify the formats that a style represents, the appearance of every cell using the style changes accordingly.

Tech Tip: If you use styles frequently, you may want to add the Style box to a toolbar. You can apply styles by simply selecting cells and then picking the style name in the Style box. If you type a new name into the Style box, Excel create a new style that applies the formatting of the current cell.

I thought pressing DEL cleared a cell. However, when I type a new entry, it has the same font and format as the old one. How do I clear the formatting when I clear the entry?

Pressing the DEL key only clears the cell's contents, not its formatting. Thus, when you place a new entry in the cell, it assumes the previous entry's formatting. To remove the formatting as well as the contents, choose Clea<u>r</u> from the <u>E</u>dit menu and then choose <u>A</u>ll. The cell should now revert to the formats set by the Normal style.

How do I format cells so that their contents are justified?

Excel's justification feature, which is just like the one used in a word processor, automatically wraps text within a cell to best fit the column width. You can also justify text in text boxes. An example of justification is shown in the following illustration.

	A	B	C	D
1	Notes:			
2	Sharon: You asked about calculating the unpaid principal. You don't. Each loan folder has its own calculation schedule printed when the loan is made. However, there are two exceptions for when you do have to make these calculations.			

To justify cell entries:

1. Select the range of cells whose text you want to justify.

2. Choose C_ells from the F_ormat menu.

3. Click the Alignment tab.

4. Check the Justify option button in the Horizontal section to apply left and right justification.

5. Click OK.

Tech Tip: To change the alignment of text in a text box, click the text box border to select the text box itself rather than the text in the box.

I need to enter long text entries in my worksheet but I keep running into the 255-character cell limit. How can I make these long text entries?

Rather than placing a long text entry in an individual cell, you can put it in a text box. Text boxes can contain as many as 10,240 characters with up to 254 carriage returns. You can also move and size text boxes within the worksheet.

To add a text box:

1. Click the Text Box button on the Standard or Drawing toolbar, as shown here:

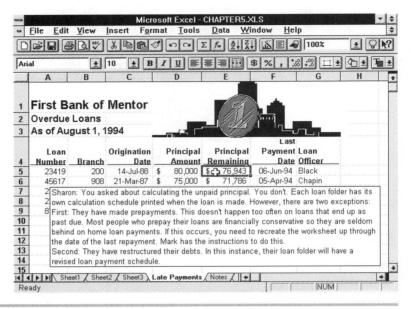

FIGURE 5-1 Text box added to a worksheet

2. Drag the mouse from where you want the box to start to where you want it to end. You can force the box to start and end at the same location as the worksheet gridlines by holding down ALT while you drag the box.

3. Release the mouse and type the text you want to appear in the box.

Figure 5-1 shows a text box added to a worksheet.

Tech Tip: When you enter or edit text in a text box, you can only set the font it uses. To add other formatting, click the text box border and then choose Object from the Format menu.

Can I put cell entries in text boxes?

Yes, you can link a text box to a cell to display its contents. This feature allows you to repeat an entry in one location in the workbook in a text box elsewhere in the same workbook. When you link a text box to a cell containing a formula, the link is actually to the formula's result, not the underlying formula. An example of a text box that is linked to a cell is shown in Figure 5-2.

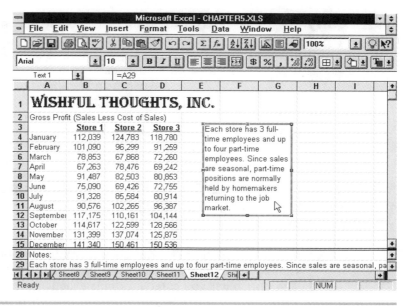

FIGURE 5-2 Linking a text box to a cell entry

Tech Tip: You cannot format individual characters in a text box linked to a cell. You can only set the overall format of the text box's contents.

To create a link:

1. Create the text box to contain the cell entry by clicking the Text Box button on the Standard or Drawing toolbar and dragging the mouse from where you want the box to start to where you want it to end.

2. Select the text box.

3. Click the formula bar or press F2.

4. Enter an equal sign followed by a cell reference. The text box now contains a link to the cell.

Tech Tip: To reference a cell on another sheet, remember to include the sheet name, followed by an exclamation point, before the cell reference; for example, =Sheet3!C4.

Can I copy column widths when I copy entire columns?

Yes. Excel 5.0 offers an improved copy and paste feature. Now, when you copy an entire column, Excel duplicates features such as column width and wrapped text. Similarly, characteristics such as row height are carried over when you copy an entire row.

When I enter a date as 12/15/93, it displays as a decimal fraction; when I enter 12-15-93, Excel subtracts the numbers. What is wrong?

You have turned on the Transition Formula Entry option, which is designed to help people convert from Lotus 1-2-3 to Excel. This option lets you enter a formula exactly as you would in Lotus 1-2-3 and is activated automatically when you open a Lotus 1-2-3 worksheet in Excel.

To disable this feature:

1. Choose Options from the Tools menu.
2. Click the Transition tab.
3. Clear the Transition Formula Entry check box.
4. Click OK.

How do I redisplay hidden columns?

There are two ways to redisplay hidden columns:

- Select the columns on either side of the hidden column. Choose Column from the Format menu and then choose Unhide from the submenu.

- Select entire columns, click them with the right mouse button, and choose Unhide from the shortcut menu. If column A is hidden, select column B and drag the mouse to the Select All button, which is the gray rectangle at the upper-left corner of your worksheet, before you choose Unhide from the shortcut menu to display column A.

To redisplay hidden rows, choose <u>R</u>ows from the <u>F</u>ormat menu and then choose <u>U</u>nhide.

Tech Tip: Excel provides several keyboard shortcuts for hiding and unhiding columns and rows. You can hide columns you have selected by pressing CTRL+0. Similarly, you hide rows by pressing CTRL+9. Pressing CTRL+SHIFT+0 unhides columns; pressing CTRL+SHIFT+9 unhides rows.

How do I check my spelling in Excel?

Spelling mistakes in your sheets look unprofessional and detract from the information you are presenting. You should always check the spelling before you print a sheet. To check spelling in the active worksheet or chart, choose <u>S</u>pelling from the <u>T</u>ools menu or click the Spelling button on the Standard toolbar.

The data Excel checks for spelling errors depends on whether you made a selection beforehand. If you have not selected cells or words in the current cell entry, Excel checks the spelling of the entire sheet, or the current cell entry if you are in Edit mode. If you preselected more than one cell or more than one word in the formula bar, Excel only checks the spelling of the selected cells or words.

As it checks the spelling, Excel displays the following dialog box whenever it encounters a word it doesn't recognize:

You can use the options described in the following table to control what Excel identifies as errors and whether or not it corrects them.

Option	Action
Ignore	Does not change the word found and continues to find the next word it does not recognize
Ignore All	Does not change the word found and ignores other instances of this word as it continues to search for words it does not recognize
Change	Replaces the word found with the word selected in the Change To box and then continues to find the next word it does not recognize
Change All	Replaces all occurrences of the word found with the word selected in the Change To box as it searches for more words it does not recognize
Add	Adds the word it has found to the custom dictionary selected in the Add Words To box and then continues to find more words it does not recognize
Suggest	Searches for words similar to the entry in the Change To box
Change To	Provides the replacement entry to be used by Change and Change All; it's also the word for which Excel looks for alternatives when you click Suggest
Suggestions	Lists possible alternatives for the word it does not recognize; selecting another word from this list replaces the entry in the Change To box.
Add Words To	Selects the custom dictionary in which Excel inserts any word you add; by default, Excel uses CUSTOM.DIC, but you can use any dictionary you created with Word for Windows if it is installed on your system
Always Suggest	Turns on and off the feature that finds words similar to the one it does not recognize
Ignore UPPERCASE	Turns on and off the feature that determines whether Excel checks the spelling of words that appear in uppercase
Undo Last	Undoes the last spelling change you have made

Tech Terror: You cannot check spelling if the Spell Checker is not installed. You select this feature in the Tools option category when you perform a Complete/Custom installation or click Add/Remove in the Microsoft Excel 5.0 Setup program.

119

Chapter 5 *Formatting*

I don't want any negative numbers to show in a range of cells. Can I prevent this?

Yes, you can create a custom number format whose negative section is blank. For example, the number format 0.00;;0 displays two digits after the decimal point for positive numbers, no negative numbers, and zero as a single digit.

Can I display my numbers in millions without dividing by a million?

Yes. Excel can format numbers to thousands or millions. For example, you can display the number 1,300,000 as 1.3. To do this:

1. Choose Cells from the Format menu.
2. Click the Number tab.
3. Type #,, in the Code box.
   Typing #, will display thousands and #,,, will display billions. You enter one comma for every three places you want to hide.
4. Click OK.

This format retains the original number (1,300,000) and displays it as 1.3.

I have heard that I can enter data quickly with the fill handle. What is it and how do I use it?

The *fill handle* quickly repeats entries. You can enter the same value in multiple cells or you can enter a series of increasing or decreasing values. You can copy a formula from one cell to others as well as fill a range of cells with entries from custom lists using the fill handle.

Before you can use the fill handle, you must first enter one or more entries, such as the ones shown here, that will act like "seeds" that determine the results Excel "grows."

	A	B	C	D	E	F	G	H	I	
1	Monday									
2	Jan	Mar								
3	Division Sales									
4	5	10								
5	1-May	8-May								
6	100000	130000								

When you want a range filled with the entries in an AutoFill list, you need to provide the first entry, such as Monday. If you want to skip some of the entries, such as adding every other month from the AutoFill list containing the months, you need to provide the first two entries, such as Jan and Mar. To create an increasing or decreasing series, enter the first few values that Excel should use to determine the pattern, such as the 5 and 10 or 1-May and 8-May. When you want text, a number, or a formula repeated in other cells, you only need to enter that particular entry, such as in Division Sales or +B6*1.3 (the formula that produces 130,000 in the illustration).

To use a fill handle:

1. Enter one or more initial entries.

2. Select the seed entries and point to the fill handle, which appears as a small square in the lower-right corner of the selection. The mouse pointer in the preceding illustration points to the range's fill handle and displays as a small plus sign.

3. Drag the fill handle to select the other cells you want to fill. In the preceding illustration, you could select each range, in turn, and then select A1:G1, A2:G2, A3:D3, A4:I4, A5:I5, and B6:I6, respectively. In the last case, you do not want to include A6 in the selection since you want to repeat the formula, not the 100000 value, in A6.

4. Release the mouse button.

Excel fills the remaining cells in the selection with entries based on the entries in the original range. For example, you might use the fill handle to produce the results shown here based on the previous illustration:

	A	B	C	D	E	F	G	H	I	
1	Monday	Tuesday	Wednesda	Thursday	Friday	Saturday	Sunday			
2	Jan	Mar	May	Jul	Sep	Nov	Jan			
3	Division Sa	Division Sa	Division Sa	Division Sales						
4	5	10	15	20	25	30	35	40	45	
5	1-May	8-May	15-May	22-May	29-May	5-Jun	12-Jun	19-Jun	26-Jun	
6	100000	130000	169000	219700	285610	371293	482680.9	627485.2	815730.7	

Besides the AutoFill lists that Excel provides, you can add other lists, as described in the following question.

I created a new AutoFill list of names, but Excel treated the first and last names as separate entries rather than keeping them together. What's wrong?

To keep first and last names together in a custom AutoFill list when they include commas, you must enclose them in single quotes using the format '*lastname,firstname.*'

To create a new AutoFill list:

1. Choose Options from the Tools menu.

2. Click the Custom Lists tab.

3. Type the entries in the List Entries box, pressing ENTER after each one. When the entries includes commas, add single quotes around the entry as in 'Doe, John'.

4. Click OK to add the list and leave the Options dialog box.

If the entries already appear on a sheet, you can save yourself time by following these steps instead:

1. Select the entries to include in the list.

2. Choose Options from the Tools menu.

3. Click the Custom Lists tab. The range of cells you selected in step 1 appears in the Import List from Cells box.

4. Click Import. Excel creates a list containing the entries in the selected cells.

   Figure 5-3 shows the selected entries and the list that Excel created from them. When you import names with a format such as Doe, John, Excel picks them up correctly.

5. Click OK.

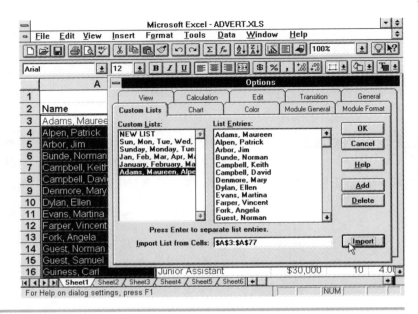

FIGURE 5-3 AutoFill entries created by importing cell entries

Can I turn the gridlines off in only part of a worksheet?

No, but you can turn off all the gridlines, and display gridlines in only a section of the sheet by adding borders, which have the same appearance as gridlines, to particular cells.

To hide all the gridlines:

1. Choose Options from the Tools menu.
2. Click the View tab.
3. Clear the Gridlines check box.
4. Click OK.

To add "gridlines" to a section of a sheet by adding borders:

Tech Tip: These "gridlines" print even if you turn off gridlines as a printing option.

1. Highlight the cells that you want to have "gridlines."
2. Choose Cells from the Format menu.
3. Click the Border tab.
4. Select the Top, Left, Right, and Bottom check boxes.
5. Click OK.

I want to type numbers into certain cells in my worksheet and have Excel add the decimal point in the correct place. I know there's a fixed decimal function that will do this for the whole sheet, but can I add this feature to only certain cells?

You can assign a number format to certain cells, which automatically adds the decimal point to numbers. To add the format:

1. Select the cells to which you want Excel to automatically add a decimal point.

2. Choose Cells from the Format menu.

3. Click the Number tab.

4. Type **0"."000** in the Code box. You must enter the quotes to make this work the way you want. (This example assumes you want three digits after the decimal point.)

5. Click OK.

 Can I remove the formulas from my worksheets without removing the values they've calculated?

You can convert formulas to their respective values by following these steps:

1. Select the range that contains the formulas.

2. Copy the range to the Clipboard by either choosing Copy from the Edit menu, clicking the Copy button on the Standard toolbar, or choosing Copy from the shortcut menu that appears when you click the selection with the right mouse button.

3. Choose Paste Special from the Edit menu or the shortcut menu.

4. Select Values and make sure Operation remains set to None.

5. Click OK, and then press ENTER or ESC.

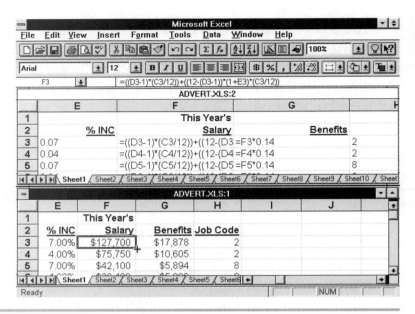

FIGURE 5-4   You can quickly display formatted and unformatted versions of a sheet

You can quickly check whether the worksheet contains formulas or their results by pressing the CTRL+' key combination. This shortcut toggles between the formatted sheet and an unformatted version. The unformatted version shows the actual text, numbers, and formulas stored in the cells. Figure 5-4 shows the difference between the two versions of a workbook that display when you press this key combination.

I have a cell that I am trying to format in two different fonts, and it is not working. Why?

The entry in the cell is probably the result of a formula. Formula results cannot include multiple character formats.

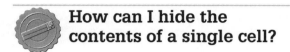

How can I hide the contents of a single cell?

Excel offers several ways to hide a cell's entry. One technique is to format the font in the cell to be the same color as the background.

To change the font color, select the cell, and then select the font color by doing one of the following:

- Click the arrow next to the Font Color button on the Formatting toolbar, shown here, and select the color that matches the background:

- Click the Cycle Font Color button, as necessary, until the font in the cell appears in the same color as the background. This button, shown here, does not appear by default on any toolbar, so you must add it to one first:

- Choose Cells from the Format menu. Click the Font tab and a select a color in the Color box. To prevent this color from being changed by yourself or others, you can then lock the cell as described in the previous question.

If the contents of the cell are strictly numeric, an easier way to hide the contents is to create and apply a ;;; number format.

When a cell entry's font matches the background color or a number has a ;;; format, you can still see the entry in the formula bar. If you want to hide the entry in the formula bar as well, you can format the cell to hide the cell's contents, whether they are text or a value, when the sheet or workbook is protected. To do so:

1. Click the Select All button in the upper-left corner of the current sheet.

Tech Tip: To display a Font Color toolbar containing the colors that can be applied to cell entries, click the Font Color button and then drag the palette away from the toolbar. You can hide this toolbar by clicking its control box.

2. Choose C**e**lls from the F**o**rmat menu.

3. Click the Protection tab.

4. Clear the **L**ocked and **H**idden check boxes.

5. Click OK.

6. Select the cell that you want to lock and hide.

7. Choose C**e**lls from the F**o**rmat menu.

8. Click the Protection tab.

9. Select the **L**ocked and **H**idden check boxes.

10. Click OK.

11. Choose **P**rotection from the **T**ools menu and then choose Protect Sheet.

12. Enter a password if necessary, and click OK.

Tech Tip: Selecting the **L**ocked check box is not necessary to hide the cell, but it does prevent anyone from accidentally making an entry in it.

Now, when you select the cell, Excel does not display its contents in the formula bar.

Tech Tip: If you want to protect an entire workbook rather than just the sheet, choose **P**rotection from the **T**ools menu and then choose Protect **W**orkbook.

Excel 4.0 had a Group Edit option so I could enter data in and format a number of sheets at the same time. I cannot find Group Edit. Is this feature still available in Excel 5.0?

To group sheets together in Excel 5.0, hold down the CTRL key while clicking the tabs of the sheets you want to include in the group. For example, if you want to group sheets 1, 4, and 5 together, hold down the CTRL key and click the three tabs. Excel selects the sheet tabs to indicate that they're grouped together. To ungroup the sheets, click the tab of any one of the grouped sheets with the right mouse button and choose Ungroup Sheets from the shortcut menu. You can also simply click the tab of any ungrouped sheet.

I work with time intervals that exceed 24 hours. Do I have to use the same complicated formulas that I used in Excel 4.0 to turn the results into text?

Excel 5.0 allows three new time number formats to correctly display times that exceed 24 hours when you're working with hours, 60 minutes when you're working with minutes, and 60 seconds when you're working with seconds. These number formats are [h]:mm:ss, [mm]:ss, and [ss], respectively.

The first of these formats is built into Excel; you must create the other two. For example, you could show that an employee worked 55 hours during a week by following these steps:

1. Select the cell to which you want to apply the format.

2. Choose C<u>e</u>lls from the F<u>o</u>rmat menu.

3. Click the Number tab.

4. Select Time in the <u>C</u>ategory box.

5. Select the [h]:mm:ss format in the <u>F</u>ormat Codes box.

6. Click OK.

7. Enter **55** in the cell to display it as 55:00:00.

Figure 5-5 shows a worksheet that uses this format to display elapsed time and total hours for billing purposes.

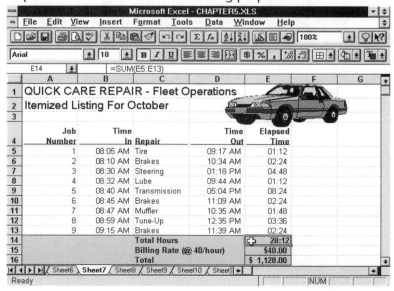

FIGURE 5-5   A worksheet that uses the [h]:mm:ss format

To use either the [mm]:ss or the [ss] format, select Time in the Category box in step 4 and then move to the Code box, type **[mm]:ss** or **[ss]**, and click OK. This number format will appear in the Format Codes list box for the Time category for the remainder of the Excel session.

I would like to have subtotals appear for my data. Is that possible?

Excel can add subtotals for you as long as you have sorted your data appropriately and included headings at the top of each column, as in a database. For example, you would follow these steps to create regional subtotals for the data shown in Figure 5-6, which has already been sorted by region:

1. Choose Subtotals from the Data menu to display the Subtotal dialog box, which will appear like the one shown here:

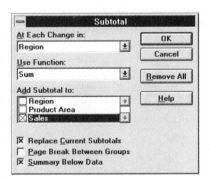

Notice that Excel automatically tries to identify the range of cells with which to work. If the range is not correct, click Cancel and then select the range you want to use before you choose the Subtotals command again.

```
┌──────────────────────────────────────────────────────────────┐
│                  Microsoft Excel - CHAPTER5.XLS            ▼│▲│
│ ▫  File  Edit  View  Insert  Format  Tools  Data  Window  Help    │▼│
├──────────────────────────────────────────────────────────────┤
│ □☞◨│🖶◙❤│✂▥▦◇│↶↷│Σ ƒ│ᴬ↓ᶻ↑│▨▤◪│100%  │▼│♀▶?│
├──────────────────────────────────────────────────────────────┤
│    A3       │  ▼  │    Region                                    │
├─────┬──────┬────────┬──────┬────┬────┬────┬────┬────┬────┬──┤
│     │  A   │   B    │  C   │ D  │ E  │ F  │ G  │ H  │ I  │▲│
├─────┼──────┴────────┴──────┼────┼────┼────┼────┼────┼────┼──┤
│  1  │Region Unit Sales in Thousands                            │
│  2  │                                                          │
│  3  │Region ⬚ Product Area │  Sales                            │
│  4  │Boston     Product 1  │  2,565                            │
│  5  │Boston     Product 2  │  4,430                            │
│  6  │Boston     Product 3  │    130                            │
│  7  │Boston     Product 4  │  8,712                            │
│  8  │New York   Product 1  │  1,890                            │
│  9  │New York   Product 2  │  9,150                            │
│ 10  │New York   Product 3  │  8,230                            │
│ 11  │New York   Product 4  │  1,100                            │
│ 12  │Dallas     Product 1  │    510                            │
│ 13  │Dallas     Product 2  │  7,842                            │
│ 14  │Dallas     Product 3  │  1,600                            │
│ 15  │Dallas     Product 4  │  9,780                            │
│ 16  │Chicago    Product 1  │  1,009                            │
│ 17  │Chicago    Product 2  │  3,590                            │
│ 18  │Chicago    Product 3  │  2,003                            │
│ 19  │Chicago    Product 4  │  2,135                            │
│ 20  │                                                          │▼│
├─────┴──────────────────────────────────────────────────────┤
│ ◀◀▶▶▌\ Sheet6 / Sheet7 \ Sheet8 / Sheet9 / Sheet10 / Sheet│◀▶│
│ Ready                                    │      │NUM│        │
└──────────────────────────────────────────────────────────────┘
```

FIGURE 5-6   Data set up to add subtotals

Tech Tip: If you make a mistake, you can immediately choose Undo Subtotal from the Edit menu to restore the data to its original form. You can also remove all the subtotals by choosing Subtotals from the Data menu and clicking the Remove All button.

2. Choose the field for which you want to show a subtotal in the At Each Change in drop-down list box. In this case, you would select Region to create regional subtotals.

3. Choose the function you want to use for the subtotal in the Use Function box. The default is the SUM function.

4. Select the check boxes for the fields whose values you want to subtotal in the Add Subtotal to list box. When you select a field's check box, Excel subtotals the field's values for each group of records that has the same value as the field selected in the At Each Change in box.

5. Click OK.

Excel adds the subtotals and automatically outlines the sheet, as shown in Figure 5-7. In this case, the AutoFormat feature was used to improve the subtotals' appearance.

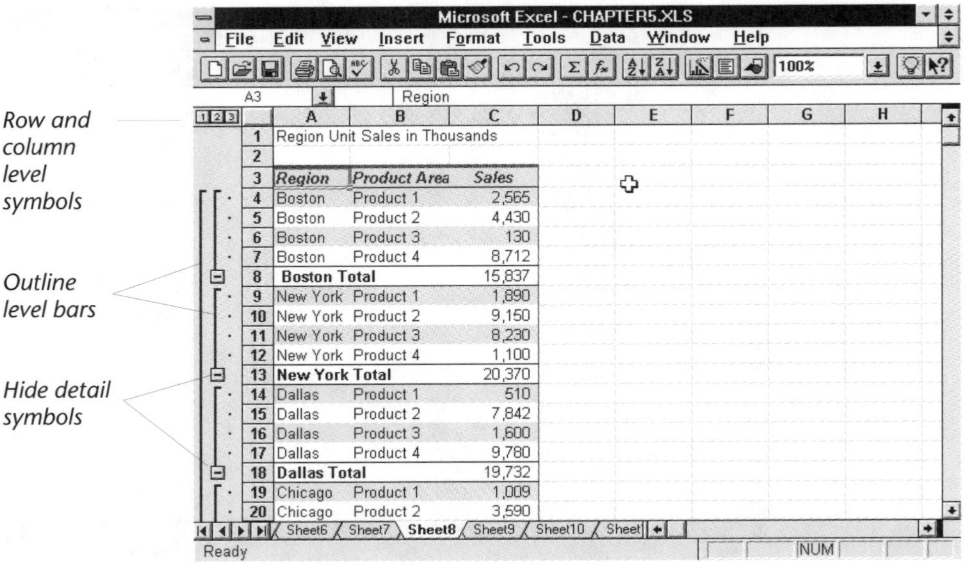

Row and column level symbols

Outline level bars

Hide detail symbols

FIGURE 5-7   Excel can add subtotals to a sheet

You can control which levels of the outlined data appear in the worksheet by clicking the row and column level symbols that appear to the left of the Select-All button. You can also hide an individual group within an outline by clicking the hide detail symbol in its outline level bar. When you hide the underlying data in the sheet shown in Figure 5-7, it looks like this:

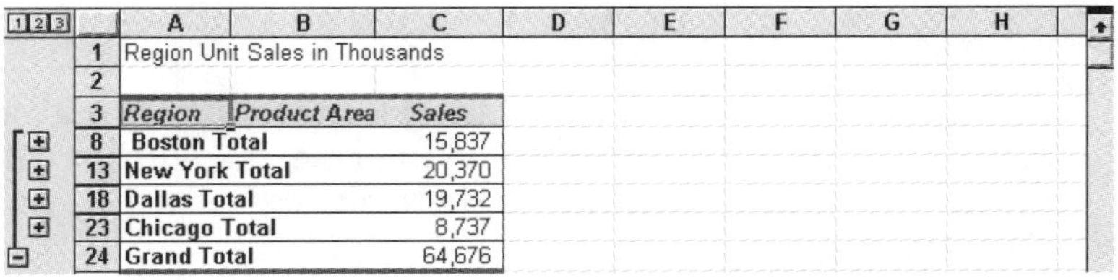

I would like to insert a tab between the data in the same cell, but Excel moves to the next cell every time I press TAB. Can I insert a tab into a cell?

To insert a tab into a cell, you must hold down both the CTRL and ALT keys, and then press TAB. Excel is really adding enough spaces so the text after the "tab" starts at what would be the next tab stop. These tab stops are located at every 1/2 inch.

I have some calculations that return a value to three decimal places. Since I only need a precision of two decimal places, I formatted the cells to display two decimals. However, Excel still shows three-decimal precision when I perform calculations with these cells. Is there a way around this?

To use numbers in calculations as they are displayed:

1. Choose Options from the Tools menu.
2. Click the Calculation tab.
3. Select the Precision as Displayed check box.
4. Click OK.

This option converts all the numbers in the worksheet to the precision at which they are displayed. For example, in a cell with a format that shows only two decimal places, Excel permanently changes an entry of 5.346 to 5.35.

Tech Terror: Be sure you want to apply this option to *all* the values in the worksheet, because it cannot be undone!

How should I format my data so that my text is distributed across a range of cells?

Perform these steps to have Excel rearrange text so that it fills a range:

1. Enter the text in a cell in the left column of the range in which you want to distribute the text.

2. Select the range in which you want to distribute the text.

3. Choose Fill from the Edit menu, and then choose Justify.

Excel distributes the text across the selected range. For example, suppose you have the following text in A2:

If you select A2:G2 and then choose Justify on the Fill submenu, the text looks like this:

Excel moves the text to additional rows in the first column so that it fits across the selected columns.

Tech Tip: You can also separate text in a cell into multiple lines within the same cell by pressing ALT+ENTER or by turning on the wrap text feature described in the answer to the question "Can I display text on several lines within a single cell?," which appears earlier in this chapter.

I added borders to cells that I want to emphasize, but after I sorted the list, the wrong entries had borders. Why aren't the borders moving when I sort?

There is no way to enable this feature in Excel 5.0. The reason that Excel no longer sorts borders is that often they are used to highlight a specific area in a worksheet, such as totals or subtotals, rather than specific entries. Therefore, Excel leaves the borders in the same locations rather than moving them with their entries.

How can I display text vertically in a cell?

Excel offers four options that let you control the orientation of the text within a cell, three of which display the cell's contents vertically. To display text vertically in a cell:

1. Choose Cells from the Format menu.
2. Click the Alignment tab.
3. Specify the desired text orientation by selecting one of the orientation boxes.
4. Select the Wrap Text check box, if you want Excel to wrap the text.
5. Click OK.

Excel adjusts the row height, as necessary, to accommodate the new text alignment. You can always set the row height yourself, and if the Wrap Text check box is selected, Excel will change how the text wraps accordingly.

Here are some examples of the different alignment options:

	A	B	C	D	E	F	G	H	I
1	Horizontal Text	Wrapped Horizontal Text	Vertical	Wrapped Vertical Text	Vertical Text	Wrapped	Vertical Text	Vertical Text	Wrapped

When you modify a cell with vertical orientation, Excel temporarily displays the cell in the default horizontal orientation to make it easier to edit the entry.

Tech Terror: If Excel changes how the cell entry wraps within a cell when you print the sheet, change the font to a TrueType font. These fonts look the same on screen as they do when they are printed.

Tech Tip: When you want vertical text to span several rows, put the text in a text box and then set the vertical alignment.

Is it possible to keep my row and column headings in place while I move around the rest of the sheet and make changes?

You can keep information displayed while you move to another section of the sheet by using either panes or worksheet titles.

Panes split the sheet into two or four parts to look at different sections of a sheet. Figure 5-8 shows a sheet split into four *panes*. To split a window like this, move to the cell that you want to be the upper-left corner of the fourth pane and then choose Split from the Window menu. You can also add *split bars* by dragging the *split boxes* to the desired locations. These split boxes add the horizontal and vertical dividers separately.

Once you've added them, you can move among panes by clicking them, in turn, or pressing F6. As you move around in a quadrant, the parts of the sheet that you see in the other quadrants change. The panes are synchronized so as you move to the left or right, the pane above or below the one you are in continues to show the same columns. As you move up or down,

Split box to add a horizontal split bar

Split box to add a vertical split bar

	A	E	F	G	H	I	J	K
1		tment						
2	DEPT.	1991	1990	1989	1988	1987	1986	
9	160	55	26	21	54	42	92	
10	175	93	46	37	17	50	45	
11	180	8	60	73	98	15	87	
12	190	76	6	9	57	94	16	
13	195	91	83	5	39	23	87	
14	200	48	87	13	32	94	16	
15	210	60	61	19	52	23	87	
16	220	65	31	20	30	94	44	
17	225	42	18	74	64	19	28	
18	228	1	49	49	57	100	23	
19	230	46	9	77	70	6	9	
20	235	73	82	4	2	57	62	
21	240	7	88	34	36	18	43	
22	245	28	1	9	76	51	28	
23								
24								
25	TOTAL	937	910	775	994	820	902	
26								

Microsoft Excel - CHAPTER5.XLS

File Edit View Insert Format Tools Data Window Help

J25 =SUM(J3:J22)

100%

Ready NUM

FIGURE 5-8   A sheet split into four panes

Tech Tip: To adjust the split bar so that it falls on a gridline rather than splitting a cell, drag the bar itself, not the split box.

the pane to the left or right continues to show the same rows. When you have finished and want to remove the split, choose Remove Split from the Window menu. You can also double-click a split bar to remove it.

The other way to keep specific columns and rows on the screen is to freeze them as titles so that they don't scroll as you move within the worksheet. Before you freeze the titles, move to the cell below and to the right of the last row and column you want to freeze on the screen. For example, if you want rows 1 through 3 and column A to always appear, you would move to B4. Then, choose Freeze Panes from the Window menu. Excel adds a heavy line to indicate that the titles are frozen. At this point, you are still moving within one area rather than separate panes.

I have several objects on my spreadsheet that overlap one another. How can I arrange them so that a certain object appears to be in front of the others?

The objects in your sheet are layered on top of one another just like papers in a pile. You can change their order by following these steps:

1. Select the object you want to appear either in front of or behind another object.

2. Choose Placement from the Format menu or display the object's shortcut menu by clicking it with the right mouse button.

3. Choose either Bring to Front or Send to Back depending upon which action you want to perform.

I have a column of data that I want to display in all uppercase. Can I do this without formatting each cell individually?

Excel includes functions that convert text from one case to another. To display a column of entries in uppercase:

1. Select an empty cell to the right of the data that you want to convert. For example, if your data is in column A and starts in A1, select cell B1 (assuming B1 is empty).

2. Enter the formula **=UPPER(A1)** in the cell. B1 should now display the contents of A1 in uppercase.

3. Copy this formula down the column by dragging the fill handle for B1 as far as you have data in column A.

4. Release the mouse button.

Two functions related to UPPER() work the same way: LOWER() converts to lowercase and PROPER() converts to proper case (the first letter of each word is capitalized). If you no longer want to see the unconverted data, you can hide the column.

You can replace the text with the results of this function by copying the result values of the function on top of the unconverted text. To do so:

1. Select the cells that contain the functions.

2. Choose <u>C</u>opy from the <u>E</u>dit menu.

3. Select the original entries.

4. Choose Paste <u>S</u>pecial from the <u>E</u>dit menu.

5. Select the <u>V</u>alues option button and click OK.

6. Press ENTER to finish the pasting.

Can I center one label across several columns?

You can use one of Excel's alignment options to center an entry across columns, as follows:

1. Enter the text in the leftmost column of the range across which you want to center the entry.

2. Highlight the columns across which the entry will appear.

3. Choose C<u>e</u>lls from the F<u>o</u>rmat menu.

4. Click the Alignment tab.

5. Select the Center <u>a</u>cross selection option button.

6. Click OK.

A shortcut for steps 3 through 6 is to click the Center Across Columns button on the Formatting toolbar. The following illustration shows a worksheet in which the text was centered:

	A	B	C	D	E	F	G	H	
A1			New Employees By Department						
1	✛		New Employees By Department						
2	DEPT.	1994	1993	1992	1991	1990	1989	19	

As you can see, the label stored in column A appears in columns B through F because it is centered over columns A through G.

 ### When I copy and paste a range of cells, does Excel duplicate everything in the new location?

When you copy and paste a range, Excel duplicates the cell contents and formatting of the cell, including the wrap text format. It does not, however, transfer the column width and row height to the destination— these attributes belong to the column or row itself, not the individual cells.

 ### Some of the Formatting toolbar buttons seem to work differently depending on how I click them. Why?

Some Formatting buttons—such as the Borders, Color, and Font Color buttons shown here—consist of both a button and an arrow:

Borders   Color   Font
                                 Color

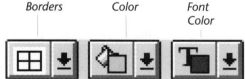

Clicking the button produces a different result than clicking the arrow. For example, when you click the Font Color button, you apply the color currently displayed on the button to whatever text is selected. When you click this button's arrow, you display a palette from which you can choose a color to apply to the text.

Certain toolbar buttons also perform the opposite function if you click them while holding down SHIFT. For example, if you click the Sort Ascending button while holding down SHIFT, you sort in descending order. This feature increases the functionality of toolbar buttons. For example, because you can use the Sort Ascending button to sort in either order, you could remove the Sort Descending button from the Standard toolbar to make room for another one. Buttons that perform this way include Delete, Insert, Delete Column, Insert Column, Delete Row, Insert Row, Paste Values, Paste Formulas, Increase Decimals, Decrease Decimals, Increase Font Size, Decrease Font Size, Zoom In, Zoom Out, Run Macro, and Step Macro.

Some buttons perform different but not necessarily the opposite function when you click them while holding down SHIFT. For example, the Print and Print Preview buttons perform each other's function when you click them while holding down SHIFT. Also, the AutoFormat button applies the next table format rather than the last table format if you click this button while holding down SHIFT.

Can I move a group of graphic objects together as a unit?

Yes, you can combine objects such as drawing objects and embedded or linked data into a group so they move as a unit. To group the objects, select each one and choose <u>P</u>lacement from the F<u>o</u>rmat menu and then <u>G</u>roup. Now, the objects will move as one. Also, the group of objects has a single set of handles rather than each individual one having its own. To ungroup the objects, select the group and then choose <u>U</u>ngroup from the <u>P</u>lacement submenu.

You can group selected objects by clicking the Group Objects button on the Drawing toolbar. The Drawing toolbar also includes an Ungroup Objects button to ungroup the selected objects. The Group Objects and Ungroup Objects buttons look like this:

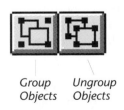

Group   Ungroup
Objects   Objects

I have a cell that has mixed formatting. Whenever I try to copy its format using the Format Painter, Excel only seems to copy the format of the first character. What's happening?

Excel 5.0 now comes with Rich Text Formatting (RTF), which allows mixed formatting in cells. However, when you copy and paste formatting to another cell, only the format that applies to the first character is copied. The information is copied on a per cell basis as opposed to a per character basis.

Printing

Printing problems in the past often revolved around trying to make your spreadsheet data look better than if you had typed it on a typewriter. Excel 5.0 can do so much more than that now! With the formatting you can add to a spreadsheet, you can present your data as a professional report, rather than as a bland collection of numbers and text. With WYSIWYG (what you see is what you get) display, Excel shows you exactly how your data looks as you enter it, which, in turn, is exactly what you see when you print your workbook. Because Excel relies on the Windows Print Manager, it's already set up to use your printer if you are running other Windows applications.

The problems discussed in this chapter range from straightforward tasks, such as selecting the data to print, to more sophisticated ones, such as changing the order of the jobs in the Windows Print Manager so you can print your Excel data first.

FRUSTRATION BUSTERS!

If you are new to printing spreadsheet data or to printing in general, you should become familiar with how Excel defines the various areas on a page. Excel uses the following terms, which are also labeled in Figure 6-1.

- The *print area* is the area selected in your workbook for Excel to print. You can set the print area every time you print or set a default for a workbook if you print the same section every time. If you do not have a print area selected when you print, Excel assumes that you want to print all the entries in selected sheets. You can prevent certain columns and rows in these sheets from printing by hiding them.

- The *header* and *footer* are text areas that appear on the top and bottom of each page, respectively. Headers and footers are common locations for inserting the workbook name, the date, and the page number. For the printed workbook shown in Figure 6-1, the top three lines are the header, and the page number at the bottom is the footer.

- *Print titles* designate one or more columns or rows that print at the left or along the top of every page. The print titles identify the contents of the workbook by serving as column and row headings. In Figure 6-1, the first column and the top two rows appear on every page.

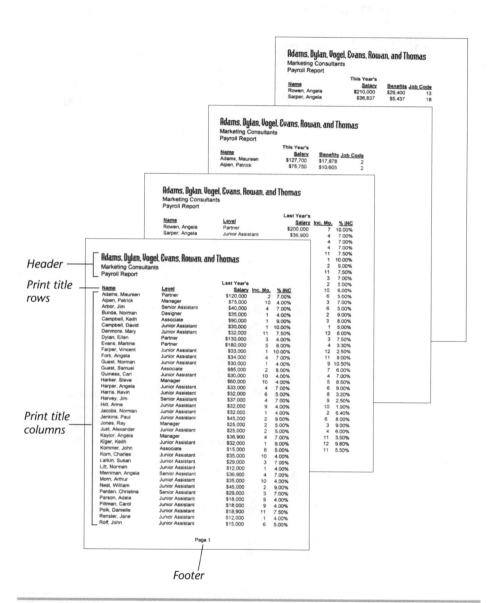

FIGURE 6-1 The terms Excel uses to describe the printed workbook

I started to print but so far nothing has happened. Why won't Excel print my data?

When Excel prints your data, the program prepares it and sends it to the Windows Print Manager, which accepts printing tasks from all Windows applications and sends them to the printer one at a time. Assuming you haven't seen an error message generated by Excel, the problem relates to the transfer of information from the Print Manager to the printer. Before you start looking for a complicated solution to your problem, check the following simple fixes. You'll be amazed how often these minor oversights cause major headaches!

- *Is the printer turned on?* It may sound simple, but it's often the culprit.

- *Does the printer have paper?* This problem also seems obvious—that is, until you've spent 15 minutes trying to solve the problem before discovering an empty paper tray.

- *Is the printer online?* Most printers have a button that puts the printer online and takes it offline. Usually, this button has a light or some other indicator that lets you know the printer is online. When the printer is offline, it cannot receive information from the computer.

- *Can another application print?* You can use the Paintbrush accessory to quickly test whether the problem rests with Excel itself or with the Windows printer settings. Open or create a text file in the Paintbrush accessory, and then choose <u>P</u>rint from the <u>F</u>ile menu. If it prints, the Windows settings for the printer are correct. You can also check the printer configuration by double-clicking the Printers icon in the Control Panel.

- *Are you printing on a network?* If so, the problem may relate to the network itself. In this case, you should contact your network administrator, who should be able to resolve the difficulty. If the printer is assigned to you exclusively, you might also try connecting it directly to your computer and printing without the network.

- *Does the printer name you see at the top of the Print dialog box in Excel match the printer you are using?* If you select the wrong printer, Windows will either send the wrong information to your printer or hold the job until the printer you selected is ready. You may also want to check that the connection that appears after the printer name, such as LPT1, matches your configuration.

Tech Tip: Check the spelling in your workbook before you print it. If you don't have Spell Checker installed, copy the data to a word processor and check the spelling with its spell checker instead. Although you cannot fix the spelling errors in the workbook this way, you can observe them and correct them manually in Excel. Alternatively, use the Excel Setup program to install Spell Checker on your system.

Is there a shortcut for printing?

A Print button appears on the Standard toolbar in Excel 5.0. When you click this button, Excel prints your document immediately using the default print options. You can also press CTRL+P to display the Print dialog box without using the menu.

Alternatively, you can hold down SHIFT while you click the Print Preview button on the Standard toolbar. When you hold down SHIFT, the button functions just like the Print button. Conversely, if you click the Print button while holding down SHIFT, you will preview the data instead of printing it. This feature makes it possible to remove one or the other button from your toolbar to make room for another one.

Can I see what my finished document will look like before I print it?

Print Preview lets you see your document as if it were printed. To switch to this view, you can either choose Print Preview from the File menu or click the Print Preview button on the Standard toolbar.

Figure 6-2 shows a preview of a document. From this view, you can see the entire page, which makes it easier to find layout errors that you might not notice in another view. To return to your previous view, press ESC or click Close on the Print Preview toolbar.

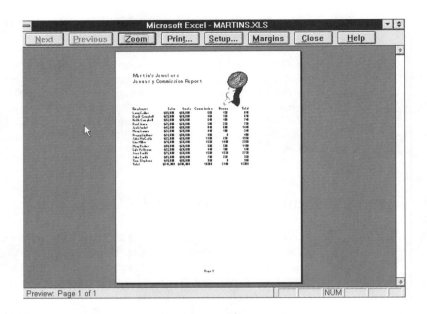

FIGURE 6-2   You can preview a document before you print it

Tech Tip: Once you print or preview a workbook, Excel adds dashed lines to the workbook sheets. These dashed lines indicate the area of the workbook Excel will print and how Excel will break up the print area into pages. Take a close look at where these lines fall so you can avoid having to reprint your workbook because Excel divided the print area into pages at undesirable locations.

Why is Excel ignoring the page break I added?

Look at the scaling set for printing the workbook. You probably have the Fit To option button selected; Excel ignores page breaks when this option is on.

To check this setting:

1. Choose Page Setup from the File menu.

2. Click the Page tab.

3. Select the <u>A</u>djust To option button.

   The <u>F</u>it to option button overrides the manual page breaks and adjusts the entire sheet or the print area, to fill the selected number of pages.

4. Click OK.

Tech Tip: You can quickly tell whether Excel is ignoring your page breaks, because if so, your sheets do not display the dashed lines that usually indicate them.

My spreadsheet does not take up the full width of the page. Can I center it within the margins?

Yes. Excel can adjust how it prints your data so it is centered on the page. From the <u>F</u>ile menu, choose Page Set<u>u</u>p, click the Margins tab, select the Hori<u>z</u>ontally and <u>V</u>ertically check boxes in the Center on Page section, and click OK. When you print, Excel will center the data on the page. This option affects the printed copy only, not the screen display.

How do I set my print area and print titles in Excel 5.0?

To set the print area and print titles:

1. Choose Page Set<u>u</u>p from the <u>F</u>ile menu.

2. Click the Sheet tab. This tab includes settings for both the print area and the print titles.

3. Move to the Print <u>A</u>rea box and either type the print area or select the area you want to print in the worksheet. (You do not have to set the print area if you only want to set print titles.)

4. Set the print titles. The exact steps to follow depend on whether you want row titles, column titles, or both.

   ■ If you want to use entries from a particular row as titles for the columns, type or select the rows in the <u>R</u>ows to

Repeat at Top box. You need to select at least one cell from each row you want to include.

■   If you want to use entries from a particular column as titles for the rows, type or select the columns in the <u>C</u>olumns to Repeat at Left box. You need to select at least one cell from each column you want to include.

5. Click OK.

Figure 6-1, shown previously, displays an example of a worksheet that has both row and column print titles. A closer look at the top of that worksheet appears in Figure 6-3. The <u>R</u>ows to Repeat at Top box on the Sheet tab of the Page Setup dialog box contains $1:$2, which repeats the contents of the first two rows. The <u>C</u>olumns to Repeat at Left box contains $A:$A to repeat the first column for all pages.

Unlike earlier spreadsheet applications, you do not have to reset the print area when you add print titles. In the past, if you did not reset the print area after selecting print titles, the columns or rows you selected for print titles would appear twice: as print titles and then again as part of the print range. Even if you use columns and rows other than the first ones as print

	A	B	C	D	E
1			Last Year's		
2	Name	Level	Salary	Inc. Mo.	% In
3	Adams, Maureen	Partner	$120,000	2	7.00
4	Alpen, Patrick	Manager	$75,000	10	4.00
5	Arbor, Jim	Senior Assistant	$40,000	4	7.00
6	Bunde, Norman	Designer	$35,000	1	4.00
7	Campbell, Keith	Associate	$90,000	1	9.00
8	Campbell, David	Junior Assistant	$30,000	1	10.00
9	Denmore, Mary	Junior Assistant	$32,000	11	7.50
10	Dylan, Ellen	Partner	$130,000	3	4.00
11	Evans, Martina	Partner	$180,000	5	8.00
12	Farper, Vincent	Junior Assistant	$33,000	1	10.00
13	Fork, Angela	Junior Assistant	$34,000	4	7.00
14	Guest, Norman	Junior Assistant	$30,000	1	4.00
15	Guest, Samuel	Associate	$85,000	2	9.00
16	Guiness, Carl	Junior Assistant	$30,000	10	4.00
17	Harker, Steve	Manager	$60,000	10	4.00

FIGURE 6-3   A workbook that uses both column and row print titles

titles, Excel knows not to print the columns or rows twice. The print area in the workbook shown in Figures 6-1 and 6-3 is $A$1:$H$77.

If the rows you specify as print titles do not appear at the top of the worksheet, Excel prints the data that appears above them first. Therefore, the titles do not appear until the page that begins after those rows appear in the worksheet. In other words, if you designate rows 59 and 60 as the print titles, Excel will print the first two pages of the worksheet (rows 1-58) and then display rows 59 and 60 as titles on page 3.

How do I print multiple sheets at the same time?

To print a selection of sheets in your workbook, press and hold down SHIFT or CTRL while you click the tabs of the sheets to print. To print more than one sheet:

1. Select the sheets to print. If the sheets are consecutive, click the first tab, hold down the SHIFT key, and click the last tab to select all the sheets in between. To select noncontiguous sheets, hold down the CTRL key while you click each tab.

   Excel displays the word "Group" in the title bar to indicate that you're in Group mode, as shown here:

   | Microsoft Excel - Book4 [Group] ▾ ◆ |

2. Choose Print from the File menu.

3. Make sure that the Selected Sheet(s) option button is selected in the Print What section.

4. Click OK.

Tech Tip: To ungroup the sheets, hold down SHIFT while you click the active sheet or click the tab of any sheet that is not part of the group.

Can I print a file without opening it?

You can print an Excel file without opening it as long as you don't need to change the workbook's default print settings. To print an Excel file that is not open:

1. Choose <u>F</u>ind File from the <u>F</u>ile menu to display the Find File dialog box.

2. Click <u>S</u>earch to open the Search dialog box.

3. Enter the filename and location (the directory in which the file is stored) in the File <u>N</u>ame and <u>L</u>ocation boxes, respectively, in the Search For section.

4. Click OK to display the results of the search in the Find File dialog box.

5. Select the file to print in the <u>L</u>isted Files list box.

6. Click the <u>C</u>ommands button and then choose <u>P</u>rint from the drop-down menu to print the selected file.

7. Click OK to print.

Can I print multiple files without opening, printing, and closing them one at a time?

Instead of opening and printing files individually, you can select several files to print all at once. To print multiple files:

1. Choose <u>F</u>ind File from the <u>F</u>ile menu.

2. Click <u>S</u>earch to open the Search dialog box.

3. Enter the filename and location (the directory in which the file is stored) in the File <u>N</u>ame and <u>L</u>ocation boxes in the Search For section.

4. Click OK to display the results of the search in the Find File dialog box.

5. When all the files you want to print appear in the Find File dialog box, select them by clicking the first filename and then holding down SHIFT while you click the last one. If you want to print files that are not listed consecutively, press CTRL as you click each filename.

6. Click the <u>C</u>ommands button and then choose <u>P</u>rint from the drop-down menu.

7. Click OK to print.

How can I print small portions of my spreadsheet without resetting the print area for each one?

You can print individual ranges by selecting the appropriate range and then simply telling Excel to print whatever is selected. To print a selection:

1. Highlight the range you want to print.

2. Choose <u>P</u>rint from the <u>F</u>ile menu.

3. Select the Selecti<u>o</u>n option button in the Print What section.

4. Click OK to print the highlighted area.

What's the easiest way to print everything in my workbook?

You can easily print the entire workbook in Excel 5.0 by performing these steps:

1. Choose <u>P</u>rint from the <u>F</u>ile menu.

2. Select the <u>E</u>ntire Workbook option button.

3. Click OK.

Is there some way to speed up printing when I just want a quick copy of my data?

Yes. You can speed up printing by printing a draft quality instead of a fully formatted version of your data. Draft quality is particularly useful when you just want to look over the contents of a workbook and you don't care what the data looks like.

To print a draft quality copy of your data:

1. Choose <u>P</u>rint from the <u>F</u>ile menu.

2. Click Page Setup.

3. Click the Sheet tab.

4. Select the Draft Quality check box in the Print section.

5. Click OK twice to print the workbook with draft quality.

You must perform these steps again to clear the Draft Quality check box when you no longer want draft quality output.

Exactly what elements appear in draft output depends entirely on the type of printer you are using. If you are using a dot-matrix printer, probably none of your character formatting will display. Most laser printers, however, will print the character formatting, but not any graphics. Postscript printers, on the other hand, will print both formatted text and graphics.

I just printed my data and now I want to reprint only a couple of the pages. Can I print just a few pages or do I have to reprint the whole thing?

When you discover a spelling mistake on a page or want to make minor changes on only a few pages, it's easy to print just the specific pages again. Because Excel divides your print area into pages, you can select and print only the desired pages.

To print only selected pages:

1. Choose Print from the File menu.

2. Select the Page(s) option button.

3. Type or use the arrows to specify the first page to print in the From box.

4. Type or use the arrows to specify the last page to print in the To box.

5. Click OK to print the selected pages.

Tech Tip: Excel prints the page numbers assuming that the first page printed is page 1. For example, if you set your worksheet to start numbering on page 3 and you want to print pages 3 and 4, which are the first and second pages in the print area, type **1** in the From box and **2** in the To box.

How do I print my charts without printing other data from the workbook?

You must open a chart, like any other embedded object, to print it separately from the workbook data. To print a chart by itself:

1. Double-click the chart to print.

2. Choose Print from the File menu.

3. Click OK.

Depending on their source, you may be able to print other embedded objects in this way also. Some source applications for embedded objects do not include printing commands. For example, if you have Word for Windows installed, you can embed WordArt objects in your Excel workbook but you cannot print them separately.

Can I move the position of the header and footer?

You can change the position of the header or footer in relation to the edge of the paper by following these steps:

1. Select the sheet or sheets that contain the header or footer you want to change.

2. Choose Page Setup from the File menu.

3. Click the Margins tab.

4. Enter the desired distances in the Header and Footer boxes.

5. Click OK.

Tech Tip: You can also access Page Setup by clicking the Setup button while you are previewing a workbook or by clicking Page Setup in the Print dialog box that displays when you choose the Print command from the File menu.

I want to see where the margins are when I preview my workbook. Can I do this?

Not only can you see markings for margins when you preview data, you can also change them. In the preview window, click <u>M</u>argins. Excel adds lines for the different margin settings, as shown in Figure 6-4. With the margin lines displayed, you can modify their positions by dragging them to a new location. You can even change column widths, because Excel also displays handles along the top of the page to indicate the columns' right boundaries. (The column width handles are the handles that do not have lines continuing downward.)

Tech Tip: Two margin lines appear at both the top and the bottom of the page to indicate the header and footer positions. You can change where the header and footer appear by dragging the lines at the very top and bottom of the page, respectively.

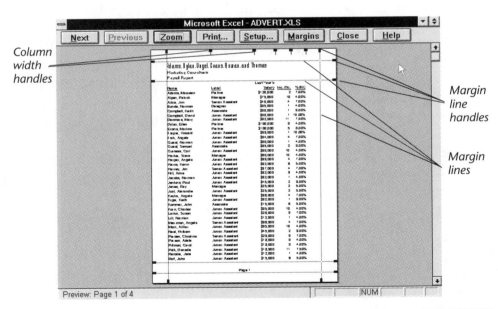

FIGURE 6-4 Handles and margin lines added to the preview window

My company name is "Dog & Cat." How do I put the "&" in a header?

Because Excel uses an "&" for special codes in the header and footer, you must insert two "&"s so that one prints out. In your case, the proper format would be **Dog && Cat**.

Tech Tip: If you select one of the predefined headers and footers that include your company name, Excel will automatically add the second "&" to the company name.

The following table lists the other codes that Excel can include in a header, their features, and the buttons you can click in the Header or Footer dialog box to add them.

Button	Code	Action
A		Displays the Font dialog box in which you can select a font for a section of a header or footer
[#]	&[Page]	Adds the current page number
[+]	&[Pages]	Adds the total number of pages
[date]	&[Date]	Adds the current date
[time]	&[Time]	Adds the current time
[file]	&[File]	Adds the filename of the current workbook
[tab]	&[Tab]	Adds the name of the sheet you select

How can I put headers and footers on every page of my workbook when I print it?

To set up headers and footers:

1. Choose Page Setup from the File menu.

2. Click the Header/Footer tab.

3. Select one of Excel's default headers or footers in the Header or Footer drop-down list boxes, or enter your own by clicking Custom Header or Custom Footer. When you select Custom Header, Excel displays the Header dialog box, shown here:

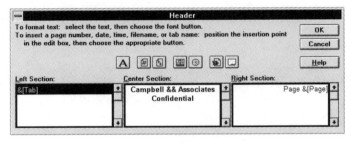

Tech Tip: A worksheet can only have one custom header or footer, although you can change it as you like.

4. In the Header or Footer dialog box, enter any text in the Left Section, Center Section, and Right Section boxes that you want to appear.

   You can use the buttons along the top to easily change the font and add codes for the page number, the current date or time, the full filename, and the sheet tab name. These buttons display an "&" plus the code in the dialog box, but the actual data appears when you preview or print.

5. Click OK until you return to the workbook or dialog box you want to use.

How can I define separate headers and footers for different parts of my sheet and print them together?

You can create views that contain separate headers and footers and then combine them by printing the views in one report. The views include options for how your workbook appears so you can quickly return to the same arrangement again. You can have more than one view for the same workbook so you can look at it in more than one way. You must define the different views in your workbook before you print them as a report.

To define a view in a sheet:

1. Choose Page Setup from File menu.
2. Click the Sheet tab.
3. Select the range to print with the specific header and footer, which will enter it in the Print Area box.
4. Click the Header/Footer tab.
5. Define the header and footer by either selecting one of Excel's defaults or creating your own.
6. Click OK.
7. Choose View Manager from the View menu.

Tech Tip: If this command appears dimmed, the View Manager add-in is not loaded. You must use the Excel Setup program to load this add-in before you can create views.

8. Click Add.
9. Type a view name in the Name box and click OK.

Repeat the steps for each part of your sheet that you want to have a separate header and footer. After you have defined the views for all the separate print areas with their headers and footers, define the report you will use to print the views.

To define and print a report:

1. Choose Print Report from the File menu. In the Print Report dialog box, Excel lists any reports you have defined for the workbook.

Tech Tip: If this command appears dimmed, the Report Manager add-in is not loaded. You must use the Excel Setup program to load this add-in before you can create views.

2. Click <u>A</u>dd to display a dialog box like the one shown here:

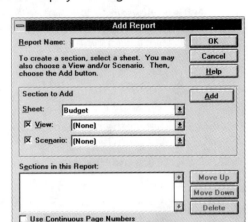

3. Type a name for the report in the <u>R</u>eport Name box.

4. Select a view name in the <u>V</u>iew drop-down list box and click <u>A</u>dd. Repeat this step for every view you want to add to the report.

5. Click OK to return to the Print Report dialog box.

6. Click <u>P</u>rint and then OK.

Once you define the report, you can print it again later by following these steps:

1. Choose Print <u>R</u>eport from the <u>F</u>ile menu.

2. Select the report you want to print.

3. Click <u>P</u>rint and then OK.

How can I import a graphic object, such as our company logo, into an Excel header or footer?

Unfortunately, there is no way to import a graphic object into an Excel header or footer. It is possible, however, to import a graphic into the header or footer of a Word for Windows (2.0 or 6.0) document, and then to import your Excel spreadsheet into that Word document as well, to produce the desired results. Other word processors may offer similar features.

Is there a way to start the page numbering at a number other than 1?

To change the page numbering for the active sheet:

1. Choose Page Setup from the File menu.
2. Click the Page tab.
3. Type the number you want to use as the starting number in the First Page Number box.
4. Click OK.

I have some shaded cells in my workbook, but they don't show up when I preview or print it. What's the problem?

You need to turn off the Black and White option in the Page Setup dialog box in order to see the shading. To disable this feature:

1. Choose Page Setup from the File menu.
2. Click the Sheet tab.
3. Clear the Black and White check box.
4. Click OK.

Why don't the gridlines in my worksheet print?

Excel only prints gridlines if you tell it to do so. The gridlines you see on the screen are designed to provide a guide when you're entering data. Most of the time, you do not want to print them. If you want them to appear in the printed output, simply follow these steps:

1. Choose Print from the File menu.
2. Click Page Setup.
3. Click the Sheet tab.
4. Select the Gridlines check box in the Print section.

	Microsoft Excel - STORERPT.XLS						

Next | Previous | Zoom | Print... | Setup... | Margins | Close | Help

STORERPT.XLS

	A	B	C	D	E	F	
1	Inventory Planner						
2	For March 31						
3							
4		Send					
5		Inventory	Trained	Posted	Preliminary	Completed	
6	Store Location	Materials	Employees	Signs	Results	Paperwork	Sto
7	20 Little Mountain Road						Trur
8	2309 Berry Drive	04-Mar	11-Mar	16-Mar	01-Apr	01-Apr	Ton
9	29671 Munson Road	07-Mar	15-Mar	23-Mar	01-Apr	01-Apr	Uta
10	3463 Stewart Street	08-Mar	23-Mar	24-Mar	01-Apr	01-Apr	Ren
11	3843 Plaza Boulevard	09-Mar	21-Mar	23-Mar			Har
12	3857 Jackson Street	14-Mar	23-Mar	28-Mar			Stor
13	3895 Pelton Drive	15-Mar	30-Mar	30-Mar			Alpe
14	423 Chilicothe Road	15-Mar	30-Mar	31-Mar			Hitt,
15	4923 Auburn Drive	22-Mar	29-Mar	29-Mar			Gui
16	4923 Turney Road	27-Mar					Star
17	5831 Johnnycake Ridge Road	21-Mar	29-Mar	29-Mar			Row
18	659 Tobbitt Avenue	28-Mar					Row

Preview: Page 1 of 1   NUM

FIGURE 6-5   Preview of a worksheet showing gridlines and row and column headings

5. If desired, select the Row and Column Headings check box to include row and column headings too.

6. Click OK twice to print the document with gridlines.

Figure 6-5 shows a preview of a workbook that will print with gridlines as well as row and column headings.

How can I cancel a print job that I've already sent to the printer?

The method you use to cancel a print job depends on how far along the print job is in the process. When you print your document, a series of steps occur:

1. As Excel tells Windows what to print and how it should print it, it displays a message like this one:

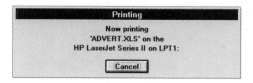

Windows uses this information to create a temporary file that stores the data it will send to the printer. (At this point, you can cancel the printing by clicking Cancel or pressing ESC.)

2. The Windows Print Manager sends the temporary file to the printer. To cancel printing at this stage you must do so from the Print Manager.

3. If the Print Manager has already finished sending the print job to the printer, you can only cancel the job by resetting the printer itself.

Tech Tip: If you are printing on a network, you must use network commands to cancel a print job from the queue.

To cancel printing from the Print Manager:

1. Open the Print Manager, shown in Figure 6-6, by double-clicking its icon in the Program Manager's Main program group window.

2. Select the print job you want to cancel, and click <u>D</u>elete.

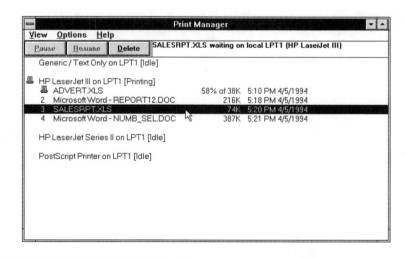

FIGURE 6-6   The Print Manager window displays the current print jobs

3. Click OK at the prompt.

4. Leave the Print Manager by closing it or switching to another application. To close the Print Manager, choose E̲xit from the V̲iew menu or double-click the Control-menu box.

   You should avoid closing the Print Manager if you have other documents printing, because doing so will cancel those print jobs as well.

How do I change the priority of a print request?

You can change the order in which your documents print by using the Windows Print Manager. The Print Manager manages all the printing you do from your Windows applications.

To reprioritize your print job:

1. Press ALT+TAB until you see "Print Manager." Windows displays the Print Manager window, shown in Figure 6-6.

2. Select the document you want to print sooner.

3. Press CTRL+UP ARROW to move it to the desired position in the list.

Tech Tip: You cannot move the "rush" print job ahead of the job that Windows is currently printing, which displays a miniature printer icon next to it.

How do I install my new printer so Excel can print to it?

There are two stages involved in setting up a printer: attaching it to your computer and installing the printer driver.

Attaching the printer consists of physically running a cable from the printer to the correct port on your computer. Your printer's documentation should explain how to do this.

The *printer driver* is a file that contains all of the information needed to let your applications communicate with the particular printer. Once you install the printer driver in Windows, all of your Windows applications will be able to print to the printer.

To install the Windows printer driver:

1. Make sure you have your Windows Setup disks handy.

2. Open the Windows Control Panel by double-clicking its program icon in the Program Manager's Main group window.

3. Double-click the Printers icon or choose Printers from the Settings menu.

4. Click Add.

5. Select your printer in the List of Printers list box.

   If your particular printer does not appear in this list box, check your printer's documentation. You need to find out whether there is another printer that yours can emulate and then select that printer in the list box, or see if an updated Windows printer driver file comes with the printer.

6. Click Install.

7. If Windows prompts you for one of the Windows Setup disks, insert it in the appropriate drive and click OK to install the printer driver. (If no prompt displays, the appropriate printer driver is already stored on your computer's hard disk.)

8. Select the new printer's name in the Installed Printers list box.

9. Click the Set as Default Printer button, if you want Excel (and all other Windows applications) to automatically print to this printer.

10. Click Close and then choose Exit from the Settings menu.

The new printer is now installed and ready to print.

Tech Tip: If you have installed more than one printer, you can change which printer is the default for all the Windows applications right from within Excel. To do so, choose Print from the File menu, click Printer Setup, select a printer in the Printer list box, and click OK.

How can I use fonts from my font cartridges in Excel?

Windows applications, including Excel, can use the font cartridges installed on your printer as long as the printer driver "knows" they are there. Once the printer driver "knows" which font cartridges you have, you can select any of these fonts whenever you format text in your document.

To install a font cartridge for a Windows printer driver, follow these steps:

1. Open the Control Panel by double-clicking its icon in the Main program group window of the Program Manager.

2. Double-click the Printers icon or choose Printers from the Settings menu to open the Printers dialog box.

3. Select the name of the printer with the cartridges in the Installed Printers list box.

4. Click Setup.

5. Select the installed cartridge in the Cartridges list box. If you have more than one cartridge, click the first one and then hold down CTRL as you click the others.

6. Click OK.

7. If you wish, click Set As Default Printer so that Excel and other Windows applications automatically print to this particular printer.

8. Choose Close.

9. Press ALT+F4, choose Exit from the Settings menu, or double-click the Control-menu box to close the Control Panel.

As long as this printer is selected as the default, all the fonts provided by the cartridges will appear in the list of available fonts whenever you format text in Excel.

Why does the list of available fonts seem to change whenever I use a different printer driver?

Excel depends largely on the current printer driver to determine the available fonts, because some printers can only print certain fonts. For example, a Generic/Text Only printer driver can print relatively few fonts; a Hewlett-Packard LaserJet III printer driver, on the other hand, supports a wide variety of fonts. When you switch to another printer, Excel looks at the appropriate driver to find out which fonts it can print. Excel, therefore, displays many more fonts in the Font list box when you select the Hewlett-Packard LaserJet III printer than when you specify Generic/Text Only.

Excel also uses software-generated fonts called TrueType fonts. These fonts are created graphically, which is why they take longer to print. TrueType fonts print on a wide variety of printers because they do not rely on the internal printer fonts.

My friend has a better printer, but she doesn't have Excel. Can I still print my Excel documents on her printer?

Yes. You can print your Excel documents on her printer, even though she doesn't have Excel. Before you can use her printer, you need to print your Excel document to a file, and then copy this file to a disk. This file contains all of the information that Excel and Windows would send to your friend's printer if it were connected to your computer. You can then take your disk to your friend's computer and simply copy the file to her printer to print your Excel document from either DOS or Windows.

To print an Excel document to a file and then print it directly from the operating system:

Tech Terror: When you create the file, you must select the correct printer driver for the printer you will use; otherwise, the final output will be gibberish.

1. Open the Control Panel program by double-clicking its program icon in the Main group window of the Program Manager.

2. Double-click the Printers icon or choose <u>P</u>rinters from the <u>S</u>ettings menu to open the Printers dialog box.

3. Select the type of printer that your friend has in the Installed <u>P</u>rinters list box and click <u>C</u>onnect. If you do not have that printer installed, you must install it on your computer first.

4. Select FILE in the <u>P</u>orts list box and click OK.

5. Click Se<u>t</u> As Default Printer to use this printer as the default in all your Windows applications.

6. Click Close.

7. Press ALT+F4, choose E<u>x</u>it from the <u>S</u>ettings menu or double-click the Control-menu box to close the Control Panel.

8. Switch to Excel.

9. Choose <u>P</u>rint from the <u>F</u>ile menu.

10. Click OK in the Print dialog box.

11. Enter a name for the file in the <u>O</u>utput File Name box and click OK.

12. Copy the file to a floppy disk.

13. Remove the floppy disk, take it to the other computer, and insert it.

14. Copy the file to the port to which the printer is attached, which is most likely LPT1. For example, you might enter

```
COPY A:\MYDOC.PRN >LPT1
```

at the DOS prompt and press ENTER, assuming the floppy disk containing your file is in drive A and the file is named MYDOC.PRN.

Customization

Excel's customization options let you tailor the application to match your individual work style and projects. You can use these customization features to change default settings, eliminating some of the tasks you perform in each new workbook. You can also retain some aspects of Excel 4.0 if you aren't quite ready to make a full switch to Excel 5.0.

You access most of Excel's customization features by choosing Options from the Tools menu. Options offers a wide range of choices with which you determine how you want to view, edit, and calculate your workbooks. In fact, there are so many items you can control in the Options dialog box that it contains ten tabs!

FRUSTRATION BUSTERS!

If you haven't yet explored the customization options, quickly review the description of each Option tab in the following table. Then, take a closer look at those features that are most likely to save you time and frustration based on how you work with Excel.

Tab	Customization Options
Calculation	Determines how Excel handles calculations, including iteration and precision
Chart	Sets options for the active chart and the default chart format
Color	Sets standard colors and provides default colors for chart fills and lines
Custom Lists	Lets you predefine lists of frequently used entries
Edit	Determines whether features such as in-cell editing, drag-and-drop, and fixed decimal places are in effect
General	Sets basic options such as the standard font, the number of sheets in a new workbook, and the default file location
Module Format	Defines the font, size, and colors for Visual Basic modules
Module General	Determines error handling, tab width, and the language or country for Visual Basic modules
Transition	Provides help tailored to 1-2-3 users switching to Excel
View	Determines window settings, whether formula and status bars appear, and how Excel handles objects

How can I change my default font in Excel?

You first need to decide whether you want to change the default font for all new workbooks that you create or just for the current workbook.

To change the default font for all new workbooks:

1. Choose Options from the Tools menu.

2. Click the General tab. You'll see the General options, as shown here:

Options

| Custom Lists | Chart | Color | Module General | Module Format |
| View | Calculation | Edit | Transition | General |

Reference Style
- A1   O R1C1

Menus
- X Recently Used File List
- Microsoft Excel 4.0 Menus

OK
Cancel
Help

- Ignore Other Applications
- Prompt for Summary Info
- Reset TipWizard

Sheets in New Workbook: 16

Standard Font: Arial   Size: 10

Default File Location:

Alternate Startup File Location:

User Name: Mary Campbell

Tech Tip: Changing the standard font only affects new workbooks. The current workbook continues to use the same default font.

3. Select the desired font in the Standard Font drop-down list box.

4. Click OK.

To change the default font for the current workbook:

1. Choose Style from the Format menu to display the Style dialog box shown here:

Style

Style Name: Normal

OK
Cancel

Style Includes
- X Number   General
- X Font   Arial 10
- X Alignment   General, Bottom Aligned
- X Border   No Borders
- X Patterns   No Shading
- X Protection   Locked

Modify...
Add
Delete
Merge...
Help

2. Click <u>M</u>odify to edit the Normal style.

3. Click the Font tab to display the options shown here:

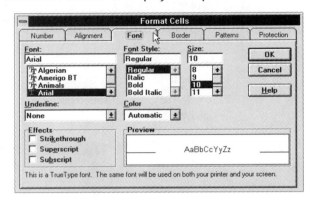

Tech Tip: Once you select the Font tab, you can also change the F<u>o</u>nt Style and <u>S</u>ize options.

4. Select the font you want in the <u>F</u>ont drop-down list box.

5. Click OK twice.

Excel changes the font for all cells except those that use a different style or have fonts that were set individually.

I prefer certain aspects of Excel 4.0 over Excel 5.0, such as the ability to double-click a cell to select its precedent cells. Can I keep Excel 5.0's features, but restore the way Excel 4.0 worked?

Yes. Excel provides many options for customizing your copy of the product. It even includes options that let you determine how some of the very basic processes work. For example, if you do not want to use the Excel 5.0 feature that lets you edit directly in cells, you can change an editing option to revert to Excel 4.0's technique of double-clicking a cell to highlight the precedent cells.

To disable Excel 5.0's in-cell editing feature:

1. Choose <u>O</u>ptions from the <u>T</u>ools menu.

2. Click the Edit tab.

3. Clear the <u>E</u>dit Directly in Cell check box.

4. Click OK.

Unfortunately, you must select one editing feature or the other—they cannot both be active at the same time.

Tech Tip: You can change other Excel 5.0 options if you are not yet ready to make a total transition to this version of the application. You can select the Microsoft Excel 4.0 Menus option on the General tab to use the old menu structure.

How do I set up a workbook so that it opens each time I run Excel?

You can set up Excel so that it automatically opens specific workbooks whenever you start it by moving these files to your EXCEL\XLSTART directory. These workbooks can contain worksheets, chart sheets, Visual Basic modules, dialog sheets, and Microsoft Excel 4.0 macro sheets. If there are no files in this directory, Excel opens a new un-saved workbook file called BOOK*n*.XLS where *n* is the next unused number.

Tech Tip: Excel does not automatically open any files in subdirectories within XLSTART at startup.

You can also store a workspace file in the XLSTART directory instead of individual workbook files. A *workspace file* contains a record of a particular arrangement of existing files. After Excel opens the workspace file, it opens all of the workbooks referenced and places them in the same positions they were in when you saved the workspace file.

You can also specify an alternate startup directory. Excel will then open any workbooks or workspace files saved in the alternate startup directory instead of the ones in the XLSTART directory. To specify an alternate startup directory:

1. Choose Options from the Tools menu.

2. Click the General tab.

3. Type the name of the directory in the Alternate Startup File Location box.

4. Click OK.

Another way to direct Excel to look in a particular directory or open a specific workbook is to use a *startup switch.* You can add a startup switch to the command line that Windows uses to launch Excel by editing the properties of the Excel program icon in the Program Manager. To add a startup switch:

1. Select the Excel program icon in the Program Manager.

2. Choose Properties from the Program Manager's File menu.

3. Edit the Command Line box to add the startup switch you want, as described in the following table, and click OK.

Entry	Effect	Example
EXCEL.EXE *filename*	Opens a specific workbook	EXCEL.EXE C:\BUDGET\YEAREND.XLS
EXCEL.EXE /E	Prevents Excel from opening Book1 at startup	EXCEL.EXE /E
EXCEL.EXE /P *directory name*	Specifies a working directory	EXCEL.EXE /P C:\BUDGET
EXCEL.EXE /R *filename*	Opens a workbook as read only	EXCEL.EXE /R C:\BUDGET\YEAREND.XLS

You can also make changes in the Working Directory box in the Program Item Properties dialog box to change which directory Excel uses by default.

Tech Tip: If you want to start Excel with a particular startup switch only once, you can choose Run from the File menu, and then enter the command to start Excel along with that startup switch in the Command Line box.

Tech Terror: If you change the working directory by choosing Options from the Tools menu, clicking the General tab, and specifying a working directory, this directory overrides the one set as a property of Excel's program icon. Make sure that you specify the working directory that you really want to use in the Options dialog box so you use the correct directory for your files.

How do I shut off the TipWizard?

The TipWizard is designed to display helpful information when the task you are completing could be done more efficiently. To see the TipWizard's advice, click the TipWizard button in the Standard toolbar.

Excel adds another toolbar that shows the TipWizard's text along with any toolbar buttons that you might want to use. To avoid seeing Excel's advice, don't click the TipWizard button, or click the button a second time to remove the TipWizard toolbar. If you're already completing your tasks efficiently, this toolbar won't often display new tips anyway.

However, if you want the TipWizard to stop displaying new tips altogether, hold down SHIFT while you click the TipWizard button. This technique doesn't hide the TipWizard; it just prevents new tips from appearing. You can turn the Tip Wizard on again by pressing SHIFT while clicking the button again.

Tech Note: You can completely remove the TipWizard button from your toolbar using the steps outlined in the question "How can I create a custom toolbar?," later in this chapter.

Can I display multiple sheets from my workbook at one time?

Yes. You can see more than one sheet from the same workbook at one time by opening a separate document window for each sheet you want to view. You can then size each window on your own or let Excel do it for you, as follows:

1. Choose <u>N</u>ew Window from the <u>W</u>indow menu until you have as many windows as sheets you want to see.
2. Choose <u>A</u>rrange from the <u>W</u>indow menu.
3. Select the <u>W</u>indows of Active Workbook check box.
4. Select the <u>T</u>iled option button.
5. Click OK.

Your workspace might look something like Figure 7-1.

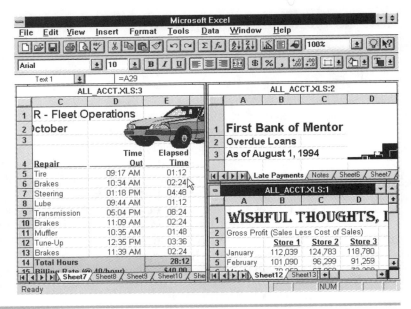

FIGURE 7-1   Multiple sheets from one workbook displayed in different windows

Can I find out the Excel 5.0 equivalents of Excel 4.0 commands?

You can use Help to identify which Excel 5.0 commands are equivalent to those in Excel 4.0. This feature can be particularly useful if you are just starting to use Excel 5.0, but are well acquainted with Excel 4.0.

1. Start Help by double-clicking the Help button in the Standard toolbar, or choosing Search for Help on the Help menu. You can also press F1 and then click Search.

2. Type the keywords **menu commands** in the first box.

3. Click Show Topics.

4. Select "Menu Command Changes In Version 5.0" in the Select a topic list box.

5. Click Go To.

I don't have much disk space. Can I remove some components of Excel to provide additional space?

You can remove whatever components of Excel that you think you can do without, including the Help system. You can run the Excel Setup program at any time to add or delete any such components from your system.

To add or remove Excel components:

1. Start the Excel Setup program in one of two ways:

   ■ Switch to the Program Manager, choose Run from File menu, click Browse, select the directory in which the Excel program files are located, select the file named SETUP.EXE, and click OK twice.

   ■ Double-click the MS Excel Setup program icon in your Excel program group in the Program Manager.

2. Click the Add/Remove button.

3. Clear the check boxes for the Excel components you want to remove. For several of the main components, you can click Change Option to further refine your selections and then click OK.

4. Click Continue and then OK to remove the components.

Tech Tip: You can also use this procedure to add components of Excel that you didn't install originally. In this case, make sure you have your Excel Setup disks on hand.

What is the easiest way to change the default directory in Excel?

Since you can change the default directory from Excel or the Program Manager, which way is easier depends on whether Excel is open when you decide to make the change.

To change your working directory from Excel:

1. Choose Options from the Tools menu.
2. Click the General tab.
3. Type the path for your new default directory, such as **C:\EXCEL\MYFILES**, in the Default File Location box.
4. Click OK.

To change your working directory from the Window's Program Manager:

1. Click the Excel program icon once to select it.
2. Choose Properties from the File menu or press ALT+ENTER to display the Program Item Properties dialog box.
3. Type a new entry in the Working Directory box to change the default directory.
4. Click OK.

I really want to have my Excel 4.0 menus back. Is there some way to do this?

Many users aren't quite ready to make the switch to Excel 5.0 when they first find it installed on their computer. It's nice to know that there is an easy way to switch back to the familiar menu structure of Excel 4.0.

To use Excel 4.0 menus:

1. Choose Options from the Tools menu.
2. Click the General tab.
3. Select Microsoft Excel 4.0 Menus check box.
4. Click OK.

Tech Terror: You can't have the best of both worlds with this one! When you make this choice, you lose some of Excel 5.0's new features until you are ready to switch back to the new menus.

I find it helpful to display gridlines when I enter data in my worksheets, but do I have to print them?

You can customize Excel to prevent it from printing your worksheet gridlines:

1. Choose the Page Setup from the File menu.
2. Click the Sheet tab.
3. Clear the Gridlines check box.
4. Click OK.

Because you are changing a printing option instead of a display option, the gridlines still appear on the screen. The print preview in Figure 7-2 shows how a worksheet might appear after clearing gridlines.

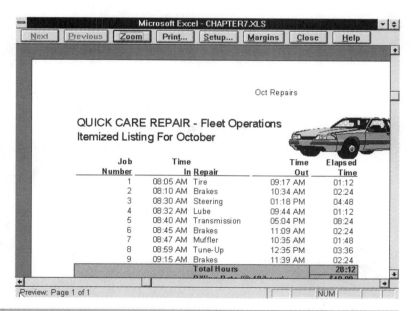

FIGURE 7-2　You can clear gridlines for preview and printing purposes

I am trying to perform statistical analysis on my data, but I can't find some of the features I used in Excel 4.0. Should I reinstall Excel 4.0 to use them?

No, Excel 5.0 offers the same capabilities but some of the features may now exist in special files, called *add-ins*. Most of Excel's statistical analysis features are part of the Analysis ToolPak add-in. To use this add-in:

1. Choose Add-Ins from the Tools menu to display a dialog box like the one shown here:

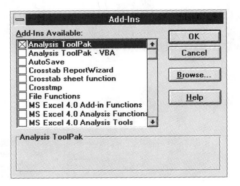

2. Select the check box for each add-in you want to use in the Add-Ins Available list box. In this example, you would select the Analysis ToolPak check box.

3. Click OK.

Tech Tip: If the Analysis ToolPak add-in is not available, you need to run Setup to install it on your computer and then perform this procedure. Start Setup, click Add/Remove, select the Add-ins check box, click Change Option, select the Analysis ToolPak check box, and then click OK to install this add-in.

How can I create a custom toolbar?

You can either customize an existing toolbar by adding and removing buttons or create a brand new toolbar.

To add a button to an existing toolbar:

1. Choose <u>T</u>oolbars from the <u>V</u>iew menu.

2. Select the check box for the toolbar you want to modify.

3. Click <u>C</u>ustomize.

4. Select a category of buttons in the <u>C</u>ategories list box.

5. Drag the button you want to add from the Buttons section in the dialog box to the position where you want it to appear on the toolbar.

6. Continue adding buttons until you have finished, and click OK.

To create a new toolbar:

1. Choose <u>T</u>oolbars from the <u>V</u>iew menu.

2. Type a name in the Tool<u>b</u>ar Name box.

3. Click <u>N</u>ew.

4. Select a category of buttons in the <u>C</u>ategories list box.

5. Drag buttons from the Buttons section in the Customize dialog box to the new toolbar.

6. When you have finished, click Close to close the dialog box and save the toolbar.

What is a floating toolbar?

Floating toolbars are located anywhere other than at the edges of your Excel window. A floating toolbar can be moved the same way that you move an application or document window.

Toolbars located at the edges of the application window are called *docked toolbars*.

Tech Tip: You can double-click the background of a docked toolbar to return it to its last floating position. Conversely, double-clicking the background of a floating toolbar docks it.

I added some buttons to my toolbar and it no longer fits at the top of the screen. Is there a way to display the toolbar in two rows?

Yes, you can make the toolbar display as two rows of buttons. To do so, drag the toolbar from the edge of the window into the worksheet area so that it changes appearance. As a floating toolbar, it now looks like a miniature workbook window with a control box and borders. If you point to one of these borders, your mouse pointer changes to a double-headed arrow. You can then drag the border to resize the toolbar to show more than one row.

Tech Tip: If your toolbar is docked at one of the edges of the application window, then it can only display as a single column or row—there is no way to change this.

Can I show more sheet tabs at the bottom of the workbook?

If desired, you can leave more room for sheet tabs at the bottom of your workbook window. There are two sections in the line that appears above the status bar at the bottom of the workbook window. The left side displays the sheet tabs, while the right side shows the horizontal scroll bar for the active sheet. By default, both of these features use half the width of the window. To devote more space to sheet tabs, point to the divider between these two sections so that your mouse pointer changes to a double-headed arrow. Drag the mouse to the right to decrease the size of the scroll bar and increase the space for sheet tabs.

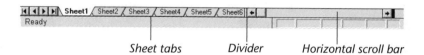

Sheet tabs   Divider   Horizontal scroll bar

After I complete a cell entry, Excel doesn't move to the next cell. I keep typing over what I just entered. What's happened?

The Move After Enter option has been disabled. To reset this option:

1. Choose <u>O</u>ptions from the <u>T</u>ools menu.
2. Click the Edit tab.
3. Select the <u>M</u>ove Selection after Enter check box.
4. Click OK.

How can I name the worksheet tabs? Are there any limitations on the names I can use?

It's helpful to assign meaningful names to your worksheets. These names not only make it easier to move to the correct sheet but to reference it.

To rename a sheet:

1. Double-click the sheet tab to open the Rename dialog box, shown here:

2. Type a new name in the <u>N</u>ame box and click OK.

There are several limitations on the names that you can use for sheets:

- Names cannot be longer than 31 characters.
- Each of the sheets in a workbook must have a unique name.
- You cannot use the special characters \ , / , * , and ? in a sheet name.

I just upgraded from Word for Windows 2.0 to Word for Windows 6.0. How can I get the button on the Microsoft toolbar in Excel to start the latest release of Word?

You need to retrain the button to get it to start the newer release:

1. Start Word for Windows 6.0 by double-clicking its program icon in the Program Manager.

2. Switch to Excel without closing Word for Windows 6.0.

3. Click the Microsoft Word button on the Microsoft toolbar.

This trains the button. The next time you click the button, it will start the new version of Word.

Help shows the steps for performing a procedure in Excel, but they disappear when I return to my worksheet. Can I keep this window visible for reference as I'm working?

To continue displaying a Help window while you are working in your Excel workbook, you must set it to always appear on top of any other application windows. If you are in the Help application window, choose Always On <u>T</u>op from the <u>H</u>elp menu so that you can still see it when you return to your Excel workbook. If the information you want to remain visible is in a How To window, click the On Top button. Excel's Help information will display on top of your worksheet until you change the option back.

Is there a way to have Excel run a macro every time I open or close a file?

You can create a new Visual Basic module anywhere in your workbook and name it Auto_Open or Auto_Close. A module with either of these names in the workbook is executed automatically.

For example, you can start the procedure with Sub Auto_Open( ) so it executes when you open the workbook, or Sub Auto_Close( ) so it executes when you close the workbook. After either statement, enter the code you want to execute. You can only have one Auto_Open or Auto_Close procedure per workbook. Auto_Open and Auto_Close macros created in the Excel 4.0 macro language also run in Excel 5.0.

Can I prevent an automatic procedure like Auto_Open, Auto_Close, or ON.ACTIVATE() from executing?

Yes. You can stop automatic procedures from running by pressing SHIFT when you open, close, or switch to or from a worksheet or workbook.

I've used AutoFill to insert days, financial quarters, and months. Can I also define a list that is tailored to my particular work needs?

You can create a custom list from entries that already appear in your worksheet or from information you type directly into the Options dialog box.

To create a custom list from entries stored in a worksheet range:

1. Choose <u>O</u>ptions from the <u>T</u>ools menu.
2. Click the Custom List tab.

3. Select NEW LIST in the Custom Lists list box.

4. Type the reference for the range that contains your entries in the Import List from Cells box.

5. Click Import.

6. Click OK.

To enter a new list:

1. Choose Options from the Tools menu.

2. Click the Custom Lists tab.

3. Select NEW LIST in the Custom Lists list box.

4. Enter the values in the List Entries list box. Press ENTER or insert a comma as a separator after you type each entry.

5. Click Add to create another new list, if desired.

6. Click OK.

I work with the same set of files all the time. Is there a quick way to open all of these files with one command?

You can open all the files at once by first saving a workspace file that indicates which workbooks to open and where to place them. To save a workspace file:

1. Open all of the workbook files you want to display when you open the workspace file.

Tech Tip: If any of the workbooks in the workspace file did not have gridlines displayed, the gridlines will reappear when you open the workspace file.

2. Position the workbook files the way you want to see them when they are opened.

3. Choose Save Workspace from the File menu.

4. Type a name for the workspace in the File Name list box.

5. Click OK to save the workspace file.

To open all the files in the workspace:

1. Choose Open from the File menu.

2. Select the name of the workspace file, which has a .XLW extension.

3. Click OK.

The same documents in the XLSTART directory open whenever a network user starts Excel. Can I set up which files automatically open when I start Excel?

Yes. You can specify an alternate startup directory, and on a network, each user can create a unique alternate startup directory.

To specify a different startup directory:

1. Choose <u>O</u>ptions from the <u>T</u>ools menu.
2. Click the General tab.
3. Type the directory name in the Alternate Startup File Location box.
4. Click OK.

A line that reads altstart=*directory* is added to the EXCEL5.INI file in the WINDOWS directory.

In Excel 4.0, I created several custom toolbars. Can I use them in Excel 5.0 too?

To use your Excel 4.0 toolbars in Excel 5.0, you must open the file named EXCEL.XLB in the C:\WINDOWS directory using the <u>O</u>pen command from the <u>F</u>ile menu. This opens your custom toolbars from Excel 4.0. When you next exit Excel 5.0, the custom toolbars are saved in EXCEL5.XLB. These toolbars will then be available whenever you use Excel 5.0.

Tech Tip: When you are ready to switch back to the standard Excel 5.0 toolbars, you can open the EXCEL5.XLB file in the C:\WINDOWS directory the same way.

I wrote an Excel 4.0 macro that adds a custom menu to the Excel menu bar. In Excel 5.0, the macro adds the custom menu but doesn't remove it. I get the message "Command or menu does not exist" when the Delete.Menu command is executed. Is this a bug?

No, it is not a bug. When you run a custom macro that adds a menu to one of the Excel 4.0 menu bars in Excel 5.0, the same menu is added to the Excel 5.0 menu bar. However, Delete.Menu does not remove this menu because, in Excel 4.0, menu bar number 1 referred to the Standard menu and 2 referred to the Chart menu. In Excel 5.0 these menu bars are instead assigned the numbers 10 and 11, respectively. Changing the bar numbers in your Delete.Menu function should remedy the problem.

When I select XLODBC.XLA using the Browse button in the Add-Ins dialog box, this error message displays: "File error, cannot find xlodbc.dll." This only happens on my network version of Excel, not on my own system. Why?

The Add-In Manager lets you control which add-ins are automatically available in Excel. Add-ins provide features to Excel that are not part of the main program. This error message appears when you are trying to install the XLODBC.XLA file (a file that lets Excel directly access external database files and use their data) as an automatically available add-in.

The message appears because the Add-In Manager does not automatically recognize the MSQUERY directory, which contains XLODBC.XLA, as an add-in directory like the SOLVER directory. Therefore, it suggests copying the add-in into the add-in library directory, \LIBRARY. If you let Excel copy the file, it copies the add-in to the add-in library directory, but doesn't copy its associated .DLL file. You then have two copies of the add-in file, one in each directory, but only one copy of the .DLL file, which is still in the MSQUERY directory. When you attempt to set this add-in as automatically available, Excel attempts to use the copy of the add-in that's stored in the add-in library. Since it cannot find the associated .DLL file, you receive the error message.

You can prevent this problem by following these steps:

1. Delete XLODBC.XLA from the EXCEL\LIBRARY directory.

2. Select <u>B</u>rowse in the Add-In dialog box and add the XLODBC.XLA file from the EXCEL\LIBRARY\MSQUERY directory.

3. When Excel displays the message, "Copy XLDBOC.XLA to Microsoft Excel Add-In Directory," click <u>N</u>o.

Excel doesn't copy the file, so it only appears in its original location, along with its .DLL file.

Can I create an Auto_Open macro that applies to an individual sheet within my workbook the way I could in Excel 4.0?

An Excel 5.0 workbook is a single file even though it can have many sheets. Only one Auto_Open macro can be associated with a file. Therefore, you cannot have an Auto_Open macro associated with each sheet in the workbook. However, you can create a Defined-Name automatic procedure that runs at the worksheet level in Excel 5.0. To do so:

Tech Note: An Excel 4.0 workbook actually contained multiple files; therefore, in 4.0 you could associate an Auto_Open macro with each file in the workbook.

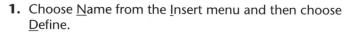

1. Choose <u>N</u>ame from the <u>I</u>nsert menu and then choose <u>D</u>efine.

2. Enter a name in the Name in <u>W</u>orkbook box that begins with the sheet's name, followed by an exclamation point and Auto_Open, Auto_Close, Auto_Activate, or Auto_Deactivate.

    For example, you could enter

    MySheet!Auto_Open_Routine*X*

3. Enter an equal sign followed by a reference to the procedure you want to associate with the defined name in the <u>R</u>efers To box.

    For example, you could enter

    =MyBook!Module1.SortRoutine

Workbook level automatic procedures take precedence over worksheet level defined-name procedures.

What do templates offer and how do I create one?

Templates serve as patterns for creating new sheets or workbooks. If you use a specific template when you create a new workbook, you automatically inherit its formatting, fonts, and other settings.

Excel also supports *autotemplates*, which are used each time you create a new workbook or insert a new sheet into an existing workbook. Autotemplates must be stored in the XLSTART subdirectory and must have specific names. For example, an autotemplate used to create new workbooks must be called BOOK.XLT. The autotemplates used to insert new sheets are shown in the following table. Excel does not use autotemplate files unless you create your own, since the defaults used to create the sheets are stored in Excel itself.

Type of Sheet	Autotemplate Names
Chart	CHART.XLT
Dialog	DIALOG.XLT
Module	MODULE.XLT
Worksheet	SHEET.XLT
Excel 4.0 macro	MACRO.XLT

To save a workbook as a template or autotemplate:

1. Create the workbook, including all the formulas and formatting that you want to appear in the template.

2. Make sure that the active sheet is the one that you want to use as the template if you are going to save the workbook as an autotemplate for a specific type of sheet.

3. Choose Save As from the File menu.

4. Type the filename in the File Name box.

Tech Tip: If you do not match an autotemplate name exactly, your changes will not affect the new workbooks and sheets as planned.

5. Select the drive in the Dri<u>v</u>es drop-down list box and the directory in the <u>D</u>irectories list box. If you are creating an autotemplate, you must save it in the XLSTART directory.

6. Select Template in the Save File as <u>T</u>ype drop-down list box.

7. Click OK.

The autotemplates will work correctly as long as they have the correct names and storage locations.

To use other templates that you have created, you need to specify the template when you create a new workbook. To do so:

1. Choose <u>O</u>pen from the <u>F</u>ile menu.

2. Select the template you want to use in the File <u>N</u>ame list.

3. Click OK.

Excel automatically creates a copy of the designated template in order to protect the integrity of the original.

I created a template named SHEET.XLT on which I based my worksheets in Excel 4.0 and saved it in the XLSTART directory. My Excel 5.0 sheets in my workbook are not based on my SHEET.XLT. What did I do wrong?

Excel 5.0 uses SHEET.XLT to create any sheets that you insert into a workbook. However, it does not use this file to create sheets when you first create a workbook. Excel uses the BOOK.XLT template instead. To insert a sheet into a workbook using the SHEET.XLT template, choose <u>W</u>orksheet from the Insert menu.

To change the default setting of new workbooks:

1. Create a workbook with any settings and formatting that you want to apply to all new workbooks. This could be your SHEET.XLT workbook.

2. Choose Save <u>A</u>s from the <u>F</u>ile menu.

3. Select Template in the Save File as <u>T</u>ype drop-down list box.

4. Type **BOOK.XLT** in the File Name box.

5. Select the XLSTART directory in the Directories list box.

6. Click OK.

Can I change the appearance of some of the buttons in my toolbar?

You can customize the image on a toolbar button by following these steps:

Tech Tip: If the toolbar you want to customize is already displayed, you can simply click it with the right mouse button and choose Customize from the shortcut menu to display the Customize dialog box.

1. Choose Toolbars from the View menu.

2. Select the check box for the toolbar you want to edit in the Toolbars list box.

3. Click Customize to display the Customize dialog box.

4. While the Customize box is open, click the appropriate button on the toolbar with the right mouse button.

5. Choose Edit Button Image from the shortcut menu to display a Button Editor dialog box like this one:

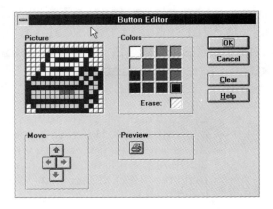

6. Make the desired changes to the image by clicking a color in the Colors palette and then clicking one or more squares in the Picture box to color them. Repeat this step until you are satisfied with the new image. (The Preview section displays a sample as you edit.)

7. Click OK for the changes to take effect.

8. Click Close.

Can I still use Excel 4.0's Dialog Editor to create custom dialog boxes in Excel 5.0?

You can copy the dialog box from the Dialog Editor and then paste it into a macro sheet. You then have to display an Excel 4.0 macro using the Dialog.Box command. You cannot, however, use the Dialog Editor to make dialog boxes on a dialog sheet.

Analysis Tools

Excel's computational abilities go well beyond the basics you might expect from a spreadsheet. Excel includes 94 additional advanced functions. These functions analyze complex financial transactions, such as calculating the yield from bonds and stocks, and perform specialized engineering calculations as well.

Excel also includes analysis tools you can use to analyze your data and create formatted reports. Advanced functions are often used with the analysis tools to calculate values and then convert these formulas to numbers. Most of the analysis features are provided by the Analysis ToolPak add-in. If you cannot find or access one of the commands described in this chapter, you must add the appropriate add-in to your system.

FRUSTRATION BUSTERS!

The Analysis ToolPak add-in provides complex analysis of data for statistical and engineering purposes. The following table describes the analysis tools included in the Analysis ToolPak.

Tool	Description
Anova: Single Factor	Calculates a simple variance analysis
Anova: Two-Factor with Replication	Calculates a two-factor variance analysis of more than one sample
Anova: Two-Factor without Replication	Calculates a two-factor variance analysis of one sample
Correlation	Calculates the correlation coefficient that measures the relationship between two sets of numbers
Covariance	Calculates the average of the product of deviations of data points from their respective means
Descriptive Statistics	Calculates many common statistics for a group of numbers
Exponential Smoothing	Calculates the forecasted values using past points to correct the prediction
F-Test: Two Sample for Variances	Calculates a two-sample F-test to compute the closeness of the population variances of two groups of numbers
Fourier Analysis	Performs a fast Fourier transform for solving partial differential equations
Histogram	Calculates a frequency distribution to measure how many times values within ranges appear in a set of data
Moving Average	Calculates a moving average
Random Number Generation	Fills a range with numbers with a selected distribution

Tool	Description
Rank and Percentile	Calculates the ranking and percentiles for a group of numbers
Regression	Calculates linear regression analysis
Sampling	Selects a sample of data from a larger population
t-Test: Paired Two Samples for Means	Performs a two-sample student t-test that measures whether the means for two samples of data are the same
t-Test: Two Sample Assuming Equal Variances	Performs a paired two-sample student t-test with the assumption that the means of both samples of data are the same
t-Test: Two Sample Assuming Unequal Variances	Performs a paired two-sample student t-test with the assumption that the means of both samples of data are not the same
z-Test: Two Sample for Means	Measures whether the means for two populations of data are the same

When I use one of the more advanced functions, my formula returns the error #NAME?. I know I entered the formula correctly so how do I get the function to work?

Many of the advanced functions are not part of the main Excel application but are available through the Analysis ToolPak add-in. The reason the formula may not return a result is that you do not have the Analysis ToolPak add-in loaded. If the <u>D</u>ata Analysis command doesn't appear on your <u>T</u>ools menu, this is your problem. Before you can use the advanced functions and other analysis tools, you must install and load this add-in.

If the add-in is not listed, follow these steps to install the Analysis ToolPak:

1. Choose Add-<u>I</u>ns from the <u>T</u>ools menu.

2. Select the Analysis ToolPak check box in the <u>A</u>dd-Ins Available box.

3. Click OK.

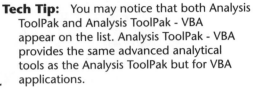

Tech Tip: You may notice that both Analysis ToolPak and Analysis ToolPak - VBA appear on the list. Analysis ToolPak - VBA provides the same advanced analytical tools as the Analysis ToolPak but for VBA applications.

To load the Analysis ToolPak:

1. Double-click MS Excel Setup program icon in the Program Manager.

2. Click the Add/Remove button.

3. Select the Add-Ins check box to install all the add-ins.

4. Click Continue.

5. At the prompts, insert the appropriate disks.

6. Click OK when Excel has finished installing the add-in.

Tech Tip: When some, but not all of the add-ins are installed, the Add-Ins check box appears selected. Double-click this check box or click Change Option to ensure you are installing all the add-ins you want.

When I use the Random Number Generation analysis tool, it seems to return values based upon a normal distribution. Are other types of distributions available in Excel?

Excel can generate seven types of distributions: uniform, normal, Bernoulli, binomial, Poisson, patterned, and discrete. The different distribution patterns determine how the values returned by this analysis tool are distributed between the two end points. You can change the distribution pattern in the Random Number Generation dialog box by selecting the desired distribution pattern in the Distribution drop-down box. The following table describes the different distributions.

Distribution	Description
Uniform	Returns values that are evenly distributed between two points
Normal	Returns values that are based on a bell curve; the bell curve assumes that one particular value—the *mean*—is more likely to occur than any other value, that values are equally likely to fall above as below the mean, and that values closer to the mean are more likely to occur than values farther away from the mean
Bernoulli	Returns values indicating the probability for success on any given trial
Binomial	Returns values indicating the cumulative successes for multiple trials
Poisson	Returns values used to estimate the occurrences of events for a period of time
Patterned	Returns values that follow a pattern using values you provide
Discrete	Returns values that recur with the frequency set by a range of cells that list the values and the probability for each value

To generate random numbers with this analysis tool:

1. Choose <u>D</u>ata Analysis from the <u>T</u>ools menu.
2. Select Random Number Generation and click OK.
3. Select the distribution type in the <u>D</u>istribution drop-down list box.
4. Supply the other values indicated in the Random Number Generation dialog box. The entries you need to provide depend on the distribution type.
5. Click OK to generate the numbers.

Tech Tip: You cannot remove the output of analysis tools with the <u>U</u>ndo command on the <u>E</u>dit menu.

In the random number generator, I saw an option for Patterned. What does this option do?

The Patterned option is a distribution method that selects the numbers that the Random Number Generation analysis tool returns. This option is a non-random number generator that yields numbers in a specific pattern you describe when you choose the parameters. You enter the upper and lower boundary of the numbers in the <u>F</u>rom and <u>T</u>o boxes that appear in the Parameters section of the Random Number Generation dialog box when you select the Patterned option. The in Steps of box indicates the distance between numbers. The values you input in the Repeating each number and Repeating the Sequence boxes tell Excel how many times you want the number to appear in a row in each pass through the sequence and how many times you want to run the entire sequence of numbers, respectively.

Can Excel calculate which number appears the most often in a series of numbers?

The MODE function returns the value that occurs the most often in a range of numbers. The function returns #NUM! if the range contains

- no values
- more than 6550 values
- the #N/A value

If no number occurs more than once, the MODE function returns the #N/A value.

What does the MEDIAN function do?

The MEDIAN function calculates the number in the middle of a set of numbers, which is called the *mathematical median*. The mathematical median is the value that has an equal number of values above and below it. Figure 8-1 shows the median calculated for homes in different areas. You can see how this number is different than the average price. If there is an even amount of numbers in your set, the median is the average of the two numbers in the middle of the set. The =MEDIAN(B5:B11) formula in B13 returns the median of the values in B5:B11.

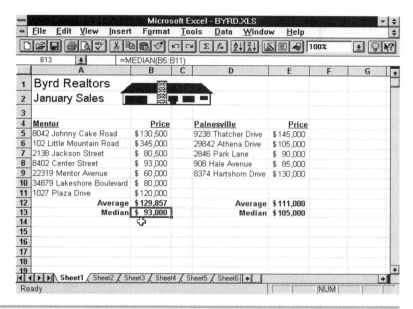

FIGURE 8-1 Using MEDIAN to determine the house price in the middle of the price range

I entered the formula =SUM(D4:D43)/40 to calculate an average of 40 cells in column D. I think the answer Excel displays is wrong but how can I check it?

Check whether there are any blank cells or cells with text in them in your range—either of these will throw off your average! When you calculate an average by dividing the total by the total number of cells, the result will be incorrect if any of the cells are empty or contain text. Instead, use the AVERAGE function. The AVERAGE function calculates the average, or *mean*, of numbers in a range, by summing the numbers and then dividing the result by the number of values. The AVERAGE function ignores blank cells and cells containing text or logical values. To find the average of the values in D4:D43, use the formula =AVERAGE(D4:D43).

I am an accountant and I want to use your product to create several depreciation schedules. What depreciation options does Excel offer?

Excel includes several functions that calculate depreciation using popular accounting methods. These functions include

- SLN (straight-line depreciation) depreciates the same amount for each year of an asset's life.

- DDB (double-declining balance depreciation) depreciates more of an asset's value when the asset is new and less as it gets older. This method depreciates assets faster than the SYD function when you use the default 200% factor.

- DB (fixed-declining balance depreciation) depreciates the asset's value at a fixed rate.

- VDB (variable declining balance depreciation) depreciates more of an asset's value when the asset is new and less as it gets older. This function lets you change the rate that calculates the amount depreciated so that, depending on the percentage used, it can depreciate assets faster or slower than DDB or SYD.

- SYD (sum-of-years' digits depreciation) depreciates more of an asset's value when the asset is new and less as it gets older.

These functions use the following syntax:

DDB(*cost,salvage,life,period,factor*)
SLN(*cost,salvage,life*)
SYD(*cost,salvage,life,period*)
VDB(*cost,salvage,life,start_period,end_period,factor,no_switch*)
DB(*cost,salvage,life,period,month*)

For each of these functions, *cost* is the initial asset cost, *salvage* is what you expect it to be worth after all depreciation is taken, and *life* is how long you expect it to last. For all but the SLN function, you must also indicate the *period* in the asset's life for which you are calculating a result since the depreciation returned

Tech Tip: Excel also includes AMORDEGRC and AMORLINC functions that calculate depreciation for the French accounting system.

depends on whether you are calculating the depreciation for the first year or the fifth. VDB uses *start_period* and *end_period* arguments to set the beginning and end of the time for which you are measuring depreciation. You can use this function to calculate depreciation for different time intervals. DDB and VDB also allow a *factor* argument so you can use a depreciation percentage other than the default of 200%. In addition, you can enter a *no_switch* argument for the VDB function to indicate whether you want Excel to switch to straight-line depreciation when it exceeds the declining balance depreciation.

Figure 8-2 shows four different depreciation methods applied to the same asset. The asset information appears in B2:B4 so all the functions reference these cells for the *cost, salvage value,* and *life* arguments. The DDB, SYD, and VDB formulas derive the *period* from the numbers in column A. These numbers have the format code "Year "#":" to show the text as well as the numbers. By looking at the results, you can see that ultimately all the functions fully depreciate the asset, but they do so at different rates.

	Microsoft Excel - DEPREC.XLS						
File Edit View Insert Format Tools Data Window Help							

Arial   10   B I U $ % ,

C6   =DDB($B$2,$B$3,$B$4,A6)

	A	B	C	D	E	F	G	H
1	Comparison of the Different Depreciation Methods							
2	Cost¹:	$12,000						
3	Salvage Value:	$2,000						
4	Useful Life:	5						
5		Straight-line	Double-Declining Balance	Sum-of-the-years' Digits	Variable Declining Balance (150%)			
6	Year 1:	$2,000	$4,800	$3,333	$3,600			
7	Year 2:	$2,000	$2,880	$2,667	$2,520			
8	Year 3:	$2,000	$1,728	$2,000	$1,764			
9	Year 4:	$2,000	$592	$1,333	$1,235			
10	Year 5:	$2,000	$0	$667	$881			
11	Total Depreciation:	$10,000	$10,000	$10,000	$10,000			
12								
13	¹ Cost is used as basis with the assumption that no section 291 deduction will be taken for the asset.							
14								
15								

Sheet1 / Sheet2 / Sheet3 / Sheet4 / Sheet5 / Sheet6

Ready   NUM

FIGURE 8-2   Different depreciation methods applied to the same asset

What functions does Excel provide to help me calculate plot lines to fit sets of data?

Excel features regression functions that can calculate the values for your plot lines. *Regression* is a statistical technique that calculates the equation that best describes a set of data. The following table describes Excel's regression functions.

Function	Description	Format
LINEST	Returns regression statistics about the straight plot line that fits the data using the "least squares" method	LINEST(*known_y's,known_x's,const, stats*)
TREND	Returns values for *y* using a straight plot line given one or more values of *x*	TREND(*known_y's,known_x's,new_ x's,const*)
FORECAST	Returns a forecasted value from a straight plot line given the set of data that creates the plot line	FORECAST(*x,known_y's,known_x's*)
SLOPE	Returns the slope of the straight plot line that fits the data using the "least squares" method	SLOPE(*known_y's,known_x's*)
STEYX	Returns the standard error of each set of *y* values for a straight plot line that fits the data using the "least squares" method	STEYX(*known_y's,known_x's*)
LOGEST	Returns regression statistics about an exponential curve plot line	LOGEST(*known_y's,known_x's,const, stats*)
GROWTH	Returns forecasted values from an exponential curve plot line	GROWTH(*known_y's,known_x's,new_ x's,const*)

Several of these functions return arrays if you set them up as array formulas. You can use Excel's Regression analysis tool to calculate regression values.

Are there any functions that will help me determine yields for securities?

Yes, Excel has three functions that calculate annual yields for securities: YIELD, YIELDDISC, and YIELDMAT. These functions return results that are percentages, as in 6%. These functions, like many of the advanced financial functions, use many of the arguments described in Table 8-1.

- YIELD calculates the annual yield for a security that pays periodic interest. The format for this function is

  YIELD(*settlement,maturity,rate,pr,redemption,frequency,basis*)

- YIELDDISC calculates a security's annual yield for a discounted security. The format for this function is

  YIELDDISC(*settlement,maturity,pr,redemption,basis*)

- YIELDMAT calculates the annual yield for a security that pays its interest at maturity. The format for this function is

  YIELDMAT(*settlement,maturity,issue,rate,pr,basis*)

For example, suppose you have a bond whose settlement date is 1/1/94, maturity date is 12/23/94, discounted purchase price is $8,000, and redemption value is $10,000. The formula =YIELDDISC(DATE(94, 1, 1), DATE(94, 12, 23), 8000, 10000) returns the value 25.57%. Since this formula doesn't include a basis argument, Excel uses 30/360 by default.

Argument	Description
settlement	The security's settlement date
maturity	The security's maturity date
issue	The security's issue date
rate	The security's interest rate at date of issue
pr	The security's price per $100 face value
redemption	The security's redemption value per $100 face value
frequency	The number of annual interest payments that the security makes
basis	A number representing the convention used to measure days
investment	The amount invested in the security
yld	The security's annual yield
discount	The security's discount rate
first_interest	The security's first interest date
par	The security's annual coupon rate

TABLE 8-1   Arguments used by several advanced financial functions

Is there a way to calculate the discount rate of securities?

The DISC function calculates the discount rate of a security based on the purchase date, maturity date, price, redemption value, and the basis of the year in days. This function uses the format DISC(*settlement,maturity,pr,redemption,basis*). See Table 8-1 for a description of these arguments.

How can I compute the interest rate for a security?

The INTRATE function calculates the rate of interest for a fully invested security based on the settlement date, maturity date, initial purchase price, value at redemption, and the day count basis of the security. INTRATE differs from the DISC function in that DISC calculates the discount rate for securities whereas INTRATE computes the interest rate for securities that pay periodic interest. INTRATE uses the format

INTRATE(*settlement,maturity,investment,redemption,basis*)

See Table 8-1 for a description of these arguments.

How do I determine the price of a security?

The PRICE, PRICEDISC, and PRICEMAT functions calculate the price of a security under three different conditions:

- The PRICE function calculates the price per $100 of face value of a security that pays interest on a periodic basis. The format for this function is

    PRICE(*settlement,maturity,rate,yld,redemption,frequency, basis*)

- PRICEDISC returns the price per $100 of face value of a security that is discounted instead of paying periodic interest. The format for this function is

    PRICEDISC(*settlement,maturity,discount,redemption,basis*)

- PRICEMAT returns the price per $100 of face value of a security that pays its interest at maturity. The format for this function is

    PRICEMAT(*settlement,maturity,issue,rate,yld,basis*)

The arguments listed are described in Table 8-1.

Is there a way to figure out how much interest will be earned on a security?

The RECEIVED function calculates the total amount received at maturity for a fully invested security, based on the settlement date, maturity date, initial purchase price, discount rate, and the day count basis of the security. The difference between this function's result and the initial investment is the interest earned. The format for the RECEIVED function is RECEIVED(*settlement,maturity,investment,discount,basis*). This function uses the same arguments as those described for other financial functions in Table 8-1.

Can Excel calculate accrued interest on securities?

The ACCRINT and ACCRINTM functions calculate accrued interest. You use ACCRINT for securities that pay interest on a periodic basis, and ACCRINTM for those that only pay interest at the maturity date. A coupon bond is an example of a security that periodically pays interest. Series H government bonds are securities that pay interest at maturity since the interest is the difference between what you paid for the bond and the face amount you receive when the bond matures. The ACCRINT function's format is ACCRINT(*issue,first_interest,settlement,rate,par,frequency,basis*). The format of ACCRINTM is ACCRINTM(*issue,maturity,rate,par,basis*). These arguments are defined in Table 8-1.

What's the difference between the DOLLARDE and DOLLARFR functions?

DOLLARDE and DOLLARFR are a pair of functions that convert fractional pricing of securities into decimal format (DOLLARDE) or decimal pricing into fractional (DOLLARFR). For example, if you have a security at 1+7/8, the formula =DOLLARDE(1.7,8) converts it to 1.875. Conversely, =DOLLARFR(1.875,8) converts to 1.7. The number after the comma in each function is the denominator of the fraction. Thus the 1.7 result equals 1 and 7 over the denominator of 8, or 7/8ths.

I do a lot of work with bonds. Are there any Excel functions I might find useful for this purpose?

The following table lists six Excel functions for bond coupons you may find very useful.

Function	Description	Format
COUPDAYSB	Calculates the number of days from the beginning of the coupon period to the settlement date	COUPDAYBS(*settlement,maturity, frequency,basis*)
COUPDAYS	Calculates the number of days in the coupon period that contains the settlement date	COUPDAYS(*settlement,maturity, frequency,basis*)
COUPDAYSNC	Calculates the number of days from the settlement date to the next coupon date	COUPDAYSNC(*settlement,maturity, frequency,basis*)
COUPNCD	Calculates the next coupon date after settlement date	COUPNCD(*settlement,maturity, frequency,basis*)
COUPNUM	Calculates the number of coupons payable between the settlement date and maturity dates	COUPNUM(*settlement,maturity, frequency,basis*)
COUPPCD	Calculates the coupon date previous to settlement date, where the settlement date is the date of purchase	COUPPCD(*settlement,maturity, frequency,basis*)

These functions' arguments are the same ones that other financial functions use and are described in Table 8-1.

Are there any functions in Excel that deal with Treasury bills?

Yes, Excel has three functions that are directly related to Treasury bills, or T-bills:

- TBILLEQ calculates the bond-equivalent yield for Treasury bills, using the format

    TBILLEQ(*settlement,maturity,discount*)

- TBILLPRICE calculates the price per $100 of face value for a Treasury bill, using the format

    TBILLPRICE(*settlement,maturity,discount*)

- TBILLYIELD calculates a Treasury bill's yield. This function's format is

    TBILLYIELD(*settlement,maturity,pr*)

Like other advanced financial functions, the T-bill functions use the arguments listed in Table 8-1.

Can Excel create a list of how frequently values appear in a range so I can create a histogram chart?

Excel will not only calculate the values you want for your histogram chart, it will create the histogram for you! A *histogram* is a chart that takes a number of measurements, and plots the frequency with which the values of the measurements occur in certain intervals. These intervals are generally referred to as *bins*. For example, in a histogram of survey responses, the bins might be the numbers 1 through 5. The bins don't have to be evenly spaced as in 1-2, 3-4, and 5-6; they could be 1-3, 4-10, and 11-12. However, the bin values must be in ascending order. Excel can even create the bins for you based on the data you are analyzing.

To create the histogram data:

1. Choose <u>D</u>ata Analysis from the <u>T</u>ools Menu.

2. Select Histogram in the <u>A</u>nalysis Tools list box and then click OK.

3. Select the range containing the values to analyze or type it in the <u>I</u>nput Range box.

4. Select or type the range containing the values to use as bins in the <u>B</u>in Range box or leave the box empty to have Excel create the bins for you.

5. Select whichever appropriate check boxes describe the options you want Excel to use to present the histogram results.

6. Select the option that describes where you want Excel to place the output of the analysis:

- <u>O</u>utput Range places the histogram results in the location you enter in the adjoining box.
- New Worksheet <u>P</u>ly adds a new sheet to the workbook to contain the histogram results. You can enter a name for this new sheet in the adjoining box.
- New <u>W</u>orkbook creates a new workbook to store the results of the histogram analysis.

7. Click OK.

Figure 8-3 shows a histogram analysis and the beginning of the data that it analyzes. This output includes a histogram chart as well as the cumulative percentages and the sorting by (or Pareto) frequency.

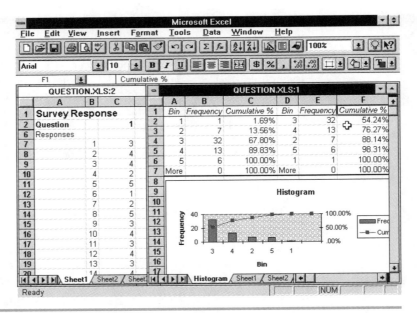

FIGURE 8-3   A histogram analysis measures the frequency of values in a range

Can I sort my histogram data output?

Excel initially shows histogram data output in the same order as the bins. Alternatively, you can sort the output according to the frequency so that Excel lists the most frequent bin first. When you select the Pareto check box in the Histogram dialog box, the histogram output includes two copies of the frequency analysis. The first one is the standard one, with the bins listed in ascending order; the second one displays the output sorted in descending order according to frequency. This second version of the frequency analysis appears in column E in Figure 8-3.

I selected the Cumulative Percentage option when I created a histogram but Excel didn't show the percentage for each of the bins. What's wrong?

The cumulative percentage option doesn't track individual bin percentages, but rather the percentage of the total of all the bins up to that point in the list. In other words, the percentages approach 100% as you get closer to the end of the list of bins. However, you can add a simple formula to your worksheet to calculate the percentages for the individual bins. A sample histogram analysis with that formula appears here:

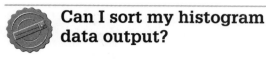

	A	B	C	D	E	F	G
	Bin	Frequency	Cumulative %	Bin	Frequency	Cumulative %	Bin %
1							
2	1	1	1.69%	3	32	54.24%	54.24%
3	2	7	13.56%	4	13	76.27%	22.03%
4	3	32	67.80%	2	7	88.14%	11.86%
5	4	13	89.83%	5	6	98.31%	10.17%
6	5	6	100.00%	1	1	100.00%	1.69%

G2 = =E2/SUM($E$2:$E$6)

The formulas in column G divide the bins' frequency by the total of the frequency of all bins. G2 contains =E2/SUM($E$2:$E$6), which was then copied to G3:G6. You must use an absolute cell reference (such as $E$2:$E$6) to ensure that Excel points to the same range when you copy the formula down the column. In this case, the first E2 in the formula adjusts but $E$2:$E$6 remains the same when copied.

Sometimes when I select a scenario, I get the message "Redefine *scenario name* scenario based on current cell values?" What does this message mean and why does it appear sporadically?

By design, Excel prompts you with this message if you try to display a scenario that already appears in the worksheet by using the WorkGroup toolbar. You can avoid this problem by examining the Scenarios box on the WorkGroup toolbar to see which scenario is current. Excel only displays the message you mention if you select the same scenario, not if you select another one. Also, it only appears when you use the WorkGroup toolbar, not the Scenarios command on the Tools menu, to select the scenario. When you use the menu command, Excel doesn't display any message.

What is the Goal Seek command?

The Goal Seek command can help you work backward through a problem when you know what you want the answer to be but you don't know one of the variables. In other words, you can use Goal Seek when you know the target result and have only one input that can change.

For example, suppose you know you need to make $1000 a week in salary after taxes, but you don't know exactly how much you must make per hour to reach this goal. Assuming you know your salary is taxed at 20%, you want to determine the hourly rate before you approach your boss about a raise.

To solve this problem using Goal Seek:

1. Set up the entries you want to evaluate in the worksheet, including the entry whose value you want to find, such as the hourly wage, and any formulas that evaluate this value, including the one you want to equal a specific value.

   In this example, your worksheet might look like the one shown here:

B2		=0.8*40*B1							
A	**B**	**C**	**D**	**E**	**F**	**G**	**H**	**I**	
1 Hourly Wage									
2 Take Home Pay	0								

Cell B2 contains the formula =.80*40*B1. This formula calculates 80 percent of your wages, assuming you are paid for 40 hours per week at the per hour rate in cell B1. At this point the result is 0 because B1 is empty. You may want to enter an initial guess in the cell whose value you don't know when you create such a model so you can make sure your formulas are entered correctly.

2. Choose Goal Seek from the Tools menu to display this dialog box:

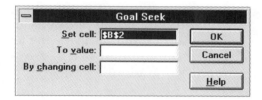

3. Enter the cell that contains the formula you want to equal a specific result in the Set cell box. In the hourly wage example, this cell is B2.

4. Enter the value you want the results of the formula to equal in the To value box. In the hourly wage example, you would enter **1000**.

5. Enter the cell containing the value you want Excel to change in the By changing cell box. In this case, B1 is the cell for which you want to find a value.

6. Click OK. Excel displays the correct value in the cell you specified; in this case, it enters 31.25 in B1. It also informs you that it has found a solution, as shown here:

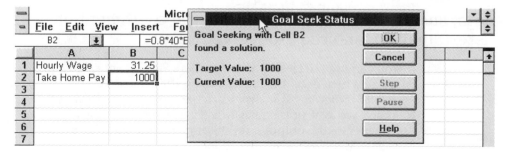

7. Click OK to close the Goal Seek Status dialog box.

I have a data set with 15 samples. When I use the Descriptive Statistics analysis tool, the confidence interval it gives is different from the one I calculate using a textbook t-table. What's wrong?

The CONFIDENCE() function, which the descriptive statistics analysis tool uses to calculate the confidence interval, assumes a large sample. In most cases, this function gives an accurate result for samples of 200 or more, but it is not accurate for smaller samples. For smaller samples, you can calculate the confidence interval by multiplying the results of the TINV() function by the standard deviation of the sample. For 95% confidence, you would use this formula:

=TINV(0.05,*number_of_samples*)*STDEV(*values*)

When I use the Regression analysis tool on my data, it gives me a negative value for R^2. I thought this value should always be between 0 and 1. What's happening?

A negative R^2 occurs if you force the constant, or y-intercept, to be zero. To fix this problem, the next time you use the Regression analysis tool, clear the Constant is Zero check box in the Regression dialog box. The same thing will happen if you create a trendline on a chart and force the constant to zero.

I've used the new Regression analysis tool in Excel 5.0, but how can I generate individual statistical regression data, such as the slope of my data, the coefficient of determination, and the F-observed value?

You can use the LINEST array function. First, select an output range. Then, enter the formula using the syntax =LINEST(*known_y's, known_x's,const,stats*). Make sure that the logical value of *stats* equals True. Finally, press CTRL+SHIFT+ENTER to generate the output array. A sample of this function's results is shown in the following illustration.

E1				{=LINEST(A3:A10,B3:C10,TRUE, TRUE)}				
	A	**B**	**C**	**D**	**E**	**F**	**G**	**H**	**I**
1	Sales	Disposable	Advertising		12.75261	0.002093	-60493.6		
2	Product A	Income	Expense		5.102854	0.000534	39282		
3	110,000	25,000,000	9,000		0.94981	13290.54	#N/A		
4	135,000	31,000,000	9,500		47.31044	5	#N/A		
5	205,000	53,000,000	12,500		67E+10	8.83E+08	#N/A		
6	215,000	58,000,000	13,000						
7	125,000	42,000,000	9,000						
8	175,000	43,000,000	11,000						
9	210,000	63,000,000	11,000						
10	250,000	67,000,000	12,000						

Tech Tip: Another advantage of using LINEST rather than the Regression analysis tool is that the function remains on your worksheet so results will change if the analyzed data changes.

 ## What is Solver and why would I want to use it?

Solver is an add-in function that adjusts the value in more than one cell to return a desired output. This output can be the largest possible result for a formula, the smallest possible result for a formula, a specific result for a formula, or simply a set of values that fits the limitations you have placed on the problem. You use Solver rather than Goal Seek when you want to vary the value in more than one cell. You can also use Solver when you are not sure what the final results you want are. Solver decides which cell values to change based on *constraints* you provide to set the limits for a value. Constraints are logical formulas you want to be True when Solver replaces values in the sheet.

To use Solver:

1. Set up the problem for which you will use the Solver. You must enter the values you expect Solver to change, the formulas that operate on the adjustable cells, and any formula for which you want Solver to find a specific value, a maximum value, or a minimum value.

    Figure 8-4 shows two views of the same sample problem. (The bottom window shows the same worksheet after pressing CTRL+` to display the formulas rather than their results.) In this problem, a company has two products and needs to decide how many to make of each type. Product A has variable costs of 4 per unit and fixed costs of 200,000. This product has a sales price of 5 per unit.

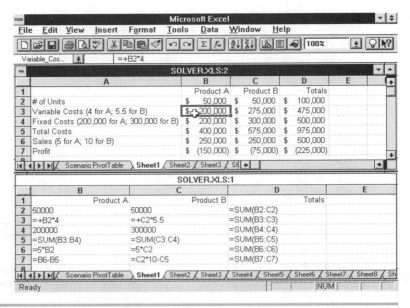

FIGURE 8-4   A problem set up for Solver

Product B has variable costs of 5.5 per unit and fixed costs of 300,000. This product has a sales price of 10 per unit. While you could try out different values to determine the best mix of the two products, Solver can quickly calculate the optimal combination for you.

2. Choose Sol**v**er from the **T**ools menu to display the Solver Parameters dialog box. This illustration shows the dialog box after it was completed for this example:

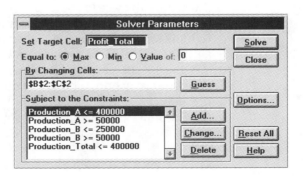

3. Select the cell containing the value you want to use as a final result in the Se̲t Target Cell box. You can also select one of the Equal to option buttons to specify that you want to find the maximum, minimum, or a specific value.

   In Figure 8-4, you want to maximize the company's total profits, which appear in cell D7 (also named Profit_Total).

4. Select or type the range of cells that Solver can change to enter it in the B̲y Changing Cells box.

   For the problem in Figure 8-4, you want Solver to change the values in B2:C2.

5. Select or type the cells that limit the solution Solver returns in the Su̲bject to Constraints box and then click A̲dd to display the Add Constraint dialog box that looks like this one:

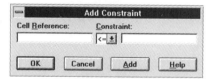

Tech Tip: It takes Solver longer to find a solution when you specify that a value must be an integer.

6. For each constraint, select or type the cell on which you want to place a limit, to enter it in the Cell R̲eference box. Select the cell's relationship to the limit in the C̲onstraint drop-down box and enter the value the cell reference is limited to in the other box on the right. You can add a limit that a particular cell must equal an integer (no digits after the decimal point) by selecting int for integer. Click A̲dd to record the constraint and continue adding another one. When you finish adding constraints, click Cancel to return to the Solver Parameters dialog box.

   The problem depicted in Figure 8-4 used the following constraints:

   ■ The total number of units of both products that can be made is 400,000.

- The company needs to make at least 50,000 units of Product A, but not more than 400,000.

- The company needs to make at least 50,000 units of Product B, but not more than 250,000.

7. Click Options if you want to change how Solver performs. Click OK to return to the Solver dialog box.

8. Click Solve.

Solver analyzes your problem and finds a set of numbers for the adjustable cells that fits the limits you have placed on the problem. Excel displays a dialog box that looks like this one:

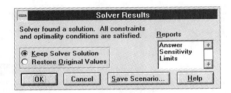

9. If you want to save the solution Solver finds, click Save Scenario and enter a scenario name.

10. To produce reports about the solution, select the reports you want in the Reports box.

11. Click OK to leave the Solver Results dialog box.

If you have asked Excel to create any reports, it adds them as separate sheets to your workbook at this time.

Figure 8-5 displays the solution that Solver found to the problem shown in Figure 8-4. Solver determined how many units of each product to make to generate maximum profits. You can also see the beginning of one of the reports that Solver created for this problem.

Tech Tip: You can enter your "best guesses" for the values of the adjustable cells in the worksheet to give Solver a head start. Solver uses these initial guesses as the starting points when it looks for a solution and therefore may need less time to find one.

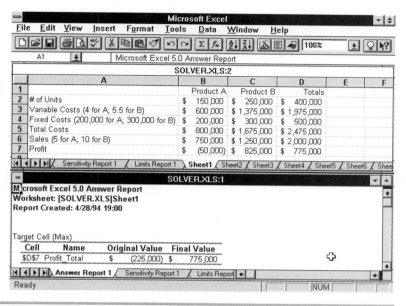

FIGURE 8-5   Solution and report created by Solver

I was using Solver and it stopped before it came to a solution. Why?

There are several reasons why Solver may have stopped:

- The target cell is changing without limit. You need to adjust the constraints or the formulas that reference the adjustable cells.

- You have assumed that the model is linear when the model is nonlinear. You need to change one option before you restart Solver. Choose Solver from the Tools menu, click the Options button, clear the Assume Linear Model check box, click OK, and then click Solve.

- You have not given Solver enough iterations to complete the problem. Increase the maximum number of iterations and resolve the problem.

- You may need to select AutoScaling because some input values may be several orders of magnitude apart.

■ You may have a complex model with integer constraints. Try increasing the maximum time allowed.

When I create a correlation or covariance matrix with the analysis tools, it produces a lower-left matrix. Can I convert this to an upper-right matrix?

To convert the matrix from a lower-left matrix to an upper-right matrix:

1. Select the cells containing the matrix.
2. Choose Copy from the Edit menu.
3. Move to the location at which you want the upper-right matrix to appear.
4. Choose Paste Special from the Edit menu.
5. Select the Transpose check box.
6. Click OK to copy the lower-left matrix as an upper-right matrix.

I have a worksheet that has a two-input data table in it. Every time I enter a number, it takes a long time to recalculate. Is there any way I can speed this up?

Yes, you can limit Excel's automatic recalculation to make it skip over the data tables and recalculate the tables only when you tell it to do so by pressing F9.

To recalculate the tables manually but the other data automatically:

1. Choose Options from the Tools menu.
2. Click the Calculation tab.
3. Select Automatic Except Tables in the Calculation section. This option automatically recalculates everything except tables when Excel calculates the sheet: Automatic recalculates the entire worksheet, including tables, whenever any data changes; Manual doesn't automatically recalculate any formulas.

4. Click OK.

Now Excel will perform faster because it won't update the tables. To recalculate the tables, click the Calc Now button on the Calculation tab of the Options dialog box, or press F9.

 Online Help for the MIRR function gives a formula for how the function is calculated that uses the NPV function. When I use that formula, I get a different result. Why?

Online Help gives the following formula:

$$\left(\frac{-NPV(rrate, values[positive]) * (1+rrate)^m}{NPV(rrate, values[negative]) * (1+frate)}\right)^{\frac{1}{n-1}} - 1$$

This formula is correct, except that the arrays containing positive and negative values must have the values in the same position as in the original array, with zeros in the other positions. For example, if you have an array of the following cash flows:

{–120000,39000,30000,21000,37000,46000}

the positive values array you would use in the NPV function is

{0,39000,30000,21000,37000,46000}

and the negative values array would be

{–120000,0,0,0,0,0}

Using these arrays, the NPV() formula above would provide the same result (12.61) as the MIRR() function.

Lists and Data Management

You will probably find yourself using Excel as a way to create and maintain lists of data such as sales results, convention attendees, and transactions in your checking account. You can use Excel to store this raw data for analysis or for use with other applications. Excel provides a wide variety of tools for managing the data in your Excel worksheets, including pivot tables for summarizing information, automatic subtotals to sum by category, filters to view subsets of the data, data forms to simplify adding new records, and sorting to organize your data in a meaningful fashion.

FRUSTRATION BUSTERS!

Creating and updating a large list can require a large investment of time, so you certainly want to manage these tasks in the most efficient manner. You need to set up your data in a way that makes sense to Excel so you can take full advantage of the many features that make working with lists easier. In particular, you want Excel to be able to recognize your list using its automatic selection capability. Here are some useful tips to help you lay out and format a list for working with Excel:

- Assign the same format to each entire column of data. Don't use different formatting in different cells in the column; doing so makes it harder for Excel to correctly identify the list.

- Avoid entering spaces at the beginning of a cell entry, since these spaces result in incorrect sorts.

- Create only one list per worksheet. Some list management features can only work with one list in a worksheet at a time.

- Enter labels in the list's first row to identify each column. Excel uses these labels when filtering, sorting, and creating pivot tables.

- Enter only one type of data in each column; otherwise, you are likely to encounter difficulties when you try to use certain features, such as pivot tables.

- Format your column labels differently than the data in your list to help Excel identify them.

- Leave one completely blank row and column between the list and any other data to help Excel correctly define the list.

- Store important data under or above the list in the worksheet. Since filtering a list hides rows, data that appears elsewhere in those rows is also hidden.

- Use cell borders under your column labels rather than a blank line or a row of dashes if you want to separate your column labels from your data. Excel interprets a blank row as a border marking the beginning of the list, and might interpret a row of dashes as part of the list.

Is there a limit to the size of a list in Excel 5.0?

No. Excel does not actually limit the size of a list. However, a list must fit on a single worksheet. Therefore, an Excel list can be as large as 256 columns by 16,384 rows, which is the size of a worksheet.

Tech Tip: If you have more than 16,384 records in your list, you may want to consider switching to a database management application such as Microsoft Access, which is designed to work with larger collections of data.

What is the easiest way to manage lists in Excel 5.0?

The easiest way to manage your lists in Excel 5.0 is to use the *data form,* which appears as a dialog box. In this dialog box, you can add, delete, and find records in your list. The data form dialog box is especially useful when you are entering data, because it provides a consistent format for the list. Using the data form can help prevent mistakes that result from entering data in the wrong column or accidentally entering data in the row above or below the correct one.

To use the data form dialog box:

1. Move to a cell in your list.

2. Select Form from the Data menu to display a data form dialog box similar to the one shown here:

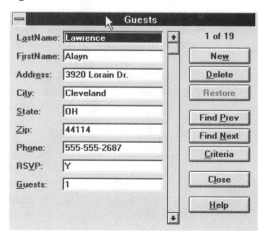

Your data form dialog box will look different than this one because you will have different fields in each record. The names of the boxes that appear on the left side of the dialog box are taken from your header row. The number of boxes depends on the number of columns of data in your list.

3. You can add, delete, restore, or move to records in your list from this dialog box by clicking the various buttons:

■ Click Ne<u>w</u> to clear the boxes on the left side of the dialog box so you can enter a new record.

■ Click <u>D</u>elete to delete the current record.

■ Click <u>R</u>estore to undo any changes you have made to the current record's entries.

■ Click <u>C</u>riteria to add search criteria to find specific records.

■ Click Find <u>P</u>rev to move to the previous record or find the previous record that matches the search criteria.

■ Click Find <u>N</u>ext to move to the next record or find the next record that matches the search criteria.

4. When you have finished working with your list, click C<u>l</u>ose to close this dialog box.

What does the new SUMIF function do?

The SUMIF function adds the values in a range if the values meet specified criteria. For example, suppose you are keeping a list for items in lay-away at your store. You may keep partial payments on items in lay-away in a separate account, and just transfer that money to your main account when the lay-away items are paid in full. In your list, shown in Figure 9-1, you want to total only those payments that are complete, to indicate how much money you should transfer from the lay-away account to your main account. You can use the SUMIF function to total the payments recorded in column E that are complete.

This function uses the syntax SUMIF(*range,criteria,sum_range*), where *range* is the range of data you want to evaluate, *criteria* is what the entries in *range* must match to be summed, and *sum_range* is the range of data you want to sum. This function can only use very simple criteria. It can compare the contents of *range*

	Microsoft Excel - XL09ART.XLS						

File Edit View Insert Format Tools Data Window Help

| E18 | =SUMIF(F2:F17,0,E2:E17) |

	A	B	C	D	E	F	G	H
1	LastName	FirstName	Item Code	Price	Payments	Owed		
2	Brianson	William	66410	$ 78.27	$ 78.27	$ -		
3	Bryan	Carol	87348	$ 109.73	$ 29.98	$ 79.75		
4	Campbell	Edward	63351	$ 60.14	$ 26.72	$ 33.42		
5	Connor	Kay	50396	$ 34.39	$ 34.39	$ -		
6	Ericson	Allen	72674	$ 82.07	$ 32.52	$ 49.56		
7	Genet	Dwayne	36682	$ 52.81	$ 52.81	$ 0.00		
8	Horace	Creta	91082	$ 115.30	$ 39.78	$ 75.51		
9	Johnson	Joanna	43055	$ 108.45	$ 64.96	$ 43.49		
10	Mann	Thomas	35630	$ 95.18	$ 26.90	$ 68.29		
11	Nichols	Shawn	27799	$ 89.59	$ 89.59	$ 0.00		
12	Richards	Marie	9399	$ 113.51	$ 60.09	$ 53.42		
13	Stuart	Laney	39170	$ 89.82	$ 80.97	$ 8.84		
14	Thomas	Timothy	99686	$ 68.20	$ 23.51	$ 44.69		
15	Torrington	Sandy	69247	$ 77.60	$ 52.58	$ 25.02		
16	Walters	Cynthia	25430	$ 73.11	$ 73.11	$ 0.00		
17	Washington	Thomas	66755	$ 94.47	$ 35.89	$ 58.58		
18					$ 112.66			

Guests \ **Layaway** / Sheet3 / Sheet4 / Sheet5 / Sheet

Ready

FIGURE 9-1   You can use SUMIF to keep track of lay-away payments

to text or to a constant. For example, in Figure 9-1, the function in E18 is SUMIF(F2:F17,0,E2:E17). In addition to matching, you can use comparison operators, as in SUMIF(C3:C10,"<10",D3:D10), which sums the numbers in D3:D10 if the corresponding numbers in C3:C10 are less than ten.

Tech Terror: It's difficult to tell at a glance whether you have entered this function correctly. Unlike the SUM function, whose result you can usually estimate, it's easy to enter arguments incorrectly with SUMIF. Using the Function Wizard can greatly simplify this task.

How does the COUNTBLANK function work?

The COUNTBLANK function counts all of the blank cells in the specified range. For example, you may want to know how many of your guests you invited have not responded yet. You can use the COUNTBLANK function to count all of the cells without entries in the column that indicates RSVP responses, as shown in Figure 9-2.

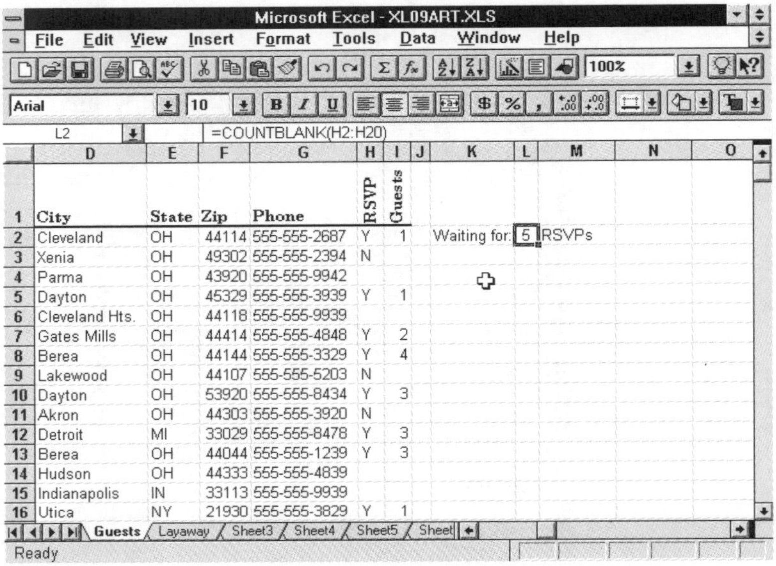

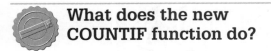

FIGURE 9-2   Using COUNTBLANK to find out how many responses are still expected

This function uses the syntax COUNTBLANK(*range*), where *range* is the range in which you want to count all the cells with no, or null string, entries. In Figure 9-2, COUNTBLANK returns 5, because five people have not responded to their invitations.

What does the new COUNTIF function do?

The COUNTIF function counts all of the entries in a range that match the criteria you specify. This function is very similar to SUMIF. However, instead of summing the contents of the range, COUNTIF simply counts the number of cells that match the criteria. As shown in Figure 9-3, you might want to keep track of how many people are paying the Patron rate instead of the Attendee rate as you maintain a list of reservations for the showing of a new film at your art museum, since patrons are invited to a special reception and dinner party before the film. The COUNTIF function in G3 counts the number of P entries in column D to determine the number of patrons that will attend the opening.

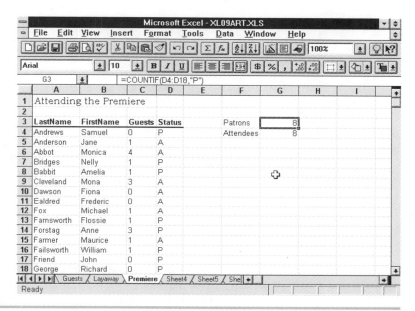

FIGURE 9-3   Tracking film premiere attendees and patrons

This function uses the syntax COUNTIF(*range,criteria*), where *range* is the range of values or entries you want to test and count, and *criteria* are the specifications an entry must match to be counted. For example, in Figure 9-3, the function reads =COUNTIF(D4:D18,"P").

Can I easily name each row in my list, using the entries in the first column?

Excel provides an easy way to name all of the rows in your list using the contents of the first column. To do so:

1. Select the entire list, including the first column you want to use for names.

2. Choose Name from the Insert menu, and then choose Create.

3. Select the Left Column check box, since the entries you want to use as names are in the left-hand column of the selected range, and click OK.

Excel now names each row of your list using the contents of the cell in the first column. You can also select Top Row to apply the entries in a header row as column names.

Is there a way to see only some of the records in my list?

You can limit which of the records in your list are displayed by filtering your list. When you filter a list, Excel only displays the records that match the criteria you specify. Excel 5.0 has a feature called AutoFilter, which makes filtering your lists even easier.

To use AutoFilter:

1. Move the insertion point to any cell in your list.

2. Choose Filter from the Data menu, and then choose AutoFilter.

   Your worksheet should now look similar the one shown in Figure 9-4. The drop-down arrows appear on top of the column labels in the header row of your list. You will use these drop-down arrows to select which of the records in your list you want to display.

3. Click a drop-down arrow to open the drop-down list box for that column. The drop-down list box shows the first 250 unique entries in that field.

4. AutoFilter offers you several ways to choose which records Excel displays:

   ■ Select a unique entry from one drop-down list to have Excel hide any record that does not contain that entry in that field. For example, select XYZ Company from the drop-down list for the Client field in Figure 9-4 to hide everything but the records for XYZ Company, as shown in the following illustration. This process is called *filtering* the list.

	A	B	C	D	E	F	G	H
1	Client	SalesRep	Sale	ItemCo	Qt	ShipDa	Via	
2	XYZ Company	Brian Fox	$ 90,535.72	4803	8	4/12/95	UPS	
6	XYZ Company	Susan Connor	$ 72,175.43	1400	2	4/14/95	FedEx	
12	XYZ Company	Brian Fox	$ 65,793.49	4868	4	4/21/95	FedEx	
17	XYZ Company	Brian Fox	$ 54,287.91	1360	9	4/12/95	DHL	
19								

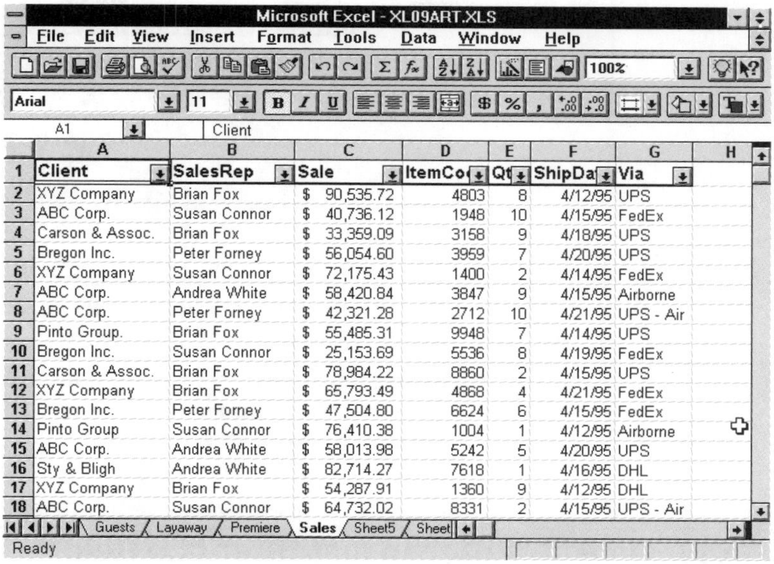

FIGURE 9-4   Using AutoFilter to select the records to display

You can continue to select entries from other drop-down lists when you want to further limit the records displayed. For example, select Brian Fox from the SalesRep field in Figure 9-4 to display only those records that include Brian Fox in the SalesRep field and XYZ Company in the Client field.

- Select All from a drop-down list to remove the filtering of that column. For example, select All from the Client field's drop-down list box in Figure 9-4 to redisplay records for other clients. Not all of your records will display, however, because you are still filtering the SalesRep field. You can tell when a field is filtered, because the drop-down arrow becomes blue instead of black.

- Select Custom from a drop-down list box to set a criterion that includes a range of values or two text entries. Selecting Custom opens the Custom AutoFilter dialog box, shown in the following illustration.

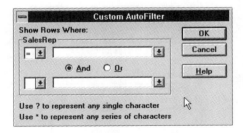

- Select NonBlanks or Blanks to display all the records with or without an entry in that field, respectively.

5. When you have finished working with AutoFilter, you can turn it off by choosing <u>F</u>ilter from the <u>D</u>ata menu and then choosing Auto<u>F</u>ilter again.

Can I use AutoFilter to just filter one field?

Yes, you can use AutoFilter and only select one field as a filter. Excel even makes it easy to only display the drop-down arrow for a single field. To do so, select the column you want to use as the filter either by moving to the heading for the column and pressing SHIFT+CTRL+DOWN ARROW or by clicking the column border. Next, choose <u>F</u>ilter from the <u>D</u>ata menu, choose Auto<u>F</u>ilter, and proceed as usual.

Is there a quick way to move to different sections of a list?

You can use AutoFilter to quickly move around in a long list that has been sorted alphabetically. To do so:

1. Choose <u>F</u>ilter from the <u>D</u>ata menu, and then choose Auto<u>F</u>ilter.

2. Click the drop-down arrow for the sorted field.

3. Type a letter and then press ENTER so the list is filtered to show only the entries that match the first entry on the list that starts with that letter.

4. Select the record you want.

5. Refilter the list to display all of the records. The insertion point will continue to be at the first cell that starts with the letter you typed in step 3.

What does the Consolidate command in the Data menu do?

The Consolidate command lets you combine data from many worksheets into one. To consolidate data using this command, the data on each sheet must be positioned in exactly the same way on each page, have the same names for ranges, and use the same row and column names. For example, you could have 12 identical worksheets used for recording monthly income and expenses. You could use the Consolidate command to create a 13th worksheet that sums all of the entries on the 12 monthly worksheets to provide yearly totals.

Tech Terror: Be very careful when specifying the ranges you want to consolidate, or use defined range names. If you accidentally identify one range incorrectly, the data on your consolidation sheet will be inaccurate.

I sorted my list and then realized that I used the wrong column. Can I fix this problem?

You can undo a sort, but only if you act immediately. Choose Undo Sort from the Edit menu, press CTRL+Z, or click the Undo button on the Standard toolbar.

If you performed another action in your document before using Undo so that it's impossible to undo the sort, you can try closing the file without saving your changes. Use this option only as a last resort—you will also lose any changes you made to the workbook since you last saved it.

Tech Tip: It's a good idea to save your workbook before performing a sort. This way, if you sort incorrectly, you can easily return the workbook to its previous state without losing any other changes.

When I filter my list using AutoFilter, the data to the right of my list disappears. Why?

Excel filters the list by hiding the rows that do not match the criteria you specify. Because entire rows are hidden, any other data in these rows disappears as well. To avoid hiding data when you apply filters, simply put your list in a worksheet of its own or place the other data above or below the list.

Are there any shortcuts for sorting my lists in Excel?

Yes. Excel provides two sorting buttons on the Standard toolbar that can sort a list in either ascending or descending order:

Sort Ascending —— —— *Sort Descending*

To sort your list, simply move to any cell in the column you want to sort by and click the appropriate button. Excel automatically recognizes the list and sorts it based on the entries in the current column.

Is there some way to break up my text files into worksheet cell entries?

This process is called *parsing.* Parsing is usually done when you import a text file that was created as output from another application, such as a database or the Windows Cardfile accessory. You must parse the data, because text files do not have the information that Excel uses to indicate which cells the entries belong in. Instead, data in text files may be separated by special characters, called *delimiters*, or by spaces.

In Excel 5.0, you use the Text to Columns command on the Data menu to parse data. Microsoft improved this command from earlier releases of Excel to let you visually change the results of the parse.

To parse your data:

1. Select all of the data; if you don't, only the current cell's contents will be parsed.

2. Choose Text to Columns from the Data menu.

3. Select either the Delimited or Fixed Width option button to indicate how the data is separated.

4. Click Next.

5. The option button you selected in step 3 determines which dialog box appears next:

   ■ If you selected Delimited, you can now specify which characters are used to separate the data and which characters are used to indicate text entries. As you make your selections, Excel applies them in the Data Preview section of the dialog box so you can make sure you have chosen correctly.

   ■ If you selected Fixed Width, you can now specify where each column's data starts. As you make your selections, Excel applies them in the Data Preview section so you can double-check your choices.

6. Click Next.

7. Select formats for each column of data and specify where the parsed data should appear.

8. Click Finish.

Excel parses your data, separating each line into columns, and inserts it at the designated location.

Tech Tip: When you open a text file, the Text Import Wizard starts automatically. The Text Import Wizard works in the same way as the Text to Columns Wizard described here.

How does Excel 5.0 know what cells to select when I sort my list?

Excel 5.0 can automatically detect and select your list when you use a list-related command. To select the list, Excel looks for the last nonblank row of data above the insertion point. If this row contains text, appears in a larger font than the rest of the data, or is boldface, Excel assumes that it is the row of headings. Excel then selects the heading row and all the rows below it until it encounters a blank one or the bottom edge of the worksheet.

Similarly, Excel selects all columns to the left and right of the current cell until it runs into either a blank one or a worksheet edge. If Excel cannot identify an appropriate block of data, it prompts you to specify the list. You always have the option to override the selection Excel makes.

What's the difference between criteria entered on one line and criteria entered on different lines?

You can create a criteria range that requires a given record to meet either all of the criteria or just one of them. Excel interprets all criteria that appear in a single row as joined by a logical AND, which means that a record must satisfy all of the criteria to be selected. If, on the other hand, you want to select all records that meet at least one, but not necessarily all, of the criteria, you enter the criteria on different rows. In this case, Excel assumes the criteria are separated by a logical OR and selects any record that matches at least one of them. In all cases, the column headings in the criteria range must be identical to those in the list itself. If you want to join two criteria for the same column with a logical AND, you can enter the column heading twice in the criteria range.

Can I use the LOOKUP function to refer to two different sheets in another workbook?

You can use the LOOKUP function in Excel 5.0 to look up information in another file as long as you use the correct syntax in the formula. For example, if the current worksheet is called ALPHA.XLS and you want to look up a value in a file called BETA.XLS, the proper syntax for the formula would be as follows:

=LOOKUP(B5,[BETA.XLS]SHEET1!A2:A50,[BETA.XLS]SHEET1!B2:B50)

If B5 in ALPHA.XLS contains the name "ABC Company," the above searches for "ABC Company" in A2:A50 of BETA.XLS, and if one entry is "ABC Company," returns the corresponding entry contained in B2:B50 of BETA.XLS in the cell that contains the LOOKUP function in ALPHA.XLS.

In Excel 4.0, only 18 fields appeared in the data form, so for larger databases I had to create my own custom data form. Do I still need to do this in Excel 5.0?

The data form dialog box in Excel 5.0 now supports up to 32 fields. Excel automatically adjusts the layout of the form so that all fields are displayed. If you already created a custom data form dialog box in Excel 4.0 using the Dialog Editor, you can still use that dialog box in Excel 5.0.

Can I sort by more than three columns?

Yes, but doing so takes several more steps than when you sort by one, two, or three columns. You sort the list first by the least important fields and then resort it as necessary until you have sorted it by the most important one. To do so:

1. Position the insertion point in the list you want to sort.

2. Choose <u>S</u>ort from the <u>D</u>ata menu to open the Sort dialog box.
   This dialog box lets you designate up to three fields by which to sort and whether to sort each in ascending or descending order. The first fields listed in the dialog box are sorted first and so on.

3. Select the least important field to sort by in the last drop-down list box, the second least important in the second to last list box, and the third least important in the first list box.

4. Click OK to sort the records by these fields.

5. Choose <u>S</u>ort from the <u>D</u>ata menu again. Repeat step 3 to sort the next three fields.
   The next three fields in the list should be your three most important fields. Ultimately, the most important, or primary, field you want to sort by should appear in the first drop-down list box the last time you sort the data.

6. Click OK to sort the list.

For example, suppose you wanted to sort your list by LastName, then FirstName, then City, then ZipCode. To do so, you open the Sort dialog box and select ZipCode in the third drop-down list box, City in the second, and FirstName in the first. You then click OK to sort the list the first time. Next, you open the dialog box again, select LastName in the first drop-down list box, and click OK. The list is then sorted by the desired fields in the appropriate order.

When I sort my data, the hidden rows are not being sorted. Why?

Unlike Excel 4.0, Excel 5.0 does not sort hidden rows or columns when you sort data. There is no way to work around this. Therefore, you need to display all of your hidden rows and columns before you attempt to sort the list in which they occur.

Tech Terror: If you sort a list in which there are hidden columns, Excel does not sort the contents of the hidden columns. Because the data in the hidden columns no longer appears in the correct rows, it becomes meaningless.

When I edit a worksheet that is stored as an OLE object in another application, I can't create a crosstab table. What am I doing wrong?

Tech Note: Pivot tables are described in more detail in the following question.

You cannot create a crosstab table in a worksheet that is an OLE object in another application. The crosstab add-in macro creates a second workbook in which to store the data, but when the worksheet is an OLE object, you cannot create a second workbook.

To solve this problem, use Excel 5.0's new feature, called a *pivot table,* instead of a crosstab table. Pivot tables are easier to work with than crosstab tables, and you can create them in the worksheet that is an OLE object. Pivot tables summarize data like crosstab tables and, in addition, include features for customizing and editing the table.

If you need to use a crosstab table rather than a pivot table, you can create and save it in Excel and then embed it in or link it to the other application.

I've heard that Excel 5.0 has a new feature called a pivot table. What is a pivot table and why would I use one?

A *pivot table* is a tool for summarizing and analyzing lists of data. A pivot table, like the one shown in Figure 9-5, summarizes data in different categories using functions such as count, sum, average, max, min, product, stdev, and var. The great advantage of pivot tables is that you can easily rearrange, hide, and display different categories in the table.

For example, suppose you are using Excel to track your checking account expenditures. You could quickly create a pivot table showing the total amount paid to each person or company to which you wrote checks in the last year.

All pivot tables have similar elements. These items include *column fields*, *row fields*, and *page fields*, which you use to organize the data that appears in the table. When you create a pivot table, you specify the fields you want to use as column, row, and page fields. You also indicate which fields to use as *pivot table items*, or data, in the pivot table.

Column and row fields appear in a pivot table as column or row headings. The individual entries provide the pivot table

	A	B	C	D	E	F
1	Sum of Sale	SalesRep				
2	Client	Andrea White	Brian Fox	Peter Forney	Susan Connor	Grand Total
3	ABC Corp.	$ 116,434.82	$ -	$ 42,321.28	$ 105,468.14	$ 264,224.24
4	Bregon Inc.	$ -	$ 103,559.40	$ 25,153.69		$ 128,713.09
5	Carson & Assoc.	$ -	$ 112,343.31	$ -	$ -	$ 112,343.31
6	Pinto Group	$ -	$ 55,485.31	$ -	$ 76,410.38	$ 131,895.69
7	Sty & Bligh	$ 82,714.27	$ -	$ -	$ -	$ 82,714.27
8	XYZ Company	$ -	$ 210,617.12	$ -	$ 72,175.43	$ 282,792.55
9	Grand Total	$ 199,149.09	$ 378,445.74	$ 145,880.68	$ 279,207.64	$ 1,002,683.15

FIGURE 9-5   Pivot tables display summary data by categories

items, which are like column headings in the table. For example, suppose you chose the Regions field as your column field. The data in the table would be organized into columns by the different regions entered in this field, such as Northern, Southern, Eastern, and Western. Row fields work the same way.

Page fields work somewhat differently. Page fields appear as drop-down list boxes above the pivot table. You can select one of the page field's entries to display data for that entry only. For example, if the page field contains the names of salespeople, you can select a specific salesperson to show data about only that individual.

To create a pivot table, create your list and then choose PivotTable from the Data menu to start the PivotTable Wizard. The PivotTable Wizard guides you through four steps:

1. You specify the type of data you are going to summarize in the table by selecting one of these options: Microsoft Excel List or Database, External Data Source, Multiple Consolidation Ranges, or Another Pivot Table.

2. You identify the actual location of the data you are going to summarize in the table, such as the external data source and filename, or the range in which the list appears.

3. You drag the field or column label buttons to the PAGE, ROW, COLUMN, and DATA areas in a sample pivot table, as shown here:

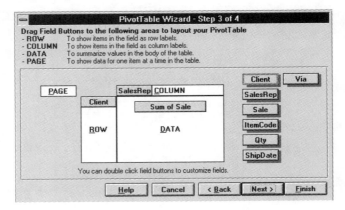

The pivot table being created has column labels created from the entries in the SalesRep field and row labels created from the entries in the Client field. The body of the table contains the sum of the Sale field entries for each combination of the SalesRep and Client field entries.

4. You specify the location where the pivot table should appear in your worksheet.

Can I create a pivot table using a closed workbook?

Yes. You can create a pivot table in your current workbook using data from another closed file by following these steps:

1. Choose PivotTable from the Data menu.

2. Select the Microsoft Excel List or Database option button and click Next.

3. Type the name of the closed workbook followed by an exclamation point and the list range in the Range box, as in **SALES.XLS!JAN!D4:X:231**, and click Next.
   Don't forget to add the sheet's name, unless the data is on the first sheet in the workbook. You can also click Browse to find and select the file, and then add the range.

4. Drag the field name buttons from the right side of the dialog box to appropriate areas in the sample table and click Next.

5. Enter the location where you want to display the table, and select the options you want to retain.

6. Click Finish to create the pivot table.

I closed the Query and Pivot toolbar and now it no longer displays automatically when I create a pivot table. Why not and what can I do to bring it back?

If you close your Query and Pivot toolbar by clicking its miniature control box, the toolbar will not reappear the next time you create a pivot table. To redisplay it:

1. Choose Toolbars from the View menu.

2. Select the Query and Pivot check box in the Toolbars list box and click OK.

This toolbar now appears when you create a new pivot table just as it did before.

Can I use the crosstab tables I created in Excel 4.0 with Excel 5.0?

You can open an Excel 4.0 worksheet that contains a crosstab table in Excel 5.0. To make any changes to the crosstab, you have to open the Crosstab Report Wizard, which came with Excel 4.0 and is located in the EXCEL\LIBRARY\CROSSTAB directory.

Tech Tip: Before opening worksheets containing crosstab tables, make sure that the CROSSTAB.XLL, CROSSFNC.XLA, and CROSSTMP.XLT files that came with Excel 4.0 are stored in the EXCEL\LIBRARY\CROSSTAB directory.

Why does the PivotTable Wizard change one of my field names from Data to Data2?

Excel changes a field named Data to Data2 automatically when you run the PivotTable Wizard. This prevents confusion in step 3 of the PivotTable Wizard when you drag fields to different areas of a sample pivot table, one of which is called DATA.

When I try to create pivot tables, I get the error message, "Not enough memory to completely display pivot table." What do I do?

Creating pivot tables uses a significant amount of memory and other system resources. To create a pivot table, Excel builds a cache of the list you are using in memory and uses this cache to retrieve information for the pivot table. If the file containing your list is open, Excel uses twice as much memory, because the cache is nearly as large as the file itself.

To use your memory and system resources more efficiently, try the following options:

- Create pivot tables from closed files.

- Select the Another Pivot Table option button in step 1 of the PivotTable Wizard when you create a second pivot table using the same data. When you select this option button, Excel uses the same cache it built for the first pivot table you created, instead of building a new cache for the next pivot table.

- Close your workbook and reopen it after you create and format the pivot tables. When you close the file, Excel deletes the cache from memory. Deleting the cache frees up a lot of memory and system resources. Excel does not recreate the cache unless you modify the pivot table.

Why does the PivotTable Wizard convert all my dates to text, and how can I return them to their original form?

The PivotTable Wizard assumes you will only use text entries as the pivot table's page, row, and column fields. Therefore, Excel converts all entries in these areas to text before placing them in the pivot table as pivot table items.

A quick way to get your dates back is to follow these steps:

1. Type **1** in a blank cell.

2. Choose <u>C</u>opy from the <u>E</u>dit menu to copy this entry to the Windows Clipboard.

3. Select the cells with dates that have been converted to text.

4. Choose Paste <u>S</u>pecial from the <u>E</u>dit menu.

5. Select the <u>V</u>alues option button.

6. Select the <u>M</u>ultiply option button and click OK.
   The dates are now serial numbers again.

7. Choose <u>C</u>ells from the F<u>o</u>rmat menu.

8. Click the Number tab.

9. Select the date format you want to use in the <u>F</u>ormat Codes list box and click OK.

What does the page field do in a pivot table?

The page field filters the view of a pivot table into separate pages. Each page shows only the data for a single entry in the page field. When the pivot table is displayed, a drop-down list box appears above the upper-left corner of your table. You display the desired category by clicking the down arrow next to the page field and selecting the appropriate entry in the drop-down list box. Excel displays only the data for the selected category in the table. When you print a pivot table that contains a page field, each category prints on a separate page.

I got the following error message: "Pivot table will not fit on sheet. Show as much as possible?" Why?

The pivot table is currently set up to show more than 256 columns of data. Therefore, there are not enough columns in the worksheet for the entire pivot table to be displayed. To work around this problem, switch the column and row headings so the pivot table can use the 16,384 rows instead.

I created a pivot table using the SUM function to summarize data. Can I quickly change the formula used to summarize data?

You can easily change the summarizing function in a pivot table. To do so:

1. Select a cell in the data area of the pivot table.

2. Choose PivotTable Field from the Data menu or click the PivotTable Field button on the Query and Pivot toolbar.

3. Select the desired function in the Summarize by list box and click OK.

Microsoft Query and ODBC

Microsoft Query is an application provided with Excel that works with databases from other applications. You can use Microsoft Query to select the source of the data you want to work with, choose the data you want, and place the data in an Excel workbook or copy it to another application. The overall process you use to bring data from Microsoft Query into an Excel workbook is summarized in the following Frustration Busters box.

FRUSTRATION BUSTERS!

If you have never used Microsoft Query before, you may not know where to begin. With these step-by-step instructions, you can avoid the frustration of a first-time user as you bring data from Microsoft Query into an Excel workbook.

1. Choose Get External Data from the Data menu to start Microsoft Query.

   If this command doesn't appear, you must first load the Microsoft Query add-in. To do so, choose Add-Ins from the Tools menu, select the MS Query check box, and click OK. If you do not see the option for MS Query in the Add-Ins dialog box, open the Microsoft Excel 5.0 Setup program, click Add/Remove, and install MS Query from your Excel setup disks.

2. Select the source of the data you want to use.

3. Select the table you want to add in the Table Name box and click Add. Repeat this step for each table you want to use in the query.

4. From the tables, add the fields you want to display in the result set.

5. Add criteria to determine which records are included in the result set.

6. Choose Return Data to Microsoft Excel from the File menu to return to Excel.

7. Make any necessary changes in the Get External Data dialog box and click OK to place the results of the query in the workbook.

What is Microsoft Query?

Microsoft Query is an application that retrieves, views, and organizes data from databases. It is not a database itself—just an easy way to view the data in one. You use Microsoft Query to select the data you want to work with from databases. You can then copy the result set into Excel or another Windows application.

What does "table" mean in Microsoft Query?

In Microsoft Query, the term *table* refers to a collection of information on one subject, organized into fields (columns) and records (rows). A table is similar to a list in Excel. Figure 10-1 depicts a table in Microsoft Query. You can have as many tables as you want in Microsoft Query. In addition, you can join the tables when you want to combine data from more than one.

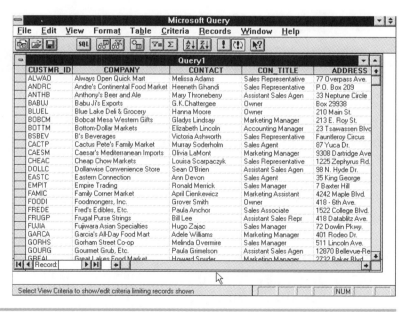

FIGURE 10-1   Table showing a collection of fields and the data for each record

What is a query?

A *query* is a question about the data in a database or table. After you define your question, Microsoft Query displays all of the data in the database or table that answers it. This group of data is called the *result set*. For example, if you want to find all the records for items that cost more than $5.00, you could define a query to examine the Cost field using the criteria Cost>$5.00. The result set would include all the records for items that cost more than $5.00.

In Microsoft Query, what is the difference between a field and a record?

A *field* is a category of information, such as "Name," "Department," and "Annual Sales." A *record* is a group of information about one event, transaction, or person. Fields in Microsoft Query are represented as columns; records are displayed as rows. For example, Figure 10-1 shows a table in Microsoft Query. This table includes the field names CUSTMR_ID, COMPANY, CONTACT, CON_TITLE, and ADDRESS. The first three records you can see are for Always Open Quick Mart, Andre's Continental Food Market, and Anthony's Beer and Ale.

Some of the data sources I use in Microsoft Query allow me to edit information, but others don't. Why?

Some data sources, such as Excel and text, do not let you edit records. You must check the documentation that came with the data source you are using to determine whether it allows editing.

Why is it that some of the expressions I use in one data source don't work in another?

The functions, operators, and literal values supported by Microsoft Query are driver specific. Microsoft Query uses different drivers to interpret data in tables and databases from different sources. For this reason, the format in which you enter an expression varies depending on the driver used with the data source. For example, if you want to find all the records that meet a certain criterion in two different databases that require different drivers, you may have to enter the expression in two ways. If you are having problems entering an expression, check the data source's documentation to make sure you are using the correct format.

What is a join?

A *join* is a multiple table query. You can join a field in one table with a field in another, to establish a relationship between the two and create a *relational database*. For example, you might join the social security number field in an employee database with the same field in a payroll database so you can search for employees' addresses when you process the payroll. Microsoft Query displays lines between connected fields to indicate any joins between tables, as shown here:

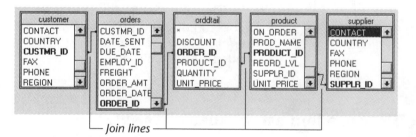

— Join lines —

What are the different types of joins you can perform in Microsoft Query?

There are three types of joins available in Microsoft Query. The type you use determines how the records selected in one table are connected to the records in another. These three types include

- An *inner join* compares the values in the joined fields and only selects records with matching entries for the result set. For example, an inner join between an employee table and a payroll table can use the social security number field to join all the records from the payroll database that have corresponding records in the employee database. This type of a join is also called an *equi-join,* and is the type created by default.

■ An *outer join* selects all the records in one table, and then selects only those records in the other table with matching entries in the joined fields. For example, an outer join of a table of museum members and a table of a local gallery's mailing list would include all the records in the museum table plus information from the gallery table for those records that match records in the museum table.

Alternatively, you could set up the join to show all the records from the gallery table with information from the museum table only when its records join with records in the gallery table. Microsoft Query lets you choose the table for which all the records are displayed.

■ A *self-join* compares values within a single table using two copies of the same table. For example, you can create a self-join for a sales summary database to find those salespeople who sold more than the average. A self-join can be either an inner or an outer join, which determines how the records must match up to be included in the result set.

How is a join established?

By default, Microsoft Query creates an inner join if one of the selected tables includes a field with the same name and data type as the primary field name in another table. If you want a different type of join between tables, follow the steps outlined in the next question.

How can I create a join in Microsoft Query?

A join determines how records in one database match those in another. Often, you don't need to create a join because Microsoft Query does so automatically when one table has a primary key that matches the name and data type of a field in another table. You can create a join using either the mouse or the menu.

To create a join using a mouse:

1. Click the data field in one table that you want to join to a field in another table.

2. Drag the data field to the other table, position it over the data field you want to create the join with, and release the mouse button. A line appears between the fields used for the join.

To create a join using the menu:

1. Choose Joins from the Microsoft Query Ta<u>b</u>le menu.

2. In the <u>L</u>eft and <u>R</u>ight boxes, select the table and fields you want to join.

3. Select the operator that matches the records between the databases in the <u>O</u>perator box. Usually, the default, which is an equal sign (=), is what you want.

4. Indicate the type of join you want to create by selecting an option in the Join Includes section. The default type is an inner join, which only shows those records from the joined tables that contain identical entries in the joined field.

5. Click <u>A</u>dd to create the join.

6. Click <u>C</u>lose to leave the dialog box.

I used to print my tables from Q + E, but I can't figure out how to do it from Microsoft Query. How do I print my tables?

Unlike Q + E, you cannot print from Microsoft Query. You must print data from another application, such as Excel 5.0 or Word for Windows 6.0.

How do I change the order of the columns in my query's result set?

To reposition a column, select the field name at the top of the column and drag it to the new location.

Tech Tip: You can control which columns appear in a query's result set table by hiding certain columns. You can hide a column by selecting it and choosing <u>H</u>ide Columns from the Forma<u>t</u> menu or by dragging the right border of the column over to the left border and releasing the mouse button. To redisplay a hidden column, choose <u>S</u>how Columns from the Forma<u>t</u> menu, select the name of the field that appears in the column in the Co<u>l</u>umns box, and click <u>S</u>how. Click <u>C</u>lose when you have finished selecting the columns you want to display in the result set.

How can I change the column width in Microsoft Query?

To change a column's width using a mouse:

1. Move your mouse pointer to the right edge of the column heading so it becomes a two-headed arrow, just like when you resize an Excel worksheet column.

2. Drag the border to the desired location.

To change a column's width using a menu command:

1. Move to any cell in the column whose width you want to change.

2. Choose <u>C</u>olumn Width from the Forma<u>t</u> menu.

3. Type a width for the column in the <u>C</u>olumn Width box and click OK.

Tech Tip: If you want to change the width of several columns at once, select them and perform one of the above procedures. Microsoft Query adjusts all of the column widths to the new specification at once.

You can also have Microsoft Query set the column's width based on its contents. To do so:

1. Select the column or columns whose width you want Query to set automatically.

2. Double-click the right border of one of the selected columns, or choose <u>C</u>olumn Width from the Forma<u>t</u> menu and click <u>B</u>est Fit.

Does Microsoft Query use the same operators that I use in Excel?

Microsoft Query offers several operators in addition to those you use in Excel, as described here:

Operator	Description	Example
Between	Determines if a number falls into the specified range	Between 1 and 10
In	Determines if a value is one of several values in a list	In('Massachusetts','Rhode Island')
Is	Combined with Null to determine if there is a value or not	Is Null
Like	Compares two values using wildcard characters	Like "BI%"

Tech Tip: Remember, the operators you can use actually depend on the source of the data. You can use those operators available in the application in which the data was created.

What wildcard characters can I use in my query criteria?

Microsoft Query includes several wildcard characters you can use in query criteria. A *wildcard* can replace one or more characters in a search. The following table describes the wildcards you can use in Microsoft Query.

Wildcard Character	Description	Example
Question mark (?)	Placeholder for any single character	Sm?th returns Smith, Smyth
Underscore (_)	Placeholder for any single character	Sm_th returns Smith, Smyth
Asterisk (*)	Placeholder for a group of characters	Sm* returns Smith, Smyth, smog, SM8754
Percent sign (%)	Placeholder for a group of characters	Sm%h returns Smith, Smyth, SM3579H, Smart Pooh
Number sign (#)	Placeholder for any single numeric digit	1#3 returns 123, 153, 133

Tech Tip: The actual wildcard characters you can use with a table depend on the source of the data. The application in which the data was created must support a wildcard in order to use it with the data in Microsoft Query.

How can I add a field to the Data pane?

You can drag and drop field names from the field list to the Data pane. Also, if you double-click a name in the field list, the field appears in your Data pane. If you double-click the asterisk (*) in the field list, Microsoft Query adds all the field names in the list to the Data pane.

What kinds of information can I use in an expression in the Criteria pane?

A criteria expression can contain operators, identifiers, functions, and literal values, as follows:

- *Operators* are instructions to perform an operation, such as arithmetic, comparison, or logic. For example, a plus sign (+) is the operator to add two values; greater than (>) is the operator that finds only those values greater than the one specified.

- *Identifiers* are names. If your table has field names such as "Name" and "Customer," Name and Customer are also identifiers. Other identifiers include database and table names.

- *Functions* are mathematical operations that return a value based on the results of calculations. Avg(Customer) finds the average of the Customer field.

- *Literal values* are values, dates, or text. Examples include "ABC Company," "56," and "#1994-12-04#" for the text ABC Company, the number 56, and the date 12/04/94.

Can I quickly select other records that match a value in the record I have found?

Yes. Microsoft Query offers a special feature that you can use once you select a value in a field to show all the other records that contain the same value. You can use this method to build a criteria expression that selects the records you want. To use this feature, move to the field value you want to add as a criterion and click the Criteria Equals button.

For example, suppose you have a Data pane that looks like this:

	CON_TITLE	ADDRESS	CITY	REGION	ZIP_CODE	COUNTRY	PHONE
▶	Assistant Sales Agen	33 Neptune Circle	Clifton Forge	WA	24422	USA	(509) 555-8647
	Owner	Box 29938	London			UK	(712) 555-8248
	Owner	210 Main St.	Port Townsend	WA	98368	USA	(206) 555-3042
	Marketing Manager	213 E. Roy St.	Seattle	WA	98124	USA	(206) 555-4741
	Accounting Manager	23 Tsawassen Blvd.	Tsawassen	BC		Canada	(604) 555-4721
	Sales Representative	Fauntleroy Circus	London			UK	(712) 555-1212
	Sales Agent	87 Yuca Dr.	Albuquerque	NM	87123	USA	(505) 555-2951
	Marketing Manager	9308 Dartridge Ave.	San Francisco	CA	94965	USA	(415) 555-6841
	Sales Representative	1225 Zephurus Rd.	Anacortes	WA	98221	USA	(206) 555-8642

Record: 3

If you want to find all the records whose COUNTRY field contains USA, move to the COUNTRY field of any record that displays USA and click the Criteria Equals button. Microsoft Query adds a criterion to select all the records with the same value, as shown here:

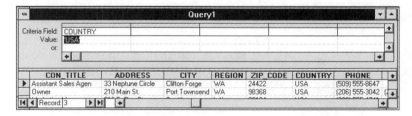

Criteria Field: COUNTRY
Value: USA
or:

	CON_TITLE	ADDRESS	CITY	REGION	ZIP_CODE	COUNTRY	PHONE
▶	Assistant Sales Agen	33 Neptune Circle	Clifton Forge	WA	24422	USA	(509) 555-8647
	Owner	210 Main St.	Port Townsend	WA	98368	USA	(206) 555-3042

Record: 3

Tech Tip: To remove an existing criterion, including one added with the Criteria Equals button, delete the appropriate column in the Criteria pane.

What are SQL aggregate functions?

Aggregate functions calculate values for a field and are the ones most often used in the Criteria pane. There are five commonly available aggregate functions:

Aggregate Function	Description
AVG	Computes the average of a set of values in a field
COUNT	Counts the number of selected records
MAX	Finds the largest value in a field
MIN	Determines the smallest value in a field
SUM	Totals the values in a field

When I use "bill" as a criterion, Microsoft Query doesn't find any records even though I know there are some that contain this name. Why can't it find my records?

Microsoft Query uses literal values exactly as they are entered in criteria. Because literals are case sensitive, you may want to check for other permutations of your entry as well, such as "Bill" and "BILL." For example, you might change your criterion to In("Bill","bill","BILL") to find the appropriate records in the result set.

Tech Tip: Some of the sample criteria in this chapter use single quotation marks and some use double quotation marks. Whether you should use single or double quotation marks in your criteria depends entirely on the source of the data you are using. The device driver of the data source determines the appropriate syntax for the criteria you use in Microsoft Query.

Why doesn't my data update when I use a multiple-table query?

Microsoft Query does not automatically update the data in a multiple-table query. If you edit the result set for a query based on a single table, however, the changes carry over to the original data.

When I create a table in Microsoft Query, I can't seem to define a primary key. How do I create one?

Because of the way Microsoft Query creates a table, it is not possible to create a primary key. However, you can sort the data in the Data pane on a field's value.

To sort the data:

1. Choose Sort from the Records menu.
2. Select a field on which to sort the data in the Column box.
3. Select the order of the sort for that field by selecting the Ascending or Descending option button.
4. Click Add to add the field and its sort order to the Sorts in Query box.
5. Repeat steps 2, 3, and 4 for each field you want to use to sort the records in the result set.
   Microsoft Query sorts the result set based on the order of the fields listed in the Sorts in Query box. For example, if the fields in the Sorts in Query box are COUNTRY, STATE, and CITY, Microsoft Query groups together all of the records for a particular country broken down by state, and then city within each state.
6. Click Close to leave the dialog box and sort the result set.

Microsoft Query's toolbar also provides Sort Ascending and Sort Descending buttons. Click one of these buttons to sort the result set by the field you have selected in the Data pane. You cannot use the Sort Ascending and Sort Descending buttons to sort on more than one field.

Sort Ascending   Sort Descending

Tech Tip: Sorting only reorders the result set based on its current contents. If you edit the result set, it may no longer appear in the correct order. To update it, simply resort it.

Why can't I change or delete my data?

There are two possible reasons you may not be able to modify the result set:

- Open the <u>R</u>ecords menu to see whether a check mark appears next to <u>A</u>llow Editing to indicate it is enabled. If not, choose the command to turn on this feature.

- Some sources, like Excel, do not allow you to change the data within Microsoft Query. You can tell whether you can edit the data by looking at the end of the result set. If you can, an empty record displays, as shown here:

Tech Note: You cannot edit a result set that is based on a multiple-table query.

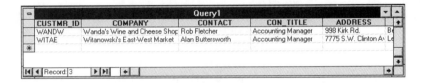

What does SQL stand for?

Microsoft Query uses *Structured Query Language (SQL)* to build the statements it uses to retrieve and manage data. You can examine the SQL statement that represents all of the selections you have made in the Microsoft Query window by choosing <u>S</u>QL from the <u>V</u>iew menu or clicking the View SQL button.

Microsoft Query opens a dialog box that contains the complete SQL statement, which indicates the fields you want to show in the result set, the source(s) of the data, and the criteria specified. A sample SQL statement might look like this:

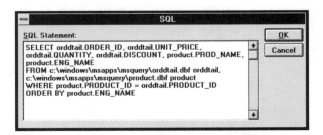

Tech Tip: If you are familiar with SQL, you can edit the SQL statement directly in the SQL dialog box. When you click <u>O</u>K, Microsoft Query updates the Table, Criteria, and Data panes to show the results of the changes you have made.

This message appeared when I was working in Microsoft Query: "SQL Query can't be represented graphically. Continue anyway?" What does it mean?

An SQL Query can display up to 28 sets of parentheses. If your query includes more than this number, Microsoft Query tells you that it cannot create a Table pane for this query. You can edit the SQL statement to simplify it, as described in the previous question.

How do I fix a mistake I just made in Microsoft Query?

How you undo the mistake depends on what you were doing when you made it:

- Choose <u>U</u>ndo from the <u>E</u>dit menu to reverse the most recent change you have made in your query.

- Press ESC to undo the last change made to a cell.

- To undo all current changes made to a record, press ESC twice or choose <u>U</u>ndo Current Record from the <u>E</u>dit menu. (This option is disabled when you move to another record or change windows.)

What is ODBC?

ODBC is an acronym for *Open DataBase Connectivity*. Microsoft Query uses ODBC drivers to access information from several different sources of data. The ODBC drivers that come with Excel include dBASE, Microsoft Access, Microsoft FoxPro, Paradox, and SQL server. You may also have other ODBC drivers on your system that came with other applications. For example,

Microsoft Access includes additional ODBC drivers that you can also use in Microsoft Query.

To see which ODBC drivers you have installed:

1. Double-click the Control Panel program icon in the Program Manager's Main program group.

2. Double-click the ODBC icon or choose OD<u>B</u>C from the <u>S</u>ettings menu.

3. Click D<u>r</u>ivers to see the list of installed drivers in the Drivers dialog box.

4. Click <u>C</u>lose twice to leave the dialog boxes.

5. Choose E<u>x</u>it from the <u>S</u>ettings menu.

This list also appears when you choose <u>T</u>able Definition from the <u>F</u>ile menu, click <u>O</u>ther, and then click <u>N</u>ew in Microsoft Query.

What ODBC drivers are shipped with Microsoft Excel 5.0?

Microsoft Query uses ODBC (Open DataBase Connectivity) drivers to import data. Excel 5.0 includes ODBC drivers for the following applications:

Microsoft FoxPro 2.0 and 2.5
Microsoft Access 1.0 and 1.1
Paradox 3.0 and 3.5
dBASE III and IV
SQL Server 1.1, 4.2, and NT
Microsoft Excel 3.0, 4.0, and 5.0

If you need to install an ODBC driver for another application, you must obtain it from the application's publisher. Microsoft maintains an *ODBC Driver Catalog*, which lists all the available ODBC drivers. For more information about this publication, call Microsoft's sales department at (800) 426-9400.

Can I use the Criteria Equals button to perform complex definitions?

While the Criteria Equals button provides the easiest way to define criteria, its use is limited to creating simple "And" and "Or" statements.

To create a complex criteria definition, you must add each element to the Criteria pane.

Tech Tip: The question, "Can I quickly select other records that match a value in the record I have found?" earlier in the chapter describes how you can create a simple criterion. You can then build on this one to create a complex criteria definition.

Why does Microsoft Query adjust other entries in the database when I make a change to my data?

When you edit data, Microsoft Query automatically changes any identical records in the result set without prompting you first. Identical records are those that contain the same information for all fields in the result's set. To avoid accidentally modifying the wrong records, add all of a table's fields that you plan to use in the query before making any changes to your data.

I installed the Excel 5.0 upgrade, but don't have an icon for Microsoft Query. How do I access this program?

Setup only installs Microsoft Query if you perform a Complete/Custom installation. If you did a Typical installation instead, you need to add Microsoft Query to your system before you can access it.

To install Microsoft Query:

1. Double-click the MS Excel Setup program icon in the Program Manager.
2. Click <u>A</u>dd/Remove to selectively install components.
3. Select the Data Access check box.
4. Click <u>C</u>ontinue.
5. Insert the appropriate disks when you are prompted to do so.
6. Click OK when Setup is finished.

Microsoft Query is now installed and the Microsoft Query program icon appears.

When I add criteria based on a date, I get the following error message: "Error in predicate: <date><=><January 15, 1994>. Incompatible type in predicate." What do I do?

Microsoft Query displays this message if you forget to enclose a date value in # signs when you enter it in your criteria definition. In this case, Microsoft Query does not interpret the value as a date. You simply need to insert # signs before and after the date, as in **#January 15, 1994#**, to use the criterion.

Can I change the column headings in my Data pane?

By default, column headings are the fields names that appear in the original data source. You can change them to other text, as desired.

For example, by renaming the column headings, you can include characters that normally are not allowed in field names, such as spaces.

To rename column headings:

1. Select the column whose heading you want to change and choose Edit Column from the Records menu. Alternatively, you can just double-click the current heading.

2. Type a new name in the Column Heading box.

3. Click OK.

How do I delete a criterion from the Criteria pane?

The easiest way to delete a criterion from the Criteria pane is to select the criterion's column heading and press DEL. If you want to remove all the criteria, choose Remove All Criteria from the Criteria menu.

Is it possible to have multiple names that refer to the same driver in the data source list?

Yes. In fact, you must define a new data source name when you want to change the data source definition. The data source definition includes the ODBC driver Microsoft Query uses, the location of the files in the database, and the data source's name and definition.

Tech Tip: For information about how to create your own data sources, see the next question.

 ## How do I add data sources for applications that are not listed?

Each data source is a collection of settings Microsoft Query uses to retrieve and manage the data you want. If you want to use data from an ODBC driver that is not already available, you must create a new data source.

To create a data source:

1. Choose <u>T</u>able Definition from the <u>F</u>ile menu, click <u>O</u>ther, and then click <u>N</u>ew to display the Add Data Source dialog box.

Tech Tip: You can also display this dialog box by double-clicking the Control Panel program icon in the Program Manager's Main program group, double-clicking the ODBC icon or choosing OD<u>B</u>C from the <u>S</u>ettings menu, and then clicking the <u>A</u>dd button.

2. Select the appropriate driver from the list of installed ODBC drivers, shown here:

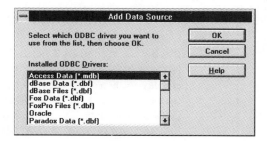

3. Click OK to open the appropriate ODBC Setup dialog box.

The exact options that appear in this dialog box depend on the ODBC driver you selected. For example, the following dialog box displays when you select the Microsoft Access ODBC driver:

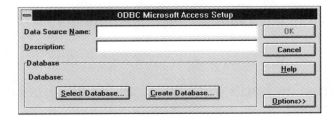

4. Enter a name and description for your data source as well as any other information requested.

5. Click OK to finish creating the data source.

To use the data source in the future:

1. Choose <u>T</u>able Definition from the File menu and click <u>O</u>ther.

2. Select the data source in the Enter Data Source box and click OK.

3. Click <u>U</u>se to select this data source and leave the dialog box. You may need to select tables for some database drivers, such as dBASE.

How do I modify a query I have already created?

There are two ways to edit an existing query:

■ Double-click any cell in the Excel workbook that includes the data supplied by Microsoft Query. This opens the Microsoft Query window with the original query displayed. Make whatever changes you desire, and then update the data on the worksheet by choosing <u>R</u>eturn Data to Microsoft Excel from the <u>F</u>ile menu or clicking the Return Data button, shown here:

■ Choose Get External Data from the Data menu and click Edit Query. Make the appropriate changes and then choose Return Data to Microsoft Excel from the File menu or click the Return Data button. To update the worksheet data, click Refresh in the Get External Data dialog box.

Why does my dBASE III file come up as a dBASE IV file when I try to save it?

When you add a new dBASE data source to Microsoft Query, you can select either dBASE III or dBASE IV. After you manipulate the data, Query saves the query in a dBASE IV file format regardless of the format in which it originated. It is not possible for Microsoft Query to save the data in a dBASE III format.

Microsoft Query doesn't adjust my row heights when I change the font for the result set. How do I fix this problem?

The row height didn't change because you set the result set's row height rather than letting Microsoft Query set it for you. When you change the fonts, the custom row heights prevent Microsoft Query from adjusting the row heights to fit the new font size, even if the font requires more or less space. You need to set all row heights back to standard, apply the new font, and reset the custom row height.

To change the row heights to the standard height:

1. Click the top record selector. It's in the same position as the Select All button on a worksheet.

2. Choose Row Height from the Format menu.

3. Select the Standard Height check box and click OK.

To change the row's height after changing the font:

1. Click the top record selector. It's in the same position as the Select All button on a worksheet.

2. Choose Row Height from the Format menu.

3. Type a height for the column in the <u>R</u>ow Height box and click OK.

I am creating a complex query with criteria that relate to several fields. It's taking a long time because Microsoft Query updates the query for each field. How can I get around this?

Try turning off the Automatic Query option. When this option is enabled, Microsoft Query performs the query every time you make a change in the Criteria pane. Therefore, you must wait for the query to update when you specify multiple criteria per field. To toggle this option on or off, choose Automatic <u>Q</u>uery from the <u>R</u>ecords menu or click the Auto Query button, shown here:

When Automatic Query is off, Microsoft Query only updates the query when you choose Query <u>N</u>ow from the <u>R</u>ecords menu or click the Query Now button, shown here:

What are the different types of DDE channels Microsoft Query uses?

Query uses two types of channels: system and query. The *system channel* gets general information about the query and the system. The *query channel* obtains query-specific information.

What is the difference between destination and source applications in DDE with Microsoft Query?

For all DDE links, the source application is the one that provides the information, while the destination application is the one that requests it. Microsoft Query is always the source application; the program to which Query supplies data—which is often Excel—is the destination application.

Is there a limit to the number of SQL servers I can connect to in Microsoft Query?

Yes. You can connect to up to 14 SQL servers. If you attempt to connect to more than 14, you get the message "ConnectionOpen(sopen()). Unable to Connect to data source." If you are connected to 14 SQL servers and attempt to connect to a dBASE source, Microsoft Query displays the message "Can't access table *path/filename*." There is no setting in either the Microsoft Query application or the ODBC drivers to change the number of connection handles available.

Charting

Excel's worksheets are terrific for working with and storing data. However, long lists of numbers don't always convey the importance of your data nor highlight significant relationships. You can present your worksheet data graphically in a chart so that it has the maximum impact. Charts can be quickly understood as a whole and can also let you easily perceive ongoing trends and relationships among data.

Excel's charting feature lets you create a wide variety of charts, so you can choose the type of chart that best communicates your information to your audience. You can use colors, graphic elements, or other features to make your charts more interesting. However, you want to be careful not to overdo your formatting, or your chart can become too complicated and therefore defeat its purpose.

FRUSTRATION BUSTERS!

There are so many different elements you can use in your charts that it can sometimes be difficult to remember all the possibilities. The example charts shown here can help you identify the items you might want to include in the charts you create.

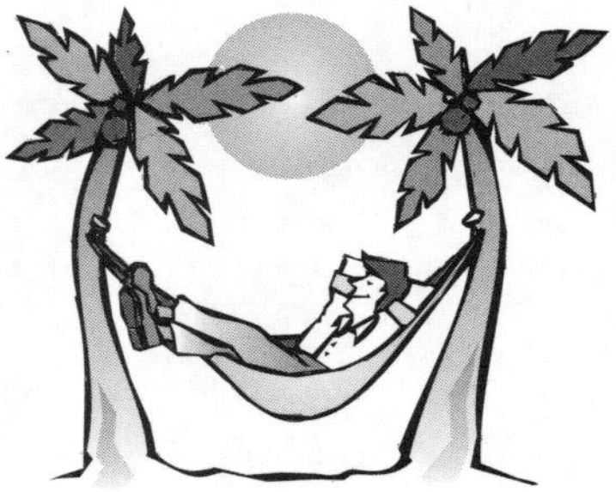

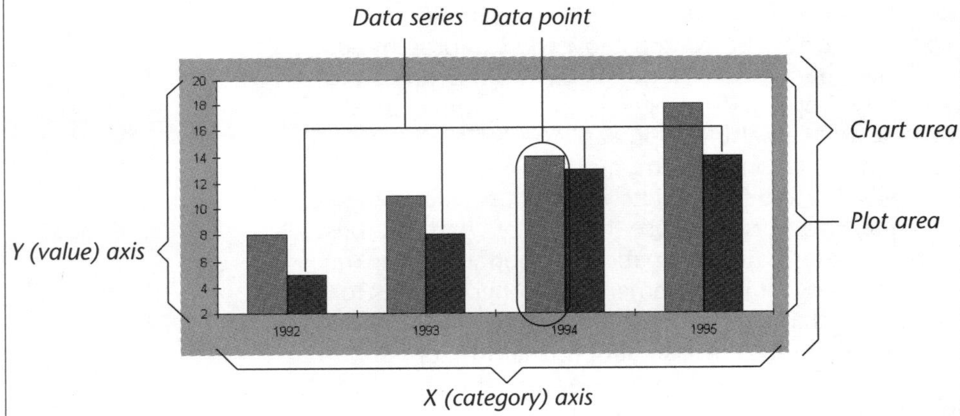

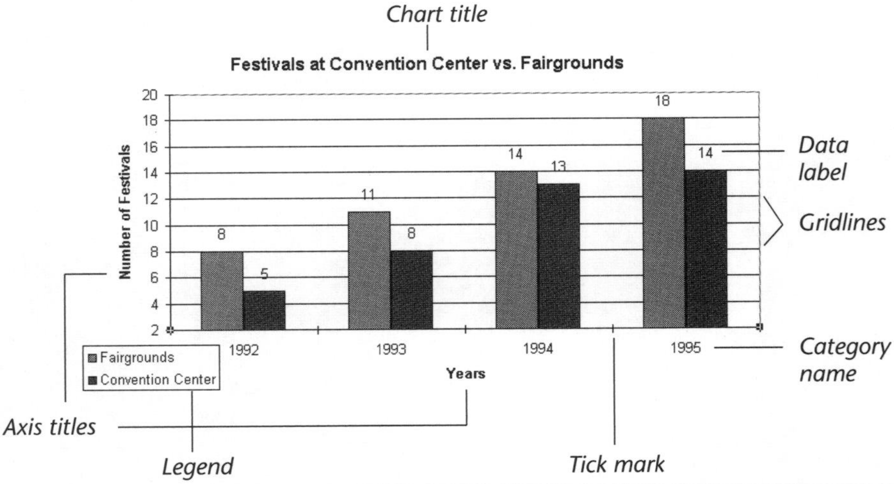

Data series
Data point
Chart area
Plot area
Y (value) axis
20
18
16
14
12
10
8
6
4
2
1992
1993
1994
1995
X (category) axis

Chart title
Festivals at Convention Center vs. Fairgrounds
Number of Festivals
20
18
16
14
12
10
8
6
4
2
8
5
11
8
14
13
18
14
1992
1993
1994
1995
Years
Fairgrounds
Convention Center
Data label
Gridlines
Category name
Axis titles
Legend
Tick mark

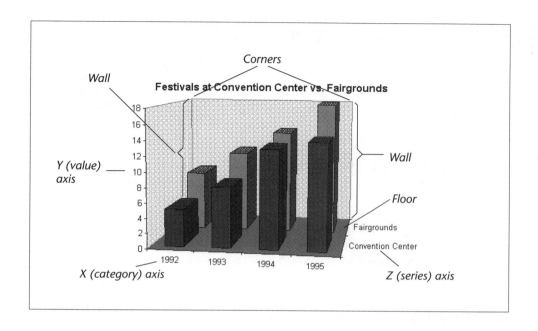

Corners

Wall

Festivals at Convention Center vs. Fairgrounds

Y (value) axis

Wall

Floor

Fairgrounds

Convention Center

X (category) axis

Z (series) axis

1992   1993   1994   1995

In Excel 4.0, when my charts had dates as X-axis labels, they sometimes displayed as serial numbers. Is this a problem with Excel 5.0?

No, you will not have this problem with Excel 5.0. You had this problem before because the first cell in your series of X-axis labels was not formatted as a date. Excel 4.0 determined the format for your X-axis labels based on the formatting of the first cell. Excel 5.0, however, displays the X-axis labels exactly as they appear in the worksheet. If a number is formatted as a date in a worksheet, it displays as a date in the chart. In short, each number on the X axis is formatted individually.

Tech Tip: If you want the X-axis labels to have a different number format than they do in the worksheet, double-click the X axis, click the Number tab, and select the format you want the X-axis labels to use instead.

Is there a shortcut for formatting an object in a chart?

Yes, there is a shortcut. Instead of selecting the object and choosing a command from the Format menu, you can just activate the chart and double-click the object. Excel opens the same dialog box you would see if you used the Format menu.

How do I change the style of a chart in Excel 5.0?

When you change the style of a chart, you are not changing the type of chart (such as a column, line, or pie chart); you are changing some of the options used to create the specific type of chart. For example, you can change the style of a column chart to use a different column arrangement, such as stacked or overlapping.

To change the style of a chart:

1. Activate the chart by double-clicking it or moving to the chart's sheet.

2. Choose AutoFormat from the Format menu to open the AutoFormat dialog box, shown here:

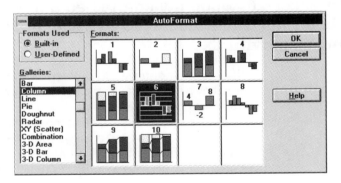

3. Click one of the formats in the Formats section and click OK.

What chart types can I create with Excel 5.0?

Excel 5.0 has 14 basic types of charts. In addition, you can assign different chart types to different data series within a single chart, creating combination charts. You can also format these charts using different colors, distances between data series, legends, gridlines, and other features to create charts of the same type that look very different. The 14 basic chart types are shown in Figure 11-1.

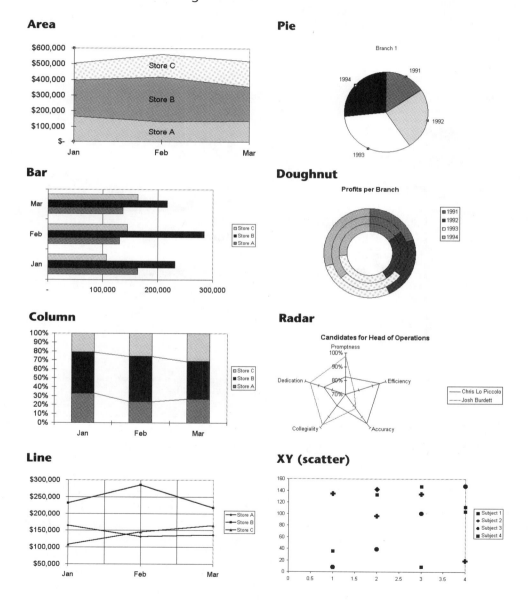

FIGURE 11-1   Excel 5.0's 14 Basic Graph Types

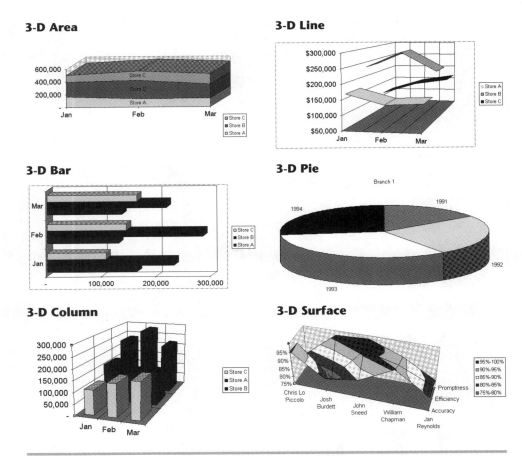

FIGURE 11-1   Excel 5.0's 14 Basic Graph Types (*continued*)

Can I get my chart sheet to match the size of the window, instead of staying one size all the time?

By default, Excel displays the chart at the current zoom. If you change the size of your window, you might only see part of your chart if the current zoom percentage displays the chart in a larger size than your window. You can tell Excel to always make an existing chart sheet the same size as the workbook window by choosing Sized With Window from the View menu. When you tell Excel to size your chart sheet to the window, you indicate that you always want to be able to see the entire chart, even if you change the window's size.

You can change this default setting for all new charts by performing these steps:

1. Choose <u>O</u>ptions from the <u>T</u>ools menu.

2. Click the Chart tab.

3. Select the <u>C</u>hart Sizes With Window Frame check box and click OK.

How do I add error bars to my chart?

Error bars indicate the probable error rate in your data series. Often, they are used in scientific and engineering applications that chart observations that have an associated error rate. You can add error bars to area, bar, column, and line charts; you cannot add them to pie charts, doughnut charts, radar charts, or 3-D charts of any type.

To add error bars to your chart:

1. Activate the chart by double-clicking it in the worksheet or moving to the chart sheet.

2. Select the data series for which you want to display error bars.

3. Choose Error <u>B</u>ars from the <u>I</u>nsert menu.

4. Select the appropriate option in the <u>D</u>isplay section to indicate how you want the error bars to appear.

5. Select the option button for the type of error you want to display and specify any settings for how you want it modified:

   - Select <u>F</u>ixed Value to specify a set value for the negative and positive error ranges.

   - Select <u>P</u>ercentage to set the percentage of the data value that is the error range.

   - Select <u>S</u>tandard Deviation(s) to set the number of standard deviations used as the error range.

   - Select Standard <u>E</u>rror to have Excel calculate the standard error for your data.

   - Select <u>C</u>ustom to specify separate negative and positive error ranges.

6. Click OK to return to your chart and display the error bars.

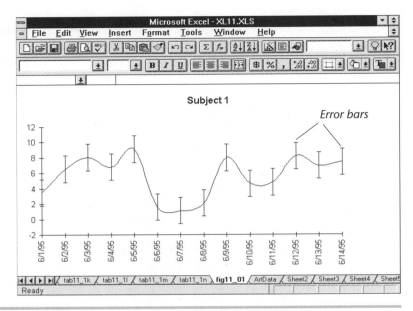

FIGURE 11-2 Error bars let you see the degree of uncertainty in your data

Figure 11-2 shows a sample chart with error bars displayed.

Can I make the columns in my chart overlap?

You can overlap the columns in your column chart by performing these steps:

1. Activate the chart by double-clicking it in the worksheet or moving to the chart sheet.

2. Choose 1 Column Group from the Format menu.

3. Click the Options tab.

4. Enter a number between –100 and 100 in the Overlap box; the larger the number, the greater the overlap. If you enter a negative number, the columns will appear separated by a space instead of side by side.

5. Click OK to return to your chart.

If you choose to overlap columns, your chart might look like the one in Figure 11-3.

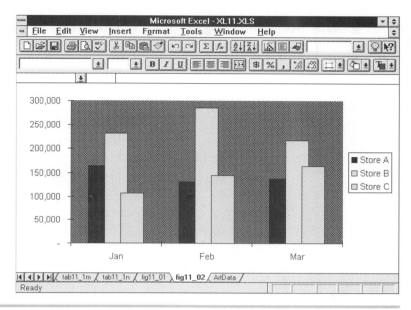

FIGURE 11-3   Overlapping columns

My charts are not updating when I edit the data on which they are based. What's wrong and how can I fix it?

At some point, you changed the recalculation setting in Excel so that it no longer recalculates formulas and charts automatically. You may have done this accidentally or used a macro that changed this setting and didn't change it back. To update your charts automatically as you change the data they depict, you need to restore the default recalculation setting.

To revert to automatic recalculation:

1. Choose Options from the Tools menu.

2. Click the Calculation tab.

3. Select the Automatic option button in the Calculation section of the dialog box and click OK.

Tech Tip: If, for some reason, you want to retain manual recalculation, you can simply press F9 to have Excel perform a recalculation once.

Can I copy an Excel chart to another application in Windows?

Yes. You can copy a picture of an Excel chart to another application in Windows. To do so:

1. Select the chart.

2. Choose Copy Picture from the Edit menu. (When you hold down SHIFT as you open the Edit menu, the Copy command becomes Copy Picture.)

3. Select the As Shown on Screen option button and click OK.

4. Switch to the other application.

5. Place your insertion point where you want the chart to appear.

6. In the other application, choose Paste from the Edit menu.

Tech Tip: You can also copy a chart as a linked or embedded OLE object to another application. For details on creating such an OLE object, see Chapter 13, "Interoperability."

How do I change the color of a bar in a bar chart?

You can change the color of an individual bar in a chart by performing these steps:

1. Activate the chart by double-clicking it in the worksheet or moving to the chart sheet.

2. Click any bar in the series that contains the bar whose color you want to change.

3. Click the individual bar whose color you want to change. If you do not select a single bar to change, you will change the color of all bars in the series.

4. Double-click the bar to open the Format Data Series dialog box.

5. Click the Patterns tab.

6. Select a new color in the Color area of the dialog box and click OK.

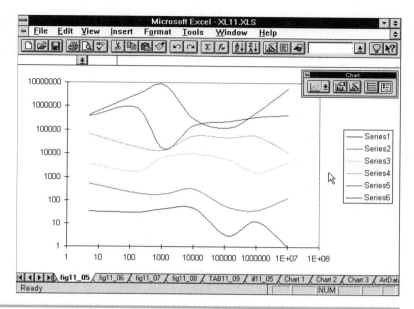

FIGURE 11-4 Using a logarithmic scale in an XY chart

Can the X axis of my line chart use a logarithmic scale?

No, it can't. In Excel 5.0, only the Y axis can use a logarithmic scale on a line chart. However, you can achieve a chart that looks like a line chart with a logarithmic X axis by creating an XY (scatter) chart. You can then use the AutoFormat feature to select a chart format that uses lines to connect the scattered points. Finally, you can change the X axis to a logarithmic scale so that the chart appears the way you want it, such as the one shown in Figure 11-4.

Can I change the colors Excel uses for a 3-D surface chart?

Yes. To change the colors used in a 3-D surface chart:

1. Select the colored square in the legend that represents the layer whose color you want to change.

2. Choose Selected Legend Key from the Format menu.

3. Select a new color in the C̲olor palette and click OK.

The change you make appears both in the legend and in the chart itself.

I want to continue using the Excel 4.0 default colors for data series in my chart even though I'm now using Excel 5.0. Can I do this?

Yes. You can use the Excel 4.0 default chart colors instead of the new Excel 5.0 chart series colors. To do so:

1. Create a chart.
2. Choose A̲utoFormat from the F̲ormat menu.
3. Select the U̲ser-Defined option button.
4. Select MS Excel 4.0 in the F̲ormats list box and click OK.

By default, Excel 4.0 used primary colors for graph elements, whereas Excel 5.0 uses muted colors.

Tech Tip: If you want to change your default colors to be the Excel 4.0 default colors, choose O̲ptions from the T̲ools menu, click the Chart tab, select MS Excel 4.0 in the D̲efault Chart Format section, and click OK.

How do I "explode" a slice of a pie chart?

Exploding a pie slice is very easy. Just activate the chart, select the slice, and drag it away from the center so that it is no longer connected to the pie. Because exploded pie slices stand out more, you can use this method to emphasize a data value. For example, in Figure 11-5, the pie slice for Jan Reynolds is exploded to emphasize her high sales volume in January.

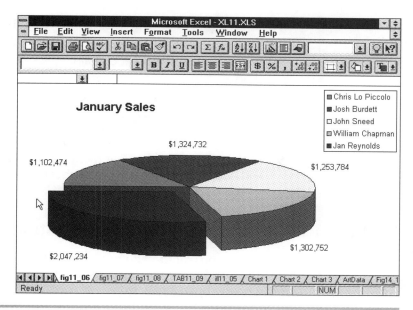

FIGURE 11-5 Exploding a pie slice

Is there any way to speed up the process of opening Excel 4.0 charts in Excel 5.0?

The TipWizard feature may be slowing down this process. You can disable the TipWizard by pressing SHIFT as you click the TipWizard button on the Standard toolbar.

Can I copy an embedded chart to a chart sheet?

Yes. Since the chart will be based on the same data whether it is embedded or not, you don't have to worry about losing any information when you copy it. Usually, you want to place a chart on its own sheet if you plan to print it by itself or if you need a full-page version of it.

To transfer an embedded chart to a chart sheet:

1. Move to the sheet containing the embedded chart.
2. Select a blank cell and choose <u>C</u>hart from the <u>I</u>nsert menu.
3. Choose <u>A</u>s New Sheet.

4. Click Finish in the ChartWizard to create a blank chart sheet.

5. Switch back to the sheet containing your embedded chart.

6. Select your chart by double-clicking it.

7. Choose Copy from the Edit menu.

8. Switch to the blank chart sheet.

9. Choose Paste from the Edit menu to paste your embedded chart onto the chart sheet.

How can I add new information to an existing chart?

You may find you want to add new information to an existing chart—for example, when your sales results for the last quarter come in or you open a new store.

To add new data to an embedded chart:

1. Select the data in the worksheet that you want to add to the chart, including the category or series name.

2. Drag the selected data to your chart. To drag the selection, you must click the border surrounding the selection, not a cell within it.

To add new data to a chart on a chart sheet:

1. Select the data you want to add, including the category or series name.

2. Choose Copy from the Edit menu.

3. Switch to your chart sheet.

4. Choose Paste from the Edit menu.

Tech Tip: You can also use this second method with an embedded chart. You simply double-click the embedded chart in step 3 instead of switching to your chart sheet.

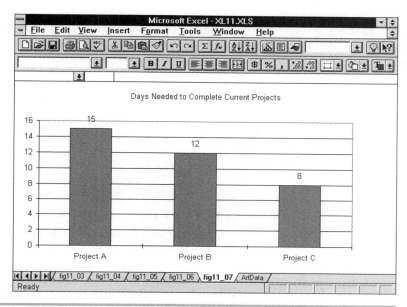

FIGURE 11-6 Using data labels

How do I add data labels to my chart?

Adding *data labels*, which display the actual value depicted in the chart, is a simple operation in Excel 5.0. To display data labels:

1. Activate the chart by double-clicking it or moving to a chart sheet.

2. Choose Data Labels from the Insert menu.

3. Select the Show Value option button and click OK.

The values for each data point now appear on the chart, as shown in Figure 11-6.

Is there a shortcut I can use if I frequently create the same type of chart?

Yes, you can create a chart template that you can use to speed up the process of formatting the chart. To do so:

1. Format a chart the way you want to format most of your charts.

2. Choose AutoFormat from the Format menu.

3. Select the User-Defined option button.

4. Click Customize and then click Add to save the current chart as an AutoFormat type.

5. Type a name for the AutoFormat in the Format Name box and a description in the Description box.

6. Click OK and then click Close.

Use the template to format the chart as follows:

1. Choose AutoFormat from the Format menu.

2. Select the User-Defined option button.

3. Select your custom format and click OK.

How do I apply a moving average to my chart?

A *moving average* is the average of a certain number of previous data points. For instance, you might create a moving average of the previous four weeks of data. You can add a moving average trendline to a bar, column, line or XY (scatter) type chart. To add a moving average trendline, follow the steps given in question 9 in Chapter 1, "Top Ten Tech Terrors." In step 4, select the Moving Average trendline on the Type tab in the Trendline dialog box, and specify the number of periods you want charted in the Period box.

Along the X axis Excel only displays every other label. The labels are long, but can I still force Excel to use all of them?

You can force Excel to use all of the labels by changing the orientation of the labels so that they fit along the X axis. To do so:

1. Activate the chart by double-clicking it in the worksheet or moving to the chart sheet.

2. Double-click the X axis.

3. Click the Alignment tab.

4. In the Orientation section, select a vertical orientation that prints the labels sideways.

5. Click OK.

Why does the ChartWizard sometimes have two steps and other times five?

The ChartWizard walks you through more steps if you are creating a chart for the first time than if you are editing an existing one. If you selected a chart before starting the ChartWizard, you are editing an existing chart, and therefore the first dialog box you see says "Step 1 of 2" in the title bar. If you did not select a chart before starting the ChartWizard, the first dialog box displays "Step 1 of 5," because Excel assumes you are creating a new chart. When you create a new chart, you need to complete additional steps to define the range and basic chart type.

I want to create a chart based on data contained within an outline. Will my chart display the hidden data as well as the visible data?

By default, only the selected visible cells are plotted on the chart. If you display additional levels of data, Excel automatically plots that data as well. Alternatively, you can tell Excel to plot all of the data—hidden and displayed—by following these steps:

1. Choose Options from the Tools menu.

2. Click the Chart tab.

3. Clear the Plot Visible Cells Only check box and click OK.

When I use a logarithmic scale for my Y axis, why does the X axis intersect the Y axis at 1 instead of 0?

The ticks that appear on the Y axis when you use a logarithmic scale are placed at even powers of 10. 1 is the same as 10 to the 0 power. On the other hand, 0 is not a power of 10. Therefore, Excel is just putting the X axis at the lowest positive logarithmic value, which is 1.

My column chart has negative values that display below the X axis. However, the columns themselves print on top of the X axis labels. Can I move the labels so they can be read?

Yes. You can move data labels so that they appear underneath or above the plotted area of the chart. To do so:

1. Select the X axis.
2. Choose Selected Axis from the Format menu.
3. Click the Patterns tab.
4. Select the Low or the High option button and click OK.

Can I change the size of my data markers in a line chart?

No, you cannot directly change the size of data markers in a chart. However, you can use a graphic as your data marker. For example, you could create a large graphic and insert it as the data marker. The steps for doing so are described in the next question.

Can I use a graphic image as a marker in a line chart?

You can use a picture in a bar, column, line, XY (scatter), or radar chart as a data marker. To do so:

1. Create an image or open an existing file in a graphics application, such as Paintbrush.
2. Copy the picture to the Windows Clipboard.
3. Select a series in the chart.
4. Choose Paste from the Edit menu.

If you are adding the graphic image to a bar or column chart, you can change how Excel uses the graphic by following these steps:

1. Select the data series.
2. Choose Selected Data Series from the Format menu.
3. Click the Patterns tab.

4. Select the option that describes how you want Excel to use the graphic in the chart:

- ■ St<u>r</u>etch expands the graphic so that it fills the entire area needed to represent the data value, as shown here:

- ■ St<u>a</u>ck stacks several copies of the graphic in its original size to fill the entire area needed to represent the data value, as shown here:

- ■ Stack And S<u>c</u>ale To stacks several copies of the graphic to fill the entire area needed to represent the data value, with each copy of the graphic scaled to equal some specific number of units on the Y axis, as shown here:

5. Click OK.

Can I protect my chart against modifications after I create it?

Yes. You can protect both your chart sheets and your embedded charts. To do so:

1. Move to the sheet containing the chart or embedded chart.
2. Choose Protection from the Tools menu.
3. Choose Protect Sheet.
4. Enter a password in the Password box.
   This password must be supplied before the chart can be modified. Although a password is optional, if you don't add one anyone can unprotect the sheet.
5. Select the Objects check box to protect an embedded chart; select Contents to protect a chart sheet.
6. Click OK.

To remove this protection later, choose Protection from the Tools menu and then choose Unprotect Sheet. If you set a password when you protected the sheet, you must enter it in order to unprotect the sheet. You can also protect your workbook. Protecting a workbook is just like protecting a sheet except that you expand the area of protection to the entire workbook.

Can I change where Excel places the Y axis in my charts?

Yes. To change where the Y axis crosses the X axis:

1. Select the X axis.
2. Choose Selected Axis from the Format menu.
3. Click the Scale tab.
4. Enter a number in the Value (Y) Axis Crosses at Category Number box to indicate the category at which you want the Y axis to intersect the X axis.
   The number you enter refers to the categories displayed on the X axis.
5. Click OK.

Can I prevent Excel from updating a chart when I edit the values the chart is based on in my worksheet?

You can prevent Excel from updating a chart when you modify the worksheet by following these steps:

1. Activate the chart by double-clicking it in the worksheet or moving to the chart sheet.

2. Select the series you want to exclude from updating.

3. Select the SERIES= function in the formula bar and press F9 to convert the arguments to a list of numbers instead of cell references.

4. Press ENTER to accept the new function.

Since there is no longer any reference to the sheet, the chart remains unchanged even when the data on the sheet changes.

Macros, Custom Applications, and Visual Basic

12

Macros are terrific productivity tools that handle repetitive tasks with ease and efficiency. You can use them to guide you through entering data, performing calculations, and formatting your worksheets. If you've had difficulties with macros in the past or have heard of problems that other people encountered, take heart! The questions and answers in this chapter can help you achieve success—whether you are creating your first macro or your fiftieth.

To make macros easier to work with, many Microsoft applications share the same macro language: Visual Basic for Applications (VBA). Visual Basic includes procedures that are stored in module sheets. Excel 5.0 also supports Excel 4.0 macros, which are stored in macro sheets.

FRUSTRATION BUSTERS!

If you are new to macros, here's a quick list of some of the basics:

- Macros are stored in *module sheets*. A module sheet can contain one or more macros.

- Macros are a collection of Visual Basic codes. The first line of a procedure is Sub, Function, or Property, followed by the macro name. Next come the instructions that tell Excel what you want the macro to do. You end the procedure with the End Sub, End Function, or End Property statement.

- Lines in the macro that start with a single quotation mark (') or "Rem" are *comments*. Comments allow you to add text that is not processed as a Visual Basic statement. You can also include comments after a Visual Basic statement by putting a single quotation mark (') and the comment at the end of the statement. Use comments liberally within your macros. This type of documentation will spare you headaches when you are looking for an error or making modifications later.

- Many of the lines in a macro represent Excel commands and features. To make entering this code easier and reduce typing mistakes, Excel can record these commands and features for you.

- A macro can include dialog boxes to receive and display information. Excel includes dialog sheets to help you create dialog boxes.

- A macro can call another macro. This second macro is called a *subroutine*. When Excel finishes running the subroutine macro, it continues with the next statement in the original, calling macro. Subroutines allow you to break up macros into smaller and more manageable sections.

What is a macro?

A *macro* is a list of instructions that Excel performs. You might think of a macro as a script for a play in which Excel is the actor. Anything Excel can do, a macro can do. Macros are very useful for carrying out tasks that you perform on a regular basis. You can create a macro in two ways. The first way is to use the macro recorder to record your actions as you perform them. These actions can then be "replayed" when you need to perform them again. The second way is to write a macro by typing code in a module sheet. For simple macros, the macro recorder is often easier to use.

What is the macro recorder and how do I use it?

The *macro recorder* is an Excel feature that lets you record actions as you perform them. The recorder then translates these actions into code so you can play them back whenever you want. Using the recorder saves time compared to writing the code yourself and ensures error-free instructions.

To record a macro using Visual Basic or Excel 4.0 macro code:

1. Choose <u>R</u>ecord Macro from the <u>T</u>ools menu, and then choose <u>R</u>ecord New Macro.

   Excel displays a dialog box that lets you name your macro as well as briefly describe it.

2. Click <u>O</u>ptions to expand the dialog box, as shown here, and then specify whether Excel should place the macro code in your own personal macro workbook, in a sheet in the workbook you are currently using, or in a brand new workbook.

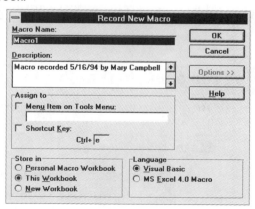

3. Select the MS Excel 4.0 Macro option button if you want Excel to record the macro instructions using Excel 4.0 macro code instead of the default Visual Basic code.

4. If you wish, add your macro as a command on the Tools menu or assign a shortcut key, such as CTRL+A (or any letter), to run your macro.

5. Click OK to start recording your macro. Excel displays this Stop Recording toolbar:

6. Perform all the steps that you want the macro to execute. For example, you might cut and paste data, set new margins and a print area, and then print the document.

7. When you have finished, choose Macro Recorder from the Tools menu and then choose Stop Recording or click the Stop Macro button on the Stop Recording toolbar.

Excel translates all your actions into code and places the code on a module sheet in the destination you indicated in step 2. By default, the macro code appears in a new sheet in the current workbook. You now have a macro that will perform a custom task for you.

Tech Tip: When you record a macro that makes selections from a dialog box, Excel records all the possible settings in the dialog box. Usually you only want to record the effect of a few changes within the dialog box. After recording the macro, you can delete the Visual Basic statements for the dialog box settings you do not want to keep.

How can I run a macro that I've written or recorded?

There are seven ways to run a macro in Excel 5.0, as follows:

Method 1

1. Choose Macro from the Tools menu.

2. Select the macro you want and click Run.

Tech Tip: You can also assign a shortcut to the macro in the Record New Macro dialog box at the time you record the macro.

Method 2

Assign and use a shortcut key to perform the macro. To assign a shortcut key:

1. Choose Macro from the Tools menu.

2. Select the macro in the Macro Name/Reference box.

3. Click Options.

4. Select the Shortcut Key check box and type the desired key in the adjacent box.

   Any shortcut key you assign here takes precedence over existing Excel shortcut keys. For example, pressing CTRL+R usually right-aligns the selected cells, but if you assign it to a macro, the macro will run instead.

5. Click OK, and then click Close to leave the Macro dialog box without running the macro.

You can now run the macro by simply pressing the shortcut key.

Method 3

Create and use a command on the Tools menu to run your macro.

1. Choose Macro from the Tools menu.

2. Select the appropriate macro in the Macro Name/Reference box.

3. Click Options.

Tech Tip: You can also assign the macro to a menu item at the time you record the macro, in the Record New Macro dialog box.

4. Select the Menu Item on Tools Menu check box and enter the text for the menu item in the adjacent box. Insert an ampersand (&) in front of the letter you want underlined in the Tools menu.

   For example, if you enter **Sa&lutation**, the command would appear as Salutation on the menu.

5. Click OK, and then click Close to leave the Macro dialog box without running the macro.

You can now run the macro by choosing the new command from the Tools menu.

Method 4

Assign the macro to an object that you can later click to run the macro. To create an object and assign a macro to it:

1. Click the Drawing button on the Standard toolbar to display the Drawing toolbar.

2. Use the Drawing toolbar to create the object.

3. Choose Assign Macro from the Tools menu or from the object's shortcut menu to display the Assign Macro dialog box. If you create a button, this dialog box appears automatically.

4. Select the macro you want to assign to this object in the Macro Name/Reference box.

5. Click OK.

You can now click the object to run the macro. If you need to select the object later to change its properties, click it with the right mouse button.

Method 5

Assign the macro to a button on a toolbar by following these steps:

1. Choose Toolbars from the View menu and click Customize. You can also click any displayed toolbar with the right mouse button and choose Customize from the shortcut menu.

2. Select a category in the Categories list box and then drag the button you want to use to the desired position on the appropriate toolbar.

3. Right-click the button and choose Assign Macro from the shortcut menu. If you choose a button from the Custom category, this shortcut menu displays automatically.

4. In the Macro Name/Reference box, select the macro you want to assign to this button.

5. Click OK to select the macro and leave the Assign Macro dialog box.

6. Click Close to leave the Customize dialog box.

Click this toolbar button whenever you want to run the macro.

Method 6

Run the macro from another macro. Use the RUN( ) function in the Excel 4.0 Macro Language or the Run( ) method in VBA. In either case, you must enter the name of the macro as text enclosed in quotation marks.

Method 7

Assign the macro to an event. When you assign a macro to a shortcut key, menu, object, or toolbar button, Excel assigns the macro to an event so that when the event (for example, clicking an object) occurs, the macro runs.

You can assign macros to other events as well. For example, when you create a dialog box for a macro, you can assign macros to run when you select items in the dialog box. You can also assign macros to events that Excel starts instead of you. For example, if you give a macro a special name, it performs automatically when the associated event occurs. The following table lists these automatic procedure names and the events that trigger them.

Macro Name	Event That Triggers Performance of the Macro
Auto_Open	The workbook containing this macro is opened.
Auto_Close	The workbook containing this macro is closed.
Auto_Activate	The workbook containing this macro is activated.
Auto_Deactivate	You switch from the workbook containing this macro to another workbook.

You can also add OnEvent procedures, or *event handlers*, to a macro that cause other macros to run when an event occurs. OnEvent procedures are dormant macros that run only if they are triggered. OnEvent procedures are set up by certain Visual Basic properties or methods.

Why do my macro entries use different colors?

Excel color codes your macro entries. This color scheme differentiates the statements, functions, objects, methods, properties, and variables in the macro. The colors, which are preset in Excel, can alert you to typing mistakes, such as when you expect an entry to appear in a specific color and it doesn't. The following table lists the default Visual Basic elements and the colors Excel displays.

Visual Basic Element	What It Represents	Default Color
Selection Text	Lines in a macro that are selected, such as when you copy code to another location	Black text
Syntax Error Text	A line in a macro containing an error	Red text
Execution Point Text	A line in a macro Excel is currently performing	Default*
Breakpoint Text	Lines in a macro that are toggled as a breakpoint	White text on a maroon background
Comment Text	Text after a ' or Rem that indicates a comment	Green text
Keyword Text	Statements and special values such as True	Blue
Identifier Text	Variable names, statements, properties, methods, and object names	Default*
Normal Text	Text not included in one of the other settings	Default*

*Default is the same color as the default that is set for cell entries.

Tech Tip: You can change the colors for the different Visual Basic elements, as described in the next question.

Can I change the colors and fonts of my Visual Basic macros, or are they standard?

Yes. You can change the colors that Excel uses to mark different parts of a Visual Basic macro by following these steps:

1. Choose <u>O</u>ptions from the <u>T</u>ools menu.
2. Click the Module Format tab.

Tech Tip: You can also select a different font for the text used in the macros. However, you should use a monospace font like Courier instead of a proportional one, so that your indentation remains obvious.

3. Select the desired font and font size in the Font and Size boxes, respectively.

4. Select a Visual Basic component in the Code Colors box.

5. Select the color in which you want Excel to display the item in the Foreground box.

6. Select the background color in the Background box.

7. Repeat steps 4 thought 6 for each Visual Basic component whose coloring you want to change.

8. Click OK.

What is an event and how does it change the way I program?

An *event* occurs whenever something changes. For instance, clicking a button is an event; changing the entry in a box within a dialog box is another event. Events are initiated by either you or Excel. In VBA, you can write code to respond to an event. The macro does nothing until the event occurs. This event-driven model is especially useful in processing a user's dialog box selections. In this case, you can specify different macros that execute depending on the items in the dialog box that are selected. Events change how you program because your planning must consider what actions Excel responds to and how it responds. Rather than viewing a macro as a simple series of instructions, think of it as sets of code that may or may not execute, depending on the actions performed by either you or Excel. This method is based on a very different concept than the one found in Excel 4.0 macros, in which the macro ends whenever the instructions finish executing.

How would a cell reference look in a Visual Basic macro?

Macros frequently need to select cells that are used by other statements in the macro. The methods Cells and Range are used in a macro to return a range of one or more cells. These methods are often used as arguments in statements that do something with the cell or range, such as format it.

The syntax you normally use for the Cells method is Cells(*rowindex,columnindex*) where *rowindex* is the number of the row you want to select and *columnindex* is the number or letter of the column you want to select. The syntax you generally use for the Range method is Range(*cell1*) or Range(*cell1,cell2*), where *cell1* is the first or only cell you want to select, and *cell2* is the cell at the opposite corner of the range this method returns. With Range, you supply the cell or range using the standard cell address format that you use in formulas, except that you encase cell references in quote marks. The following are examples of valid and invalid references to cell A1:

Not Recognized	Recognized
Cells("A1")	Cells(1,1)
Cells("A",1)	Range("A1")
Range("A1":"A1")	Range("A1:A1")

What is a good way to learn how to program in Visual Basic for Applications?

The macro recorder is an excellent tool to help you see how Excel sets up a Visual Basic procedure to run as a macro. You can use the macro recorder as a tutor by displaying the procedure you are recording while you create macros.

To show the macro recorder's entries as you record a macro:

1. Choose <u>M</u>acro from the <u>I</u>nsert menu, and then choose <u>M</u>odule to insert a module sheet in your workbook.

2. Choose <u>N</u>ew Window from the <u>W</u>indow menu.

3. Choose <u>A</u>rrange from the <u>W</u>indow menu, select <u>T</u>iled, and click OK. Excel displays two windows showing the same workbook.

4. Continue to display the module sheet in one window; in the other, move to the sheet you want to use to record the macro.

Now when you use the macro recorder, you will see the lines of code generated as you complete your steps. The window showing the recorded macro will even scroll so you can see the

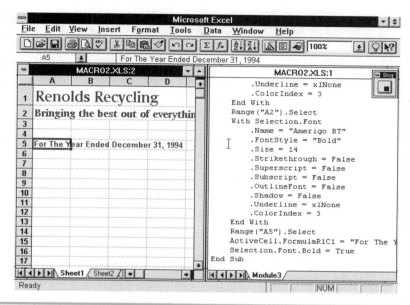

FIGURE 12-1   You can display two views of a workbook to see the Visual Basic statements Excel records

entries the macro recorder is making. Figure 12-1 shows two views of the same workbook; the one on the left shows the worksheet in which you're recording the macro, and the one on the right shows the actual code Excel records.

How do I store more than one macro on a sheet?

A module sheet can contain multiple macros. For example, the module sheet in Figure 12-2 shows several macros. A module sheet contains a *declarations section,* followed by the macros or procedures on the sheet. The declarations section is where you provide overall direction to all of the macros on the sheet, as well as set up variables that other macros in other workbooks can use. You might think of a declarations section as where you set up rules that the macros will follow. A declarations section is not necessary, however, and you can easily have module sheets that do not have them.

Each macro on the module sheet includes a pair of Sub and End Sub, Function and End Function, or Property and End

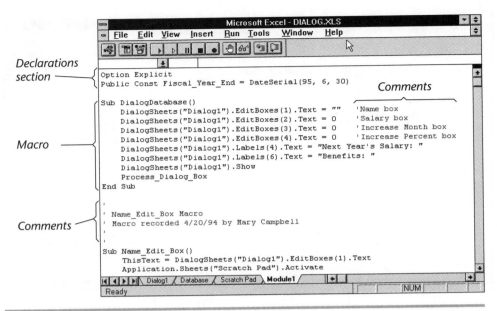

```
Declarations
section ───────► Option Explicit
                Public Const Fiscal_Year_End = DateSerial(95, 6, 30)    Comments

                Sub DialogDatabase()
                    DialogSheets("Dialog1").EditBoxes(1).Text = ""    'Name box
                    DialogSheets("Dialog1").EditBoxes(2).Text = 0     'Salary box
                    DialogSheets("Dialog1").EditBoxes(3).Text = 0     'Increase Month box
                    DialogSheets("Dialog1").EditBoxes(4).Text = 0     'Increase Percent box
  Macro ───────►    DialogSheets("Dialog1").Labels(4).Text = "Next Year's Salary: "
                    DialogSheets("Dialog1").Labels(6).Text = "Benefits: "
                    DialogSheets("Dialog1").Show
                    Process_Dialog_Box
                End Sub

                '
                ' Name_Edit_Box Macro
Comments ──────► ' Macro recorded 4/20/94 by Mary Campbell
                '
                '
                Sub Name_Edit_Box()
                    ThisText = DialogSheets("Dialog1").EditBoxes(1).Text
                    Application.Sheets("Scratch Pad").Activate
```

FIGURE 12-2   Module sheet containing multiple macros and a declarations section

Property statements with the instructions that the macro performs in between. The macros on a sheet are listed one right after another. Interspersed among the declaration section and the macros on the sheet are comments, which are the lines beginning with Rem or '. Excel ignores anything that appears on a comment line when it performs the macro, allowing you to insert descriptive text for documentation purposes.

Tech Tip: You can move from one macro on a macro sheet to another by pressing CTRL+UP ARROW and CTRL+DOWN ARROW. These shortcut keys move to the Sub statement of the previous or next macro, respectively.

Can I copy a macro from one workbook to another?

Yes. The easiest way to copy macros between workbooks is to use the Windows Clipboard:

1. Open the workbook containing the Visual Basic code you want to copy and the workbook you want to copy it to.

2. Select the Visual Basic code you want to copy from the module sheet.

3. To copy the selection to the Clipboard, choose Copy from the Edit menu or Copy from the shortcut menu, or click the Copy button on the Standard toolbar.

4. Move the insertion point to the location in the second workbook's module sheet where you want the Visual Basic code to appear.

   If there is no module sheet in the second workbook, choose Macro from the Insert menu, and then choose Module to insert one first.

5. To paste the selection from the Clipboard to the second module sheet, choose Paste from the Edit menu, choose Paste from the shortcut menu, or click the Paste button on the Standard toolbar.

Does Excel include any sample Visual Basic code?

Yes. Excel provides two sources of sample Visual Basic code. First, your EXCEL\EXAMPLES subdirectory includes a SAMPLES.XLS workbook that contains several macros. This workbook contains sample macros written in both the Excel 4.0 macro language and in Visual Basic. You can open this workbook and look at how these samples use Visual Basic keywords to run the macros.

Another source of sample Visual Basic code is the online Help feature. Choose Contents from the Help menu in Excel and then double-click Programming with Visual Basic to access this information. In most cases, when you display Help for a Visual Basic keyword, you can also view an example of that keyword's use. Click "Example" at the top of the Visual Basic Reference window and a Visual Basic Reference Example window opens.

What data types does VBA support?

VBA supports the following data types:

- *Boolean* to equal True or False
- *Integer* for whole numbers, such as 31111 and −270

- *Long* for large whole numbers, such as 2000000 and −75000

- *Single* (single-precision floating point) for numbers that contain a decimal point and are not as large as Double data types

- *Double* (double-precision floating point) for large numbers that contain a decimal point

- *Currency* for numbers with up to four decimal places (more efficient than using the Single data type)

- *Date* for dates, such as 7/4/94

- *Object* for any object reference

- *String* for text, such as "string example"

- *Variant* to hold any of the other types

- *User-defined* for a data type that includes more than one of the above data types

The Variant data type can hold any of the other VBA types. This is useful if you don't know the variable's data type ahead of time or if you expect that the type will change as the macro is performed. However, because Variant is the largest data type, and therefore uses the most memory, it's prudent to try to define a more specific data type if you can.

Tech Tip: You can set the variable type by declaring it or by entering a type-declaration character as the last character in the variable name. The type-declaration characters include % for Integer, & for Long, ! for Single, # for Double, @ for Currency, and $ for String.

What functions does Visual Basic include to convert one data type to another?

Excel provides nine functions to transform data from one data type to another. The following table lists each conversion function and its resulting data type.

Conversion Function	Data Type of Result
CBool	Boolean
CCur	Currency
CDate	Date
CDbl	Double
CInt	Integer
CLng	Long
CSng	Single
CStr	String
CVar	Variant

All these functions use the format *function name(expression)*. The expression must equal something that can be converted to the function's data type. For example, the expression you use with CDate must represent a date.

Can I hide a module sheet?

You can hide a module sheet when you do not want someone who is using the workbook to see the procedures it contains. The command for hiding a module sheet is different than the one you use to hide a worksheet. To hide the module sheet you are on, choose Sheet from the Edit menu and then choose Hide.

The command you use to redisplay the module sheet depends on the type of sheet you are currently using. If you are working in a worksheet, choose Sheet from the Format menu, and then choose Unhide; if you are working in another module sheet, choose Sheet from the Edit menu, and then choose Unhide. In either case, in the Unhide dialog box, select the module sheet you want to display, and click OK.

You can also hide a module sheet from within a VBA macro. The following macros hide and display a module sheet named "Module1". You can include these statements between the Sub and End Sub statements in your own macros when you want to hide and display module sheets.

```
Sub HideMacro()
    Sheets("Module1").Select
    ActiveWindow.SelectedSheets.Visible = False
End Sub
```

```
Sub ShowMacro()
    Sheets("Module1").Visible = True
End Sub{par}
```

Is there a built-in utility to translate my Excel 4.0 macros to VBA?

No, and this is not necessary. You can run Excel 4.0 macros directly using the same Excel features you use to run Excel macros written in VBA. You can also run any Excel 4.0 macro from within a VBA module. To run an Excel 4.0 macro from within a VBA module, use the Run method, as shown here:

```
Mac_Result = Application.Run("MY_MACRO.XLM!Generate_Report", 1, 2)
If Mac_Result = True Then
    MsgBox ("Excel has finished generating reports. Print the
    new workbook")
Else
    MsgBox ("Excel could not generate the reports. You have
    incomplete data. Fix your data then run the macro again.")
End If
```

This macro runs the Excel 4.0 Generate_Report macro in the MY_MACRO.XLM macro sheet. The Generate_Report macro returns a value that the macro shown here stores in the variable Mac_Result. Depending on the value of this variable, the macro displays one of the two messages you see above.

Can I record additional Visual Basic code and add it to an existing macro?

Yes, you can use the macro recorder to add more code to an existing macro. However, you use different steps than when you initially record a macro.

To add Visual Basic code to an existing macro using the macro recorder:

1. Click the module sheet's tab to display it.

2. Move the insertion point to where you want the additional Visual Basic statements to appear.

3. Choose <u>R</u>ecord Macro from the <u>T</u>ools menu.

4. Choose <u>M</u>ark Position for Recording.

5. Switch to where you need to be to record the code you want to add to the macro. If the macro has already set up certain conditions before the point where you want to add code, you need to create those conditions. For example, if the macro selects a range, and you are adding the codes to format that range, you should select a range in a worksheet before starting to record the formatting steps.

6. Choose <u>R</u>ecord Macro from the <u>T</u>ools menu.

7. Choose Re<u>c</u>ord at Mark to begin recording.

8. Perform the Excel actions to record them. Excel inserts the Visual Basic instructions in the macro.

9. When you have finished performing the actions, click the Stop Macro button on the Stop Recording toolbar.

At this point, you can return to the macro and edit the Visual Basic instructions you have added, as necessary.

On my Forms toolbar, some of the buttons beep and don't do anything when I click them. Why?

These buttons beep to let you know that you are trying to use them in a situation in which they have no effect. For example, the Combination Drop-Down Edit and Combination List-Edit buttons on the Forms toolbar can only be used when you are creating a custom dialog box in a dialog sheet. Other buttons that may not respond include Run Dialog, which only responds if a dialog box is present; Edit Code, which only responds if there is macro code associated with the selected object; and Control Properties, which only responds if an object is selected.

Where can I get help on all of the commands available in the VBA language?

You can look in Excel's online Help to find out how to use individual VBA commands and view their syntax. In addition, the Visual Basic User's Guide that comes with Excel contains general information about and guidelines for using VBA.

To view online information about VBA:

Tech Tip: If you press F1 while you are working in a module sheet, the Visual Basic Reference window opens automatically.

1. Choose <u>C</u>ontents from the <u>H</u>elp menu, or press F1.

2. Click Programming with Visual Basic in the Microsoft Excel Help Contents window to open the Visual Basic Reference window.

3. From this window, select a topic to display more information about it. You can also click <u>S</u>earch to look for information about a specific feature or Visual Basic statement.

How long do my macro variables last?

Variables are changing values that are stored and used by a VBA procedure. How long a macro variable keeps its value depends on its type. There are three types of Excel VBA variables, which have different scopes:

- *Public variables* are available to every procedure in all open workbooks. They are listed in the declarations section of a module, in statements that include the word "Public", as shown here:

```
Public CurrentSheet As Object      'Set up CurrentSheet public variable
Public Production As Integer       'Set up Production public variable
```

Tech Tip: The declarations section appears at the top of a module sheet above the first Sub statement that is not a comment.

- *Module variables* are available to all procedures in the module sheet in which the variable is declared; in other words, they can be used by any macros that appear on the same sheet with them. Module variables are declared in the general declarations section on a macro sheet and require a Dim statement, as shown here:

```
Dim CurrentSheet As Object      'Set up CurrentSheet module variable
Dim Production As Integer       'Set up Production module variable
```

- *Local variables* are only recognized within the procedures in which they appear. Local variables are defined with either a Static or a Dim statement, and come after the Sub statement for the macro that uses the variable. Variables declared with Static statements retain their value the next time the procedure uses the variable; variables declared with Dim statements are reinitialized at the end of the procedure, clearing any previous values. Any variables that are not declared are also treated as local variables.

What are objects, methods, and properties and how are they used in VBA?

Excel Visual Basic macros are created using a combination of functions, methods, objects, properties, and statements. Objects, methods, and properties are like parts of speech, such as nouns, verbs, and adjectives:

- *Objects* are like nouns; they have properties and methods. Objects include cells, ranges, and charts that represent the data with which you want to work.

- *Methods,* like verbs, are the actions an object can perform.
- *Properties,* like adjectives, are the traits of an object.

For example, if we had a bird object, the method might be fly, while a property might be blue. In VBA, the code to make a bird fly would be BIRD.FLY. The VBA code to change the color of the bird would be BIRD.COLOR=BLUE.

What is a collection and how is it useful to me?

A *collection* is a set of similar objects and is designated by a plural name, such as "Worksheets". Collections are very useful when you want to perform the same action on each object in a group. You achieve this by using the For Each looping structure. The loop might look like this:

```
For Each object In collection
    commands
Next
```

You don't define the collections; you use the ones Excel has already created. Some of these collections include your available worksheets or add-ins.

I have a series of statements that deal with the same object. Is there a quicker way to address the object than typing out its name each time?

Yes. You can use the With statement to have one object perform several methods. The code might look like this:

```
With object_name
    .method_1
    .method_2
    .method_3
End With
```

Note that you *must* include the period at the beginning of each method.

You can also use this technique with properties or other statements that you want to repeat on the same object. For example, the following code shows the With ... End With statements used to apply formatting to a group of selected cells:

```
With Selection.Font
    .Name = "Book Antiqua"
    .Size = 14
End With
```

What does the Option Explicit line at the beginning of my modules mean?

Tech Terror: If Option Explicit is off, Excel assumes any misspelled keywords are variable names.

When this line is included, it forces you to declare any variables before they are used, which reduces typing errors. Also, when you declare variables first, Excel reserves less memory for them and can perform macros faster. If you try to use a variable that has not been declared, you will get an error message.

Follow these steps to have Excel automatically insert the Option Explicit line in new module sheets:

1. Choose <u>O</u>ptions from the <u>T</u>ools menu.
2. Click the Module General tab.
3. Select the <u>R</u>equire Variable Declaration check box.
4. Click OK.

Are there any operators you can use in Visual Basic expressions that are not used in cell entries?

Yes. Macros can include several operators that you cannot use in cell entries, as described in the following table. These operators are all unique to Visual Basic expressions.

Operator	Description
\	Divides two numbers and returns an integer as the result; unlike the / operator, which returns a floating point number
Is	Compares two object reference variables and returns True if the objects are the same
Like	Compares two strings and returns True if the strings are the same; you can include wildcards in the string to match patterns
Eqv	Compares two expressions: if both are true or both are false, returns the value True; if one is true while the other is false, returns the value False
Imp	Performs a logical implication on two expressions; uses the first expression to decide if it implies that the second expression is true
Xor	Compares two expressions and returns True if one—and only one—expression is true; if both are true or both are false, returns False

Tech Tip: You can also use the plus sign (+) in VBA macros to concatenate strings, just as you use the ampersand (&).

What is the difference between a Sub and a Function procedure?

Both Sub and Function start sections of Visual Basic code. When the section is done, Sub and Function return to the place they were called from. A Function procedure returns a value, the result of the procedure. A statement at the end of a Function procedure makes the function name equal to the value calculated by this procedure, and then returns this name to where the Function procedure was called. This value can then be used by other sections of code. Also, a Function procedure can be called from a worksheet as well as from another procedure.

A Sub procedure, also called a command procedure, must be called by a macro. It does not calculate and return a value; instead, it performs actions in the worksheet.

When I use the macro recorder, Excel records Visual Basic instructions. I am very comfortable with Excel 4.0 macros. Can I make the recorder use this language instead?

To have Excel record the instructions for what you are performing using the Excel 4.0 macro language:

1. Choose <u>R</u>ecord Macro from the <u>T</u>ools menu, and then choose <u>R</u>ecord New Macro.

2. Click <u>O</u>ptions in the Record New Macro dialog box.

3. Select the MS <u>E</u>xcel 4.0 Macro option button in the Language section.

4. Click OK to start recording the macro using the Excel 4.0 macro language.

In Excel 4.0, I used the Dialog Editor to create custom dialog boxes for my applications. Is this feature still available in Excel 5.0?

The Dialog Editor has been incorporated into the Excel features that you see when you are working in a dialog sheet. In other words, the Dialog Editor is no longer a separate application but is built right into Excel.

How do I create my own dialog boxes?

Macros use dialog boxes to display and receive information to and from the macro's user. To streamline the creation of a dialog box, you can create a dialog sheet that contains the dialog box that a macro will use. You will have a dialog sheet for every dialog box you need. On a dialog sheet, you lay out the dialog box and add the dialog box components, called *controls*, that you want to see in the completed dialog box. You also assign the actions Excel performs when you select or change any part of this dialog box.

To create a dialog box:

1. Choose <u>M</u>acro from the <u>I</u>nsert menu, and then choose <u>D</u>ialog to add a dialog sheet.

   An empty dialog box appears on a sheet along with the Forms toolbar. You can resize this dialog box by dragging its borders just as you would the borders of a document or application window.

2. Click a button on the Forms toolbar to add the desired item to the dialog box.

   Excel displays a default item of the type you select in the dialog box. You can modify the text that appears on the item, its size, and position. After hiding the grid, the completed dialog box might look like this one:

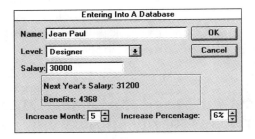

3. Set any properties for the control.

   Properties you may want to set include the type of entry to make in text boxes and whether controls are linked with individual cells. You can also enter a letter to use in combination with ALT as a shortcut to select the control.

4. Assign macros to the controls.

   These macros determine what the control does when you use it. For example, a text box control may set a variable to the value of the text box or another cell. Each control (except for a label) usually has its own macro. For example, the Name_Edit_Box macro in Figure 12-3 contains the instructions Excel performs as you update the Name box in the custom dialog box shown in the previous illustration.

A macro that uses a dialog box sets up everything that should occur until the dialog box appears and then lets the dialog box handle everything until it closes. Once the dialog box closes, the macro that displayed the dialog box can continue to perform other macro instructions.

5. Create or edit the macro that will call the dialog box.

Figure 12-3 shows the DialogDatabase macro that displays the dialog box. This macro only sets up the initial values in the dialog box and displays the box. The "Dialog1" references tell Excel which dialog box to use. (Dialog1 is the name of the dialog sheet that appears on the sheet's tab.) Once the dialog box appears, the dialog box controls process the entries in the dialog box. When the OK button is clicked, the record entered in the dialog box is copied to the end of the database, the dialog box controls are reset, and the dialog box is ready to display the next record. When the Cancel button is clicked, the dialog box closes and returns to DialogDatabase to finish the original macro.

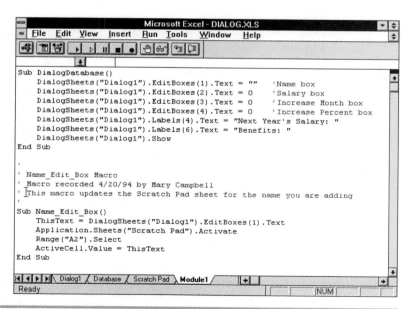

```
Microsoft Excel - DIALOG.XLS
File  Edit  View  Insert  Run  Tools  Window  Help

Sub DialogDatabase()
    DialogSheets("Dialog1").EditBoxes(1).Text = ""      'Name box
    DialogSheets("Dialog1").EditBoxes(2).Text = 0       'Salary box
    DialogSheets("Dialog1").EditBoxes(3).Text = 0       'Increase Month box
    DialogSheets("Dialog1").EditBoxes(4).Text = 0       'Increase Percent box
    DialogSheets("Dialog1").Labels(4).Text = "Next Year's Salary: "
    DialogSheets("Dialog1").Labels(6).Text = "Benefits: "
    DialogSheets("Dialog1").Show
End Sub

'
' Name_Edit_Box Macro
' Macro recorded 4/20/94 by Mary Campbell
' This macro updates the Scratch Pad sheet for the name you are adding
'
Sub Name_Edit_Box()
    ThisText = DialogSheets("Dialog1").EditBoxes(1).Text
    Application.Sheets("Scratch Pad").Activate
    Range("A2").Select
    ActiveCell.Value = ThisText
End Sub

    Dialog1 / Database / Scratch Pad \ Module1 /
Ready                                               NUM
```

FIGURE 12-3   Macros used for and by a dialog box

I am trying to place a drop-down list box in my VBA macro dialog box. How do I enter the list of items in the box?

First, enter the text for the items you want to appear in the list box in a range in one of your worksheets. Then follow these steps to display them in the list box:

1. Move to the dialog sheet for the dialog box.

2. Open the Format Object dialog box by double-clicking the list box to which you want to assign the data.

3. Click the Control tab.

4. In the Input Range box, specify the range of cells that contains the text you want to appear in the drop-down box.
   For example, to use the entries in the cells H1:W20 on a sheet called Dialog Input, you would either type **'Dialog Input'!$H$1:$W$20** or select the range H1:W20 using your mouse or keyboard.

5. Click OK.

What is an add-in macro?

An add-in macro is an application that can contain macros that you have already created in an Excel workbook. Excel loads these applications on demand, so that each part of the add-in is loaded only when it is needed. Using an add-in macro gives you the flexibility to only load the macro when it's needed. You can create add-ins from the macros in normal module sheets in workbooks.

To create an add-in macro from the macros you have stored in an existing workbook:

1. Choose Make Add-In from the Tools menu.
   Excel sets the Save File As Type box to Microsoft Excel Add-In and the extension to .XLA.

2. Type a name for the add-in file.
   You may also want to change the directory location. Most add-ins are stored in the LIBRARY subdirectory within the Excel program directory.

3. Click OK to save the workbook as an add-in.

Tech Tip: Add summary information to the workbook before you save it as an add-in. The workbook's description becomes the name of the add-in you see in the Add-Ins dialog box when you select it to load, and the work-book's title becomes the longer description you see in the Add-Ins dialog box.

4. Click <u>Y</u>es when you close the .XLA file so you still have an up-to-date version of the workbook saved in a workbook file. Having the workbook file allows you to make changes at a later time.

> **Tech Tip:** Excel stores the add-ins in an unreadable form, so be sure to keep a backup copy of your original workbook file.

After you create the add-in, you can make it available by following these steps:

1. Choose Add-<u>I</u>ns from the <u>T</u>ools menu.

2. Select the check box for the add-in in the <u>A</u>dd-Ins Available box.

3. Click OK.

Can I use some of the .XLA files that were in Excel 4.0 with Excel 5.0?

Yes. These files are functional with Excel 5.0 as long as you have access to them. To access them:

1. Choose Add-<u>I</u>ns from the <u>T</u>ools menu.

2. Select the check box for the name of the .XLA file add-in you want to load.

3. Click OK.

How can I combine two or more strings together in a macro and place the results in a variable?

Concatenation statements combine two or more strings and can take the following forms:

■ You can concatenate two strings into one by using an expression such as MVP = "Will" & " "& "Howarth", which makes MVP equal Will Howarth.

■ You can concatenate a string and a string variable into one by using an expression such as MVP = "Mike" & Last_Name$, which makes MVP equal Mike, a space, and the contents of Last_Name$.

■ You can concatenate two string variables into one with an expression such as MVP = First_Name$ & " " & Last_Name$, which makes MVP equal the contents of First_Name$, a space, and the contents of Last_Name$.

In addition, the plus (+) symbol may be used to denote concatenation. For example, you can use the expression MVP = "Larry" + " " + Last_Name$ to make MVP equal Larry, a space, and the contents of Last_Name$.

Interoperability

One of the great advantages of Windows is that you can easily exchange data between different applications using the Clipboard or Object Linking and Embedding (OLE). A simple cut and paste operation makes it easy to combine graphics, spreadsheet data, and text into one attractive document. You can enter and format each type of data in whatever application is most suitable, and then use it in any of your other applications whenever you want.

FRUSTRATION BUSTERS!

The easiest tool for exchanging data between applications is often overlooked—the Windows Clipboard. You can use the Clipboard to move and copy data not only within Excel but to and from other applications. Whether you're cutting and pasting plain data, a fully formatted 3-D graph, or an embedded OLE object, the Clipboard provides a quick-and-easy way to achieve your goal.

To add Excel data to a document in another application, simply cut or copy it from an Excel workbook and paste it into another file, just as if you were moving the data to another area of a worksheet in Excel. When you use this method, if the other application does not support OLE, you create a simple copy of the data; if it does, you create an embedded object. Using the Clipboard is ideal when you want to insert a "snapshot" of your data in another application but don't want it to update whenever your workbook changes.

You can copy data from another application into an Excel workbook in the same way. You cut or copy the data from another application to the Windows Clipboard, and paste it into your Excel workbook. Again, if the source application does not support OLE, you create a simple copy; if it does, you embed an OLE object.

What's the difference between embedding and linking?

Object Linking and Embedding (OLE) lets you share data between applications. With OLE, you can create a file, such as a graphic or spreadsheet, in one Windows application and then either link it to or embed it in another file created in the same or a different application. Linking and embedding objects differ in terms of what you can do with the data and where it is stored.

For example, the graphic shown in Figure 13-1 is an embedded OLE object created with WordArt. You edit this object with WordArt, but it appears in your Excel worksheet.

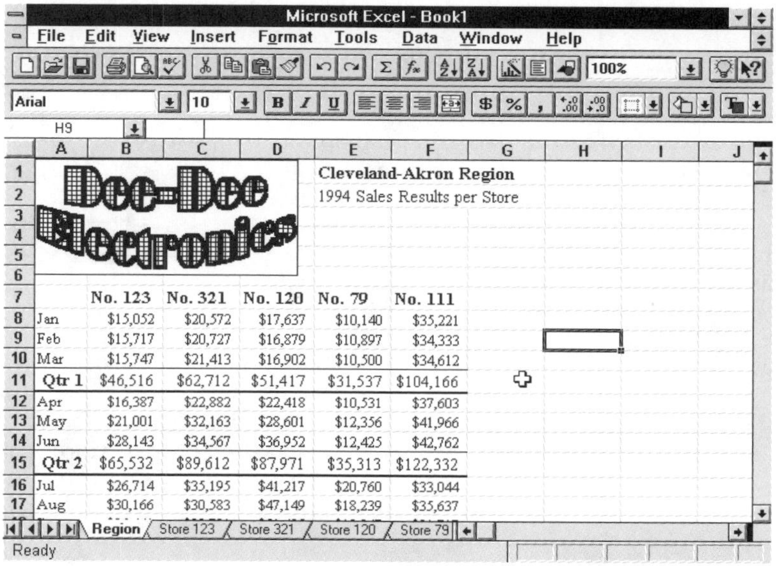

FIGURE 13-1   You can embed data in a workbook

With *linking*, the data remains in its own file. Your Excel document simply contains a connection, or *link*, that tells it where to find that object. For example, suppose you design your company logo with the Windows Paintbrush accessory and save it in a file called LOGO.BMP. If you add a link to this logo to your Excel workbook, the logo itself is still stored in LOGO.BMP; Excel simply displays and updates the image in the document by referring to that file. When you edit the logo, all the links to the file are automatically updated. In this case, if you choose a different background color for the logo in Paintbrush, this change appears in your Excel document when you next open it. You can create many different links to a single file, and changing the data in the file changes all of the linked objects.

Embedding stores the data for an object in its original format in the Excel file itself. For example, if you embed the company logo you created with Paintbrush in an Excel workbook, the graphic actually becomes a part of your Excel file; in other words, there is no file called LOGO.BMP. Because the logo is contained in your Excel document, you cannot use it in other documents or applications. Also, you can only edit the image by starting Paintbrush from within Excel.

Tech Tip: You can embed an object and also save it separately as a file. When you do so, you end up with two completely separate copies of the object: one that is part of your Excel document and another that is stored in its own file. Editing the logo in the Excel document does not affect the other file; likewise, editing the logo in its own file does not affect the logo in the Excel document.

The advantage of linking and embedding objects over just copying data is that you can edit them in the application in which they were created without leaving Excel. For example, assuming you want to edit the company logo you embedded in your Excel document, all you have to do is double-click the object to open Paintbrush and make your modifications.

Tech Tip: Two terms you frequently hear when discussing OLE objects are server applications and client applications. *Server applications* are programs that contain the data for linked or embedded objects. *Client applications* are programs that let you place linked or embedded objects in them. In the logo example, Paintbrush is the server application you used to create your company logo and Excel is the client application that accepted the embedded or linked object.

How do I create a link or embed an OLE object using Excel?

To create a link or embed an OLE object created in another application:

1. Start Excel (the client) and open the workbook in which you want to show the linked data or in which you want to embed the object.

2. Start the other application (the server) and open the document you want to create a link to or that you want to embed in the workbook. If you plan to create a link, this document must be saved as a file. If you want to

embed the data, you can create and format the data without saving it.

3. In the server application, select the data you want to create a link to or that you want to embed.

4. Choose Copy from the Edit menu to copy this data to the Clipboard.

5. Switch to Excel.

6. Move your insertion point to where you want the linked data to appear.

7. Choose Paste Special from the Edit menu.

8. To create a link, select the Paste Link option button and click OK to create a link. To embed the data, select the Paste option button and click OK.

    If the Paste Link option button is not available, then the application used to create the document cannot be a server for linked data.

Figure 13-2 shows a company logo that is linked from a Paintbrush file.

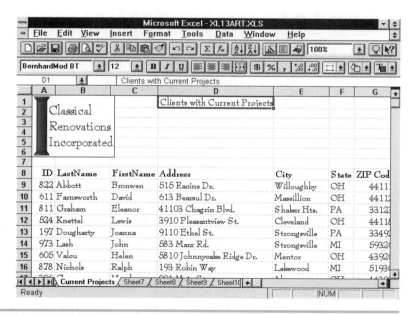

FIGURE 13-2   Linking your company logo makes it easy to update it in many different documents at once

Tech Tip: You will notice that the Object Type list box lists many applications. This list box displays all of the applications on your system that can be used to create embedded objects. If you select a file on the Create from File tab, you can easily create links as well.

You can also create objects in other applications and embed them in Excel without leaving Excel.

To create and embed an object:

1. Choose <u>O</u>bject from the <u>I</u>nsert menu.

2. Click the Create New tab.

3. Select one of the applications in the <u>O</u>bject Type list box and click OK.

4. Create the object in the application.

5. Click outside the object in the workbook, or choose E<u>x</u>it and Return from the <u>F</u>ile menu.

The steps you use to link data from an Excel workbook to another application vary depending on the application containing the data for the linked or embedded object. In most cases, you select the data in Excel, choose <u>C</u>opy from the <u>E</u>dit menu, switch to the client application, choose Paste <u>S</u>pecial from the <u>E</u>dit menu, select an option to indicate whether you want to paste the data as a link or embed it, and click OK.

Tech Tip: Excel 5.0 offers an easy solution for creating a link to another application: Open both applications, position their windows side by side on the screen, select the appropriate data in Excel, and simply drag it to the other application.

Does Excel 5.0 support .WK4 files?

No. Excel cannot read .WK4 files, which are files from Lotus 1-2-3 Release 4.*x*. However, Excel can read .WK1 and .WK3 files. If you need to open a .WK4 file in Excel, first save it as a .WK3 file in 1-2-3, and then open it in Excel.

Can I eliminate the prompt to update links when I open files with links?

You can tell Excel not to prompt you to update links each time you open a document that contains OLE links, in which case Excel will automatically update the links every time you open a file. To turn this prompt off:

1. Choose Options from the Tools menu.
2. Click the Edit tab.
3. Clear the Ask to Update Automatic Links check box and click OK.

Tech Tip: If you don't want to update your links each time you open a workbook, you must leave this feature turned on and click No at the prompt.

I can't open my .WB1 files even though the documentation says Excel can open Quattro Pro files. Why?

Excel 5.0 supports only .WQ1 files, which are in the Quattro Pro for DOS format. Your .WB1 files were created by Quattro Pro for Windows. To import a .WB1 file, you need to first save it as a .WK3 file in Quattro Pro, and then open it in Excel.

I have some 1-2-3 worksheets that contain macros. When I open these worksheets in Excel, will these macros still work?

Yes. Excel can successfully interpret most 1-2-3 macros. However, certain 1-2-3 macro commands and Lotus-specific functions do not translate well.

Why can't I open my Microsoft Works 3.0 files in Excel?

Excel 5.0 does not support the Works 3.0 format. To work around this problem:

1. Open the file in Works that you want to bring into Excel.
2. Choose Save As from the File menu.
3. Select Lotus 1-2-3 WK1 in the File Formats list.
4. Click OK to save the file in the new format.
5. Close the file.
6. Switch to Excel and open the .WK1 file.

Which Lotus file formats can Excel 5.0 open?

Excel can open and save any file in the formats listed here:

Extension	File Format
.WKS	Lotus 1-2-3 Release 1.*x*
.WK1	Lotus 1-2-3 Release 2.*x*
.FMT	Lotus 1-2-3 Release 2.*x* format files
.WK3	Lotus 1-2-3 Release 3.*x*
.FM3	Lotus 1-2-3 Release 3.*x* format files
.ALL	Lotus 1-2-3 Release 1.*x* Allways format files

When I open a file saved by Excel for the Macintosh, all of my dates are off by four years and a day. Why?

Excel stores a date as a serial number. In Excel for Windows, this serial number represents the number of days since 1/1/1900. In Excel for the Macintosh, the serial number represents the number of days since 1/1/1904.

You can change the date system used in an Excel for Windows workbook by performing the following steps:

1. Choose <u>O</u>ptions from the <u>T</u>ools menu.
2. Click the Calculation tab.
3. Select the 1904 <u>D</u>ate System check box and click OK.

Tech Terror: If you are moving worksheets from a workbook that uses the 1900 date system to one that uses the 1904 date system, your dates will be off by exactly 1462 days—the number of days between 1/1/1900 and 1/1/1904 plus 1, because the 1904 date system starts counting at 0, whereas the 1900 date system starts at 1.

Can I display part of an Excel worksheet as a table in Word for Windows 6.0?

Yes. The easiest way to add Excel data to your Word document is by using the Windows Clipboard:

1. In Excel, select the data you want to display in your Word document.
2. Choose <u>C</u>opy from the <u>E</u>dit menu.
3. Switch to Word.
4. Move the insertion point to where you want the Excel data to appear as a table.
5. Choose <u>P</u>aste from Word's <u>E</u>dit menu.

Word automatically formats the data as a table when you paste it into the document.

If you want to embed or link the Excel data as an OLE object rather than copy it:

1. In Excel, select the data you want to display in your Word document.

2. Choose Copy from the Edit menu.

3. Switch to Word.

4. Move the insertion point to where you want the Excel data to appear as a table.

5. Choose Paste Special from the Edit menu.

6. Select a format in the As list box.

Although every option will display the Excel data in columnar format, the only choice that will paste the data as a true Word table is the Formatted Text (RTF) option.

7. To embed the data, select the Paste option button; to link the data, select Paste Link.

8. Click OK.

Figure 13-3 shows a Word for Windows 6.0 table that includes data from an Excel worksheet.

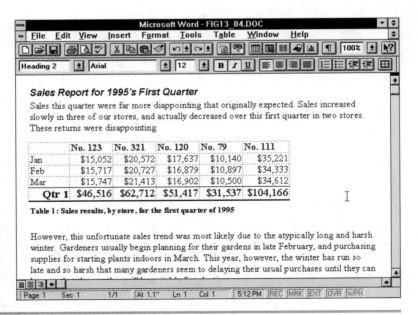

FIGURE 13-3   Displaying Excel data in a Word table

When I opened a text file that contained ZIP codes in Excel 4.0, the first character in the ZIP codes disappeared if it was a zero. Can I avoid this in Excel 5.0?

Yes. When you import a text file in Excel 5.0, the new Text Wizard starts automatically. This wizard lets you control the format of each column of the text file before Excel opens it. You can specify which columns contain text, dates, and general data, as well as which columns should be skipped. In your case, in step 3, you would select the column that contains the ZIP codes and then click the Text option button in the Column Data Format section. By specifying Text instead of the default General option, you avoid losing the zeros at the beginning of the ZIP codes.

Tech Terror: If you leave the General option selected, the Data Preview still displays the leading zeros in the ZIP codes, even though they will disappear when you import the file. You must select the Text option to retain the zeros.

When I save an Excel file in dBASE format, I lose some of my data. Why?

The dBASE file format stores lists of data. Excel can save only one list in each dBASE file. When you save a workbook as a .DBF (dBASE) file, Excel automatically selects the current list and saves that as the .DBF file. Any data outside of this list is not saved in the .DBF file. Also, if Excel does not correctly determine the limits of your list, it does not save all of the data. To prevent this problem, construct your list using the guidelines outlined in the Frustration Busters box at the beginning of Chapter 9, "Lists and

Data Management." For starters, make sure you select a cell within the appropriate list and that no blank columns or rows appear amid the data.

Tech Tip: If a range with the name "Database" exists in your workbook, Excel saves only that range in the .DBF file. This name is commonly found in files that were created in Excel 4.0 since this is the name Excel 4.0 automatically gave to the selection when you chose Set Database from the Options menu.

When I close an Excel 4.0 file in Excel 5.0, Excel asks me if I want to save it in the new format, which I do. When I use File Find, however, I can't see a preview of this file. Is there a setting I need to change?

No, you don't need to change any settings. The previews you see in Find File, like the one shown here, are created when you enter information into the Summary Info dialog box.

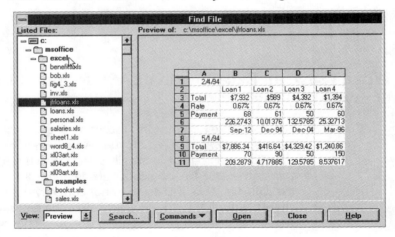

By default, all Excel 5.0 files will have a preview, because Excel automatically prompts you for summary information when you first save the file. However, when you save an Excel 4.0 worksheet as an Excel 5.0 workbook, the Summary Info dialog box does not appear. Therefore, you must enter summary information before you can see a preview of such a file in the Find File dialog box.

To create the preview for the Find File feature:

Tech Tip: To create a preview of a workbook you *already* saved in the new format, open the file, choose Summary Info from the File menu, click OK, and save it again. The summary information will be empty except for the preview of the workbook you have created.

1. Display the Excel 4.0 file.
2. Choose Save As from the File menu.
3. Select Microsoft Excel Workbook in the Save File as Type list box to save the worksheet as an Excel 5.0 workbook.
4. When Excel 5.0 prompts for the summary information, enter the appropriate title, subject, author, and comments.
5. Click OK.

Excel saves the workbook as a 5.0 file and creates a preview.

 I have both Excel 4.0 and 5.0 installed on my computer and I want to be able to use either one. Whenever I click either Excel icon in the Program Manager, I get Excel 4.0. How can I run both versions?

To run both versions of Excel on the same system, you need to change the name of the executable files so they're not identical. Because both Excel 4.0 and Excel 5.0 use files named EXCEL.EXE, you must rename one of them so Windows knows which application to launch. For example, you might change the name of the EXCEL.EXE file in the Excel 5.0 directory to EXCEL5.EXE.

You must also edit the properties of the Excel 5.0 program icon accordingly so it points to the new filename. To do so:

1. Select the Excel 5.0 program icon in the Program Manager, which is shown in the following illustration.

Microsoft
Excel

2. Press CTRL+ENTER, or choose <u>P</u>roperties from the Program Manager's <u>F</u>ile menu.

3. Edit the entry in the <u>C</u>ommand Line box to indicate the new filename.

You should now be able to run both versions of Excel without a problem.

Can I export my Excel data to a space-delimited text file?

Yes. You can save your Excel data in a text file, using spaces to separate entries in different columns. This type of file is accepted by nearly all other applications, which allows you to share your data with others who use neither Excel nor Windows.

To save your Excel data as a text file delimited by spaces:

1. Choose Save <u>A</u>s from the <u>F</u>ile menu.

2. Enter a filename in the File <u>N</u>ame text box.

3. Select Formatted Text (Space Delimited) in the Save File as <u>T</u>ype list box.

4. Click OK.

How can I bring my Excel for Macintosh files into Excel 5.0?

You must transfer the file through the Apple File Exchange utility, which translates between Macintosh and DOS-based file formats. To do so:

1. Start the Apple File Exchange on your Macintosh.

2. Insert a disk formatted for DOS in the Mac Super Drive.

3. Choose Mac To MSDOS and select the default translation.

4. Click the Translate button to save the file on the disk in a DOS format.

5. Open your file in Excel for Windows as you would any other file.

Can I call a macro originally created in 1-2-3 from a new Excel macro?

No, you cannot. You can only run existing Lotus macros that use the assigned shortcut key in a worksheet. One possible way to execute a Lotus macro from an Excel macro is to use the Send.Keys statement. However, unlike when you use the Run command, there is no guarantee that the entire Lotus macro will execute before Excel returns to the Excel macro.

I want to place an Excel chart in another Windows application that does not support Excel charts. Is there a way to do this?

Yes. You can copy a bitmap picture of the chart to the Clipboard and paste it into the other application by following these steps:

1. Display the chart in Excel.

2. Press SHIFT while clicking Edit on the menu bar, and then choose Copy Picture.

3. Click OK.

4. Switch to the other application.

5. Move the insertion point to where you want the picture to appear.

6. Choose Paste from the Edit menu.

Since you are copying a bitmap picture of the chart, instead of creating a link, the image in the other application will not be updated if you edit the chart in Excel later. The only way to update the pasted image is to delete it and repeat this procedure to add a new picture of the chart.

What is the SYLK format and how is it useful to me?

SYLK stands for SYmbolic LinK, which is a plain file format that saves only data and formulas. It does not store any formatting information whatsoever. SYLK can be very useful if you are trying to recover data from corrupted workbooks. Sometimes, saving the data without the formatting information in the SYLK format lets you recover the bare data, which you can then reformat.

Because of the nature of SYLK, you may get unexpected results if you save a document that contains groups of similar formulas as a .SLK file. When you reopen the document in Excel 5.0, you may find that these similar formulas have been translated into a single array formula. But *don't worry*—you haven't lost any data!

To avoid this problem, perform the following steps before you save the file in the .SLK format:

1. Choose Replace from the Edit menu.
2. Type = in the Find What box.
3. Type '= in the Replace With box.
4. Click Replace All.

These steps convert all of your formulas to text so Excel will not misread them later as an array. After you reopen the file:

1. Choose Replace from the Edit menu.
2. Type '= in the Find What box.
3. Type = in the Replace With box.
4. Click Replace All.

If you receive the message, "Cannot find matching data," follow these steps:

1. Choose Replace from the Edit menu.
2. Type = in the Find What box.
3. Type = in the Replace With box.
4. Click Replace All.

Workgroups

The technology changes in recent years make it possible to form workgroups of people who are geographically dispersed across the city, the country, or even the world! Individual workgroup participants are now selected solely for the skills they bring to a project. Some of these individuals may work together in the same location and have face-to-face meetings about a project. Others may rely totally on electronic communications to ensure that the project progresses smoothly to completion.

Excel includes many features that support workgroup efforts. In particular, its ability to interface with popular electronic mail systems allows people to share information easily.

FRUSTRATION BUSTERS!

Is your workgroup taking full advantage of Excel? Are there features that might help you work together more productively and efficiently? The following table lists some of the features you may want to consider using in your workgroup.

Feature	Description
File protection	Assigns a password to a workbook so it cannot be opened unless the password is correctly supplied
Locking cells and graphic objects	Prevents overwriting of formulas and graphics
Read-Only recommendation	Suggests using read-only access when a user opens a workbook
Hiding unneeded information	Information is made available on a need-to-know basis, reducing the potential for damage to data
Annotation	Adds notes to explain information to users who did not design the application
Find File	Searches for a file created by another workgroup member when you don't know where it's stored
Templates	Provides a consistent design and approach as workgroup members create and edit workbooks
Autostart options	Performs a series of tasks automatically when Excel opens a workbook, making it easier for all users to work effectively and efficiently

Which e-mail systems does Excel support?

Microsoft Excel supports mail systems that comply with MAPI (Messaging Application Programming Interface) or VIM (Vendor Independent Messaging). These include Microsoft Mail (MAPI-compliant) and Lotus cc:Mail (VIM-compliant). If you use Microsoft Mail, you can activate it by clicking this button on the Microsoft toolbar:

The Send Mail and Routing Slip commands don't appear on my menus. Why not?

For these menu options to appear, Excel must detect a MAPI-compliant e-mail system when you first install it. Excel's Setup program looks for a line that reads MAPI=1 in the [Mail] section of your WIN.INI file. If this line exists, Excel displays the Send Mail and Routing Slip commands.

If you added your mail system after installing Excel, you need to start the Excel Setup program and reinstall the application files. You do not need to reinstall the ancillary files, such as the ODBC drivers. Setup will check for and recognize the presence of the e-mail program and provide these commands.

Alternatively, if you know your mail application is MAPI-compatible, you can insert the MAPI=1 statement in the [Mail] section of your WIN.INI file and restart Windows. If you are not sure about your mail application's compatibility, or do not feel comfortable editing your WIN.INI file directly, simply reinstall the application files.

It's also possible that Excel doesn't support your particular e-mail application. Excel only works with MAPI-compliant and VIM-compliant e-mail systems, such as Microsoft Mail and Lotus cc:Mail, respectively.

I am concerned that confidential information in workbooks may be accessed by network users who are not working on the project. How can I restrict access to a workbook so that only the other members of the workgroup can see it?

You can use Excel's password features to protect the workbooks. For example, you can assign a password to each workbook that must be entered in order to open it. You can also require users to enter a

Tech Tip: You can also work with your network administrator to create a security group for all the workgroup users.

password before saving a workbook with its original name. This method prevents others from saving changes to the original copy of a workbook. If you assign such passwords, you can control who can access and modify your workbooks.

To add password protection to a workbook, follow these steps:

1. Display the workbook.

2. Choose Save As from the File menu.

3. Click Options to display the Save Options dialog box, shown here:

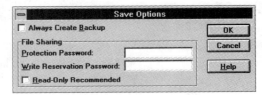

4. Type a password in the Protection Password box that you want a user to supply to open the workbook, and/or type a password in the Write Reservation Password box that a user must supply to save the workbook with the same name.

5. Click OK.

6. Type the password(s) again as prompted in the Reenter Protection Password and Reenter Write Reservation Password boxes, and click OK. (You must enter the password(s) exactly as you did the first time.)

7. Click OK again to save the workbook with the passwords.

When you next open the workbook, Excel will prompt you for the protection password you assigned. Similarly, it will prompt you for the write reservation password when you try to save the file.

Tech Tip: Password entries can be up to 15 characters long, are case-sensitive, and must match exactly when entered.

Tech Tip: If your workbook contains links to data in another workbook and that other workbook is protected with a password, you need to supply that password to access the linked data.

To remove a password:

1. Open the workbook from which you want to remove the password.

2. Choose Save <u>A</u>s from the <u>F</u>ile menu.

3. Click <u>O</u>ptions.

4. Select the password you want to remove and press DEL.

5. Click OK twice to remove the password selection and save the workbook without the password.

Tech Terror: A workgroup member who cannot supply the correct password cannot access the file. There is no way around this Excel feature. Therefore, make sure you give the password(s) to everyone who needs to work with the file and that you store a copy of these passwords in a safe place in case you forget them!

In Excel 4.0, when someone else opened a workbook that I was working with, I couldn't save my changes, because Excel locked me out of the file. Did Microsoft correct this problem in Excel 5.0?

In Excel 4.0, the file remained locked until the second user closed the Open as Read Only? dialog box by clicking either OK or Cancel; Excel 5.0 releases the file as soon as it retrieves the name of the second user. The file is therefore locked for only a brief period of time, after which you shouldn't have any problems saving it. Excel 5.0 also allows multiple users to open the same read-only file simultaneously.

I don't have any WorkGroup buttons on my Standard toolbar. Is there any way to add them?

Excel includes a WorkGroup toolbar, shown here, that you can display on your screen:

Follow these steps to add the toolbar:

1. Choose Toolbars from the View menu.
2. Select the WorkGroup check box in the Toolbars list box.
3. Click OK.

Alternatively, you can click any displayed toolbar with the right mouse button and choose WorkGroup from the shortcut menu that appears.

When I click the buttons on the WorkGroup toolbar, they don't work properly. What's wrong?

Your e-mail system must be active before the toolbar buttons for mailing and routing documents will function correctly. Press CTRL+ESC to display the Task List and see if your e-mail system is active. If it isn't, switch to the Program Manager and double-click the program icon for your e-mail application to start it. Now the WorkGroup toolbar buttons should work properly.

Each of my team members tends to format the workbooks a little differently, which makes it difficult to combine the information in them. What can I do to prevent this?

You can create templates for all the team members to use when they create and modify workbooks. The templates you create can contain text, formulas, graphics, formatting, and macros. The team members can simply enter their data in these "prefab" workbooks to ensure a consistent and compatible format.

Creating a template is easy. Just create a model workbook that doesn't contain any data and then choose Save As from the File menu. Enter the filename as you would normally, but select Template in the Save File As Type drop-down list box.

Your team members can then open this template to use as a model when they enter their data. The workbook they create is saved to another name. If you save templates in the EXCEL\XLSTART directory, Excel prompts your team members to select which template to use whenever they create new workbooks.

Tech Tip: You can also save your template as an autotemplate by saving it as BOOK.XLT in the XLSTART subdirectory. Excel then uses this template by default whenever a user starts Excel or opens a new workbook.

 Even when I know the name of a file that a member of my workgroup created, it can be difficult to find it. Is there a feature that makes searching for workbooks easier?

You can use Excel's Find File feature to help you locate files that workgroup users may have stored in different directories. To look for a workbook file:

1. Choose Find File from the File menu. Click Search, if necessary, to display the Search dialog box, shown here:

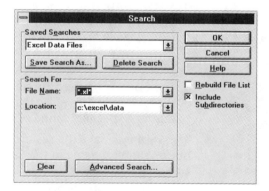

2. For a simple search, type a filename in the File Name box, and select or enter a drive and path in the Location drop-down list box. To perform a more sophisticated search, click the Advanced Search button, enter the appropriate information on the Location, Summary, or Timestamp tab, and click OK.

■ The options on the <u>L</u>ocation tab let you select additional directories in the <u>D</u>irectories list box or additional drives in the Dri<u>v</u>es drop-down list box, as shown here:

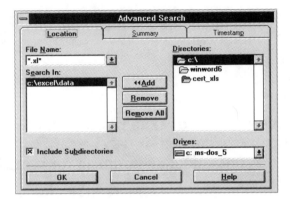

If you select the Include Su<u>b</u>directories check box, Excel also searches any subdirectories within the specified directories. Click the <u>A</u>dd button to add these locations to the S<u>e</u>arch In box.

■ The options on the <u>S</u>ummary tab let you search for files with specific entries in the summary information or with specific text in the workbook itself. Select the <u>M</u>atch Case check box to perform a case-sensitive search for the indicated text.

■ The options on the Timestam<u>p</u> tab let you search through only those files that were saved or created during a specified range of dates.

3. If you want to save the search, click the <u>S</u>ave Search As button, enter a name in the Save Search As dialog box, and click OK.

4. Click OK to process the search and display the results in the Find File dialog box like the one shown in the following illustration.

Tech Tip: To make it easier for workgroup members to locate shared files, you may want to create a directory for this very purpose. Then, all the people in the group will know exactly where to look for the information they need.

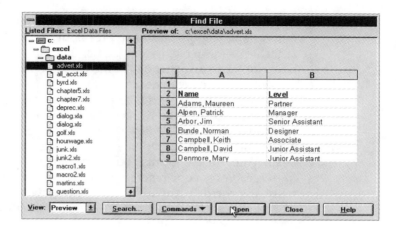

Highlight a file to see a preview of its contents in the dialog box.

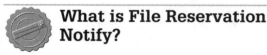

What is File Reservation Notify?

When you attempt to open a file from the server, Excel checks to see if the file is already in use. If so, Excel displays the File Reservation dialog box to notify you that the file is being modified by a specific user, as shown here:

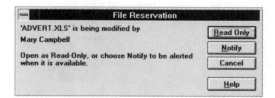

You can choose to open the file as read only or, if you prefer, you can ask to be notified when the other user finishes working with the file. To open the file immediately, click <u>R</u>ead Only to open the file as read only. In this case, you cannot save the workbook with the same filename; you must use a different one. If you click <u>N</u>otify, Excel opens the workbook as read only and prompts you when the file becomes available.

You can also click the Toggle Read Only button on the WorkGroup toolbar to request the file reservation for the read-only file that is currently open.

If the file reservation is unavailable, Excel displays the File Reservation dialog box, shown previously. If the file reservation is available, "Read-Only" in the title bar disappears, provided you have not made any changes to the workbook and another user has not saved any changes to the file. If the file reservation is available but your copy is different than the saved one because you either modified the workbook or it was modified and saved by another user, the File Reservation dialog box appears with a Read-Write button instead of a Notify button. When you click Read-Write, Excel prompts you to save any changes you made to the read-only copy before you close it. To save your edits, you must supply a different filename for this version of the workbook. Excel then opens both the original and modified versions as read-write files.

What does the new menu selection Add Routing Slip on the File menu do?

This option enables users of Microsoft Mail or any MAPI-compliant mail program to send Excel files to each other. The routing slip specifies which users will receive the file and in what order. You can send the file to all users at once or allow each user to make changes as it progresses along a specified route. You can also execute this command by clicking the Routing Slip button, shown here, on the WorkGroup toolbar:

What is the difference between mailing and routing a document?

When you *mail* a document, a copy of the document is attached to an electronic mail message and sent to others; this is a one-way process. Figure 14-1 shows a diagram of a document mailed from one user to two others.

When you *route* a document, the document is sent to others for review and editing, and then the modified version is sent back to the originator of the document; this is a two-way process. There are two ways to route a document from the

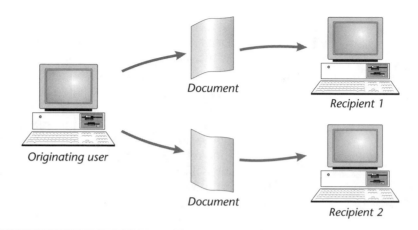

FIGURE 14-1 Mailing a document to two users

Routing Slip dialog box, which appears when you choose Add
<u>R</u>outing Slip from the <u>F</u>ile menu or click the Routing Slip button
on the WorkGroup toolbar:

- You can send copies of a document to a list of people all at
  once, and each one can then be sent back to you. Figure 14-2
  is a diagram showing the process of routing copies of a

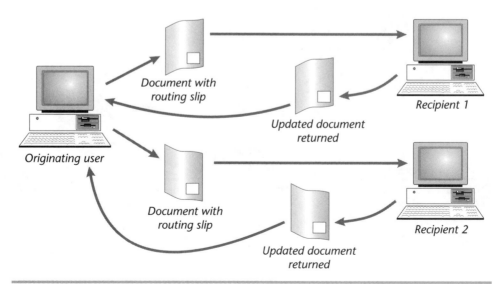

FIGURE 14-2 Routing to all recipients at once

document to two recipients and then returning the modified versions to the original user. The original user receives two copies of the document.

■ You can send a document to a list of people one after another. After the first user in the list receives and modifies the document, he or she then forwards it to the next person, who forwards it to the third person, and so on until the document reaches the last user in the list. Excel then returns the modified document to the user who originally sent the workbook. Figure 14-3 is a diagram showing the process of routing one copy of a document to two recipients before it comes back to the original user. When the original user receives the modified document, it reflects the changes made by both colleagues.

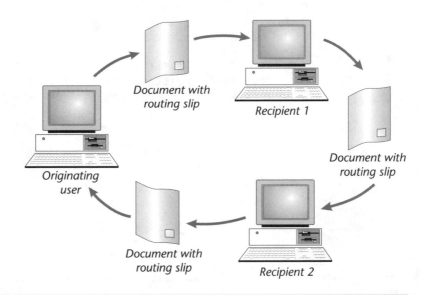

FIGURE 14-3   Routing a document in sequence

I have a predefined mailing list in my mail package. I added a routing slip addressed to this list to my workbook and selected the One After Another option to send the file sequentially to the list members. However, when I sent the file, it went to everyone at once. Why?

Excel treats a mailing list or alias as a single name and thus sends the file only once—to the name of the list itself. Your mail application then recognizes the list's name and sends the document to everyone on the list, which is why each person received a separate copy of the workbook. To avoid this problem, list each user's name individually in the Routing Slip dialog box, and select the One After Another option to route the file sequentially.

When I add a routing slip to my document, Excel adds a message at the end of it that prompts the recipient to choose Send when he or she finishes working with the file. Can I get rid of this?

No. Excel does not give you the option to change or delete this message; it was designed to remind each user to send the file to the next person when he or she finishes editing it.

Why does the command Edit Routing Slip sometimes appear instead of Add Routing Slip?

If a file already has a routing slip attached to it, then the command on the File menu changes from Add Routing Slip to Edit Routing Slip.

Every time I try to save a file I received through e-mail, Excel asks me if I want to forward it. What's happening?

The file has a routing slip attached to it and you are not the last person on the list. This message was built into Excel as a reminder to send the document to the next person on the list when you finish editing it.

I have Excel 4.0, and every time I try to open a file I created, I get the message "Cannot open binary file." Did the person to whom I mailed the file corrupt it?

More than likely, the person who sent you the file has Excel 5.0. When they rerouted the file to you, it was automatically updated to Excel 5.0's file format. This occurs because previous versions of Excel could not maintain some of the important routing information. To avoid this problem, you must include a note in the file asking everyone to save it in the Excel 4.0 format to ensure that you can read the final version. Also, each user will have to mail the file directly to you, because the Excel 4.0 file format will not incorporate the automatic routing information that returns the document to the original sender.

How can I send a single sheet through e-mail instead of the entire workbook?

You can send only the active sheet if you save it in a different file format. Choose the Save As command from the File menu, select Microsoft Excel 3.0 Worksheet in the Save File as Type drop-down list box, and click OK to save only the current sheet in the file. You can then send this single-sheet file to another user.

Index